CURVEBALLS
AND
SCREWBALLS

CURVEBALLS AND SCREWBALLS

By

JEFFREY LYONS AND DOUGLAS B. LYONS

Curveballs & Screwballs: Over 1,286 Incredible Baseball Facts, Finds, Flukes, and More!
Copyright © 2001 by Jeffrey Lyons and Douglas B. Lyons

Visit the Random House Puzzles & Games Web site at www.puzzlesatrandom.com

Typeset and printed in the United States of America.

Library of Congress cataloging-in-publication data is available.

First Edition
0 9 8 7 6 5 4 3 2 1
March 2001

ISBN: 0-8129-3315-X

New York Toronto London Sydney Auckland

TABLE OF CONTENTS

INTRODUCTION

―――――

By Robert Redford

IT'S ODD, REALLY, that facts can engage us so. Even if baseball is a universal language, why do we take interest in Moe Berg's dying words, or for whom Perryton, Ohio names its high-school field? Some of these facts are fun, even hilarious. Some are more mundane, but none are meaningless—they tell us about a time and a place and a sport. They tell us the story of baseball.

A big part of that story is told by the records. What would baseball be without them? The records and the stats fuel rivalries among children, adults, and players alike. They aren't just facts. The numbers are the standards by which the gods are created and judged. In part, they define our baseball heroes.

As far as heroes go, Ted Williams has always been mine. Though I admired Williams for his athletic brilliance, I was prejudiced by the fact that he was also a Californian, and left-handed. That partially made him the man behind the myth. And so our fascination with that—the man vs. the myth—drives our fascination with what might otherwise be mundane. What might otherwise be trivial suddenly becomes meaningful.

But enough analysis. Enjoy learning more about your heroes and the wonderful sport they play.

INTRODUCTION
& ACKNOWLEDGMENTS

———

THE UNIQUE PLACE THAT BASEBALL continues to hold in America can be demonstrated by a story told by the late *Washington Post* sportswriter Shirley Povich about Walter Johnson—"The Big Train." It is reprinted here with Povich's permission.

> "The reverence in which the Big Train was held was typified one day by Edward T. Folliard, Pulitzer Prize–winner of the *Washington Post* [1947, *Telegraphic Reporting*] and historian of virtually all important national and international events of the past 20 years. Speaking before a brilliant assemblage in the National Press Club, Folliard was introduced as a famous war correspondent, an on-the-spot reporter at White House conferences when history was made, and an authority on national affairs. When asked what was his greatest thrill, he said unhesitatingly: 'That was the day [February 22, 1936] when I covered Walter Johnson's attempt to throw a silver dollar across the Rappahannock River, as George Washington had done. As a small boy in Washington, I was a Johnson fan. That day, when Johnson threw the dollar across the Rappahannock, I got my greatest thrill. You see, I was the fellow who held Walter Johnson's coat.'" [See *SPORT* magazine, January 1950, page 50.]

# # #

Since *Out of Left Field* was published in 1998, we have pored over hundreds of e-mails, letters, media guides old and new, books, magazine articles, video and audio tapes, and myriad other sources to create *Curveballs and Screwballs*.

Where else can you read about the only woman murdered because she did not want to watch the Mets? Men buried in their baseball uniforms? Umpires' license plates? A ballplayer who was a mink farmer and three others who were Christmas tree farmers? As long as the game has new stories and new players (e.g., Wiklenman Gonzalez) we'll try to find the unusual, offbeat, odd facts and anecdotes that you just can't find anywhere else.

I am not a "walking encyclopedia of baseball." While I am as fascinated by statistics as other serious fans, I always draw a blank when someone asks me "Who led the National League in triples in 1996?" I don't know and I really don't much care. I can look that up. We're more interested in—Where is he from? Big Cabin, Oklahoma, like Ralph Terry? Nowhere, like Ed Porray? Did he play baseball in high school? How many siblings does he have? How many children? Do their names start with the same letter? Do their names rhyme? Was he a high school teammate of another future big leaguer? What's his dog's name? How many balls can he hold in one hand? Is he a pig farmer in the off-season? What does his license plate say? Does he like bow hunting? Was he married at home plate?

Many people ask us "Where do you find this stuff?" Our most valuable sources—besides brothers George and Jeffrey's vast knowledge of the game—include friends in the media relations departments of many teams—major and minor—and members of the Society for American Baseball Research.

Our other major sources include *Total Baseball*, by John Thorn, Pete Palmer, Michael Gershman, and David Pietrusza; Jonathan Fraser Light's *The Cultural Encyclopedia of Baseball; SABR Presents the Home Run Encyclopedia*, edited by David Vincent and Bob McConnell; *Baseball America's The Baseball Autograph Collector's Handbook*, media guides, *Baseball Weekly, Baseball America, Baseball Digest*, and *The Baseball Encyclopedia*. But some of our sources are of a more arcane nature. They include *Catholic New York*, the record room at Supreme Court, Criminal Term, Queens County, New York, *Modern Bride*, and license plate collectors' Web sites.

Additionally, readers of *Out of Left Field* from all over the world sent us their favorite baseball questions and answers. Many have been included here.

I made frequent use of the extensive baseball collection at the Public Library in Scarsdale, New York, and I am fortunate to work two blocks from the main branch of the New York Public Library on 42nd Street.

In ways that seem to multiply daily, the Internet has become an indispensable baseball research tool—from locating ballplayers to verify that they were married at home plate, to finding experts on vanity license plates, inventions by ballplayers, unusual minor and major league promotions, orthopedic surgeons, and baseball-related restaurants. The Internet provides virtually instant access to information that is simply not available elsewhere.

Most of the questions and stories here deal with men who played in the major leagues since 1900. Only a few deal with the minors, the Negro Leagues, 19th-century players, college, and amateur ball. Statistics are up to date through the end of the 1999 season.

# # #

If you sat down to write the complete history of the sport of curling, it might include the origins of the game, the evolution of uniforms, rules, and equipment, great players of the past, funny incidents, quirky players, champions, and the Curling Hall of Fame. But that would be it—the definitive history of curling, complete in one volume.

Such a volume of baseball is inconceivable. One of the things Jeff and I love about the game is that there is not now, nor can there ever be, a definitive, complete, and all-encompassing book of baseball. Like the universe, baseball is constantly expanding. The very nature of the game generates dozens of new baseball books every year—new analyses of old controversies and scandals; "instant" books about this year's World Series; autobiographies of today's stars; unauthorized and perhaps unflattering biographies of yesterday's stars; chronicles of a year in the minors; an analysis of baseball's numeric history; a collection of funny anecdotes; the reminiscences of a retiring umpire; a look at the economics of the game . . . the list goes on and on, and regenerates each year, because baseball renews itself annually. Is this the year of the pitcher? Has the ball been juiced up? Is pitching diluted? Why are the Mets hitting so many home runs this year? Why are the Rockies hitting so few home runs this year? How many times have you heard, "Do you think ____ will break ____'s record for ____ this year?" or "Did you ever see that play before?"

# # #

Our friends at the National Baseball Hall of Fame in Cooperstown have gone out of their way to provide us with support and encouragement, along with specific information (e.g., "For which orchestra did Eddie Basinski play the violin?"). We are especially grateful to Tim Wiles, Director of Research; Scot Mondore, Manager of Museum Programming; Senior Researcher Bruce Markusen; Tom Shieber, Manager of Internet Services; Curator Peter Clark; Pat Kelly, Director of the Photograph Collection; Jeffrey Idelson, Vice President of Communications and Education, and Library Director James L. Gates, Jr. for their generous assistance. We've been helped, too, by Dan Bennett, Jeremy Jones, Bill Francis, Sarah Quinn, Jimmy Knodel, and Dan Santameria. Our visits to Cooperstown are greatly anticipated and fondly remembered. Thanks also are due to our style proofer, Robin Perlow.

Members of the Society for American Baseball Research (SABR), 812 Huron Street, Suite 719, Cleveland, Ohio 44115 (www.sabr.org) and its many committees and publications have given us numerous leads and advice in writing and by fax, phone, and e-mail. Through the *SABR Bulletin* and other publications, SABR national and regional meetings, and the SABR-L daily e-mail message board [Bill Mazeroski either should or should not be in the Hall of Fame, and here are 20 pages of text and statistics to back up both sides; what name should be given to a gathering of umpires—how about a "Klem" of umpires?], our requests for assistance have been answered by total strangers in great volume, with good humor, and with wonderful anecdotes, many of which have been included here. If you like this book, you'll love SABR. To our SABR pals: Thanks. We appreciate it.

Special thanks to our diligent agent, Alfred Geller, and to our editor, Stanley Newman at Random House, for his continued efforts and direction, his sage advice, and his deft organization. Also at Random House, our thanks to Heidi North and Beth Levy.

Others deserving acknowledgment are Robert Redford; Julio Cruz; Willie McCovey; Dave Winfield; Gerry Myerson; Lyle Spatz, Chairman of SABR's Baseball Records Committee; Marty Appel; Dan Schlossberg; Don and Soot Zimmer; Yankee broadcaster Beto Villa; the authors' older brothers Warren H. Lyons and George M. Lyons—still the greatest living font of baseball information we have ever encountered; Virginia A. Hurley; David Vincent, co-editor of *SABR Presents the Home Run Encyclopedia;* David W. Alm, Larry Fritsch; Marion and Robert Merrill; Paula Homan, curator of the St. Louis Cardinals Hall of Fame Museum; Cardinal historian Erv Fischcer, Herb Bloomenthal; Kurt Pickering; Dick Bresciani of the Boston Red Sox; Jim Casey; Jules Tygiel; Jack Riley; Paul D. Cassetta; Ed McSweeney; Bob Bogart; B. W. Radley; Joseph Ronson; Tom McRoberts; Tim Samway; Denis Repp; Joe Williams; Bob Timmerman; Larry Salvato; Peter Henrisi; Dan Avey; Jorgen Rasmussen; Jay Sanford, who provided us with the off-season and postseason occupations of a number of 19th-century big leaguers; Daniel Levine; Gene Sunnen; Dave Stevens; Bobby Taute; Steve Thompson; Alex Semchuck; Jeff Cloud; Mike Selleck of the Oakland A's; Jon Greenberg of the Milwaukee Brewers; Howard Rosenthal; Steve Geitschier of the *Sporting News;* Richard Vang; Stephen Ferenchick; Len Zaslowski; Eddie Deezen; Brian Lepley; Andy Weiss; Bob Adams; Troy Soos; Katherine Wolff; Eugene N. Harley; Alan Heatin; Steve Matesich of the Tampa Bay Devil Rays; Steve Fink of the Kansas City Royals; Ron Selter; Chris Leible of the New York Mets; Marty Adler; Jack Weaver; Ted Williams; Bob Feller; Chris Granozio of the New York Mets; Stephen E. Milman; umpires Al Clark, Drew Coble, Rick Reed, Rocky Roe, and Don Denkinger; Joe Wasielewski of the Scranton/Wilkes-Barre Red Barons; Jerry

Mezerow; Rick Cerrone of the New York Yankees; Scott Brandon; Steve Fields of the San Jose Giants; Jason Carr of the Seattle Mariners; Dennis Burbank; John Matthew IV; Mike Kennedy of the Pittsburgh Pirates; Pat Campbell; Jim Smith; Jim Charlton; Vincent F. Scully; Glen Serra of the Atlanta Braves; Carolyn A. Serra; Paul Howland for his diligent and intrepid efforts to find every single hall of fame in Michigan; Bob "Woody" Freyman; J. Von Bushberger; Sandy Genelius of CBS Television; Jerry Malloy; and my understanding wife, Nancy.

# # #

If your favorite baseball question is not here, or if you have information about a baseball license plate, a statue of a ballplayer, a baseball player's restaurant or invention, a home-plate wedding, or a ballplayer in your city's Hall of Fame, or wish to contribute to our next book, please write us c/o Random House Puzzles & Games, 280 Park Avenue, New York, NY 10017-1216, or e-mail us at BASBALINFO@aol.com. We'll respond.

—Douglas B. Lyons

T HE REACTION TO OUR FIRST BOOK, *Out of Left Field*, was overwhelming, from inside the baseball establishment and from fans. "How on Earth did you find this stuff?" was a common reaction. We also got lots of: "You have a lot of time on your hands" reactions, too. But all with big smiles.

Most of the "grunt" work was done by my brother Douglas—the phone calls, the treks to the library, the correspondences with everyone imaginable who might provide insight, trivia, confirmations of obscure facts, and keys to other questions. That is a long and sometimes lonely process.

I had the easy part: going over the questions, using my lifelong baseball addiction to weed out the questions that seemed too familiar, doing endless radio and TV promotions for the book, plugging it wherever possible. The people who made this book possible, besides my brother, who did most of the work, were mentioned, for the most part, in our first book: my family. (My wife, Judy, holds the record for most consecutive years married to someone who constantly misplaces things, forgets people's names, prefers listening to the Red Sox on radio over dining with friends, and . . . well, you get the idea. She is my General Manager, Director of Player Development, MVP, and my life's companion.) The real stars on our team (can you STAND this baseball analogy?) are Ben and Hannah, even though Ben is a White Sox fan and Hannah likes the Yankees, especially you-know-who at shortstop.

Others to whom I dedicate this book include, once again, Joe Castiglione and Jerry Trupiano, the Red Sox's brilliant radio announcers, who welcome me into the booth at Fenway, as well as here in New York and around the league. Two more solid professionals simply do not exist. Baseball has been the catalyst for the friendship, especially between the Lyons and Castiglione families, and long may it and they endure!

The Red Sox always welcome us and treat us like royalty at Fenway; I felt like MacArthur returning to the Philippines when I attended the Pedro vs. Clemens ALCS game on that glorious day in October 1999. Thanks to Dan Duquette, Kevin Shea, Glen Wilburn, and Dick Bresciani, as always. And to Howie Sylvester for putting up with my laughter in the booth, which occasionally bleeds into the broadcasts.

Others to whom I dedicate this book include Duke Castiglione, New York's newest and most eager sportscaster. Welcome and a long career! On the Yankee side of the microphone, to John Sterling, Michael Kay, Jim Kaat (and your 16 Gold Gloves; you belong in Cooperstown), Ken Singleton, Bobby Murcer, and former Red Sox James Timothy McCarver. Thanks for making me feel welcome.

Chris Granozio of the Mets loved the first book so much he put questions up on the scoreboard all season in 1999 and 2000—an enormous compliment. Thank you so much, Chris.

My late father-in-law, Frank Kracher, lived to see the first book, and I thank this U.S. Soccer Hall of Fame member for letting me drag him to endless Red Sox–White Sox games at old Comiskey Park.

My teammates in the N.Y. Showbusiness League continue to be my "Boys of Summer" and although we are three years older since our first book, we have that much more "experience" and know-how to position ourselves against the twentysomethings we occasionally beat. We will play as long as we can walk!

Thanks also to my agent, Alfred Geller, and everyone in his office for believing in me and what abilities I may have, and to my colleagues and bosses at WNBC. To Dennis Swanson, our President and General Manager, who has seen more movies and theater than I think I have, and to Paula Madison, our News Director, and Joel Goldberg, who put up with my Red Sox affliction. It is a joy working with and for you.

Also to fellow Red Sox fans Jonathan Schwartz and Bruce Breimer. And to John Sparks, who fills me in on Texas Rangers trivia, Bob Campbell and Lewis Hart on the Phillies, Maurice Dubois, the quintessential Yankee fan, and the two closest Red Sox fans at WNBC, Rob Morrison and Phil O'Brien. United we stand! Someday, our ship will come in.

Enjoy!

—Jeffrey Lyons

DEDICATION

By Douglas B. Lyons

A
S THE IMMORTAL WES WESTRUM SAGELY OBSERVED, "Baseball is like church: many attend, few understand."
Part of the lore of baseball is its pull on our youth. Baseball can be
learned young—as a player and as a fan—and can be savored and shared for a
lifetime, first with parents, then with one's own children. The more you put in,
the more you get out.

I coached my three daughters' softball teams (to winning and occasionally
undefeated seasons) and pitched batting practice until my nose was broken
when a third grader hit a comebacker right at me. (I did get some leather on
it.) Now, I coach my son Anthony's first grade Little League team. ("I'm on
double deck!") We're Dodgers!

I took Susie to her first ballgame when she was about four. Our seats were
behind third base at Shea Stadium, and we watched Graig Nettles, then with
the Padres, show us how it's done. When everybody stood up for the seventh-
inning stretch, Susie shouted at them: "Sit down! I can't see the baseball show!"
In 1998, during her first year in college, she called me five minutes before the
Yankees' Opening Day to ask which channel she could watch the game on. I
was thrilled.

Once day when Margaret was seven, I knew I was bringing her up right. I
was pitching batting practice. Margaret came up to the plate in the severest
crouch she could manage and said "Pop, look! I'm Eddie Gaedel!"

Nora reminded me of our father, Leonard Lyons, a syndicated newspaper columnist. He pitched to my brothers and me* in Central Park every weekend during the season but would NEVER try to catch one of those spinning balls that were always popped up between the plate and the mound. "Those are my typing fingers!" he'd exclaim, knowing that it did not much matter whether he caught the ball, or waited for it to drop and stop spinning, lest he injure the fingers he needed to work. Nora is a flutist. She was also an excellent third basewoman. I was always afraid that she might make a great catch of a hot smash and injure her B-flat finger.

One night, Tony and I were talking about the Black Sox—how players had been accused of losing games on purpose. Happy Felsch's name came up. Tony loves to hear the great nicknames of old ballplayers. I explained how one player, a former pitcher, "saved" the game of baseball, by drawing disenchanted fans back to the ballparks with his prodigious home runs—the first man to hit 30, 40, 50, and then 60 in a single season. You can't cheat a home run. I said, "Tony, this is a player whose name you know. Who do you think it was?" His first guess was Mark McGwire—pretty astute for a five-year-old, I thought. But his next two guesses reassured me that I was raising him correctly: "Pretzels Pezzullo? Pickles Dilhoefer?" He finally guessed Babe Ruth, but I wondered how many five-year-olds let the names Pretzels Pezzullo and Pickles Dilhoefer roll trippingly off their tongues.

Tony is now seven. His favorite player is Tino Martinez of the Yankees. But it's never just "Tino." "No, Pop, it's Tino MARTINEZ!" One night toward the end of the 1998 season, we were watching *This Week in Baseball*, and the Orioles' fine second half of the season was described. The narrator said, "The Orioles just might be the best team in baseball." Not really knowing what he would say, I asked, "Tony, which is the best team in baseball?" Without missing a beat, he said "The Bronx Bombers!"

# # #

*My three brothers and I once chipped in to purchase a catcher's mask for our mother, Sylvia. She wrote about this in "Mother Wore a Catcher's Mask," *Parade Magazine*, September 13, 1953.

My family's team was the subject of a previous article by my mother, "She Made the Team," originally printed in *This Week Magazine* and reprinted in the June 1949 issue of *Reader's Digest*. "Because of the shortage of players, I was drafted as a catcher. I served faithfully behind the plate until the day their teammates complained to George and Warren [my oldest brothers, then age about 10 and 8] about my unorthodox catching style. My sons explained that the new baby [Jeffrey] which would arrive in a few weeks, made it difficult for me to ape the peculiar crouch of Walker Cooper..."

My own slo-pitch softball team, the Eagles, had nine straight losing seasons. I was the manager, general manager, director of softball operations, scout, trainer, director of media relations, traveling secretary, attitude coach, team historian, equipment manager, and corresponding secretary. If we'd had a bus, I'd have been bussie, too. We finished last or next to last every year. But in my defense, I must say that I never had the same lineup two nights in a row. The Eagles were primarily men in their thirties and forties (and some older than that), who had families and commuted. It was tough for them to be free for 6 PM games twice a week. What we needed was five single, unemployed 20-year-olds who could run. I always packed my cellular phone next to my glove, as I knew I'd have to call players from the field to beg them to get there in the next eight minutes.

# # #

Is there a more enjoyable experience for a parent than watching a ballgame with your children—on television or at the stadium—and perhaps remembering watching with your own parents?

And so this book is for my children, Susan Elizabeth, Margaret Rose, Nora Jane, and Anthony Edward, who put up with its creation, who understood what I was doing when I watched a ballgame and said "I'm *working,*" and who let me share my love of the game.

Pass it on.

CURVEBALLS
AND
SCREWBALLS

MARK MCGWIRE

THE ANSWER TO MOST BASEBALL trivia questions involving home runs used to be "Babe Ruth," so mightily did he tower over nearly everyone except Hank Aaron. No more. Mark McGwire has earned his own chapter.

# # #

During their historic race for the single-season home run record in 1998, Mark McGwire finished the season with 70, and Sammy Sosa with 66. For how long during their season-long battle for supremacy was Sosa actually ahead of McGwire in the race?

110 minutes.

# # #

In 1995, Mark McGwire—then of the Oakland A's—became the first player with at least 250 at bats to have more home runs than singles in one season. He hit 39 homers that year, but only 35 singles. He duplicated this feat in 1998 with the Cardinals, when he hit a historic 70 home runs but had just 61 singles.

# # #

McGwire's triple on August 2, 1999, was his first since June 20, 1988—4,618 at bats before—when he was with Oakland.

# # #

McGwire's two-year total of 128 home runs (1997–98) put him atop the "Most Home Runs in Two Consecutive Seasons" list, surpassing Babe Ruth's 114, in the 1927–28 seasons. The next year, McGwire broke his own record with 135 in 1998–99.

# # #

McG's 65 homers in 1999 gave him the most home runs in three consecutive years—193.

# # #

And in case you're wondering who holds the record for the most home runs in four consecutive years, the answer is Mark McGwire—245, from 1996 to 1999.

# # #

On August 20, 1998, McGwire became the first man to hit at least 50 home runs in a single season for three consecutive seasons. On that date, he hit his 50th home run of the season for the St. Louis Cardinals; in 1997, when he had played for both the A's and the Cardinals, he hit 58 home runs. The previous year, he hit 52.

In 1999, McGwire became the first man to hit 50 home runs in a single season four years in a row.

# # #

On April 14, 1998, Mark McGwire became the first Cardinal to hit three home runs in one game at Busch Stadium.

# # #

Big Mac reached 400 home runs in the fewest at bats in history—4,726.

He also hit 500 home runs in the fewest at bats—5,487, and in the fewest games—1,639.

# # #

How many All-Star home runs has Mark McGwire hit?

Through 2000 the authors are tied with Mark McGwire for All-Star Game home runs—none.

# # #

Mark McGwire's father, John, is a dentist. One of his patients surrendered Big Mac's first major league hit. Who is he?

Tommy John. As a Yankee, T. J. surrendered Big Mac's first hit, on August 24, 1986.

# # #

McGwire, at 23, hit the most home runs in a single season before the age of 24 with the 1987 Oakland A's, for whom he hit 49.

# # #

In 1997 McGwire accomplished a feat that had probably never been anticipated, much less accomplished by anyone else: he hit more than 20 home runs in both leagues in the same season. He hit 34 for the A's and 24 for the Cardinals—becoming the first man to hit more than 50 home runs in consecutive seasons since Babe Ruth in 1920 (54) and 1921 (59).

# # #

What did McGwire do on March 31, 1998, that no Cardinal had ever done before?

He hit a grand slam on Opening Day, homering off Ramon Martinez of the Dodgers in the fifth inning.

# # #

Mark McGwire hit the most home runs in a single season before June 1 when he hit number 27 at San Diego on May 30, 1998.

Later that year, he tied Reggie Jackson's 1967 record for the most home runs (37) before the All-Star break. Jackson tailed off in the second half, finishing with "just" 47, while McGwire just kept going, and going, and going, on to 70.

McGwire hit number 47 on August 11, 1998—the most home runs in the National League in a season before September 1.

# # #

In 1998 he hit homer number 40 on July 12, in his 281st at bat of the season, in his 90th game—the fastest that 40 home runs had ever been reached in a season (by both measures).

# # #

In 1999 Mark McGwire became the only man to hit home run number 500 the year after he hit number 400. He hit number 400 on May 8, 1998, at Shea Stadium; number 500 occurred on August 5, 1999, at Busch Stadium.

# # #

On August 22, 1999, at Shea Stadium against the Mets, McGwire hit home runs number 49 and 50 of 1999. At age 35, McGwire thereby became the oldest man to hit 50 homers in a single season. Whose record did he break?

His own, set the previous season.

# # #

McGwire's second-base steal on August 20, 1998, against the Mets in the third inning of the second game of a doubleheader came in the game in which he hit home runs number 50 and 51. It was his first steal of the season, and the 11th of his career. As Tom Keegan wrote in the following day's *New York Post,* "McGwire needs only 49 more stolen bases to become the first member of the 50/50 club."

# # #

In 1995 McGwire had 39 homers but just 87 hits for the Oakland A's—the fewest hits in a season for anyone who had hit at least 30 home runs.

# # #

In 1998 McGwire hit the most two-run home runs in a single season—28.

# # #

In 1997 McGwire scored only 86 runs to go with his 58 homers—the fewest runs scored in a season by a batter who hit at least 50 home runs. Clearly, he had little power batting behind him.

# # #

What was the winning number in the Missouri state lottery on September 8, 1998, when Mark McGwire hit his record breaking 62nd home run of the season?

062.

# # #

Only three men have hit 400 home runs over the course of a decade. Who are they?

Babe Ruth, 467 in the 1920s.
Jimmie Foxx, 415 in the 1930s.
Mark McGwire, 405 in the 1990s.

# # #

Everybody likes home runs—everybody except pitchers, that is. An examination of Mark McGwire's 1999 season shows that he homered in 56 different Cardinal games. How many of those games did the Cardinals win?

The Cardinals had a 24–32 record in games in which McGwire homered. That is, he hit more home runs in games the Cardinals lost than in games they won. Hitting 32 home runs in 32 losing games is also a record—one which we're sure he'd love to have someone break.

# # #

How close did Mark McGwire come to hitting .300 in 1998?

He finished the season at .299, just one hit shy of a .300 season.

# # #

In 1999 McGwire drove in 147 runs with only 145 hits, thus becoming the first player to have more RBIs than hits in a single season.

# # #

In 1993 Mark McGwire hit nine home runs in 84 at bats, ranking him number two on the all-time list of most home runs in 100 or fewer at bats. Who is number one on that list?

Ted Williams. In 1953 he hit 13 home runs in just 91 at bats.

# # #

McGwire's 70 homers in 1998 broke what Cardinal's single-season home run record?

Big Johnny Mize. He smacked 43 homers for the Cards in 1940.

Thanks to Stan Newman for this question.

# # #

McGwire is the only player with twice as many career home runs as doubles [minimum 500 home runs]. Through 2000, Big Mac has hit 554 homers, with only 248 doubles. Compare these numbers with Babe Ruth (714 homers, 506 doubles), Mickey Mantle (536 homers, 344 doubles), Frank Robinson (586 homers, 528 doubles), and Willie Mays (660 home runs, 523 doubles).

# # #

In 1996, Mark McGwire became the first man to hit 50 home runs in a single season in fewer than 140 games—52 homers, 130 games.

WHERE ARE YOU FROM?

—

WHICH CANADIAN HAS HIT the most home runs in the big leagues?

Larry Walker. The Maple Ridge, British Columbia, native hit his 195th career homer (his 42nd of the season) on September 6, 1997, which pushed him past Jeff Heath's total of 194. Through 2000, Walker has hit 271 round trippers.

# # #

A number of big leaguers were born in Europe, then came to America and learned baseball here. Bobby Thomson (Glasgow, Scotland) and Elmer Valo (Ribnik, Czechoslovakia) come to mind. Who was the first major leaguer born in Europe who played baseball in Europe before coming to the major leagues?

Wilhelmus "Win" Remmerswaal. Born March 8, 1954, this native of The Hague, the Netherlands, played in the Dutch Little League, Babe Ruth champions, and the Dutch All-Stars and won a European amateur title before going to the majors, compiling a 3–1 record for the Red Sox, where he pitched from 1979–80.

# # #

If you took a poll to determine ballplayers' opinions about the future of the game, who might be the best choice to conduct the poll?

Willie Adams (Oakland, 1996–97) of Gallup, New Mexico.

# # #

Who is the best ballplayer to come out of Wurzburg, West Germany?

Mike Blowers. (1989–99, Yankees, Mariners, Dodgers, A's.)

# # #

One of the most infamous incidents in baseball history occurred in the 12th inning of the 1970 All-Star Game, when Pete Rose bowled over American League catcher Ray Fosse to score the winning run in a 5–4 National League victory.

Fosse was never the same. Yet he achieved a sort of revenge years later, when Rose entered a plea of guilty to tax evasion and served time at the federal prison in Marion, Illinois—Fosse's hometown.

# # #

Who is the best player from Granada?

Dennis Martinez, from Granada, Nicaragua.

# # #

Who is the only Argonaut in the big leagues?

Ted Kluszewski, from Argo, Illinois.

# # #

Who may be the cleanest player in the game?

Mark Clark, from Bath, Illinois.

Who is the dirtiest?

Charlie Schmutz, perhaps a friend of Sloppy Thurston.

# # #

Which team broadcasts its games to Jupiter?

The Florida Marlins. Their games are heard on WJNO in Jupiter, Florida.

# # #

Which team broadcasts its games in Norway?

The Portland, Maine, Sea Dogs (the Florida Marlins affiliate in the Class AA Eastern League), on WOXO, Norway, Maine.

# # #

CALLING SUPERMAN, CALLING SUPERMAN

Which team broadcasts all of its games in Metropolis?

The Chicago Cubs, on WMOK, Metropolis, Illinois.

# # #

Through extended radio networks, baseball games, both major and minor, are broadcast in Malta, Lisbon, Canton, Lebanon, Odessa, Dublin, Carthage, Sparta, Holland, Naples, Thermopolis, Lyons, Florence, Mexico, Dover, Calais, Paris, and Lake Geneva—all American towns.

# # #

Who was the only Sardinian in the majors?

Jayhawk Owens, a resident of Sardinia, Ohio.

# # #

Who was the first Okinawan big leaguer?

Bobby "Bloop" Fenwick, a native of Naha. He hit .179 for the Astros and Cardinals, 1972–73.

# # #

Who is the only Singaporean to play in the major leagues?

Robin Jennings, Cubs, 1996–97.

# # #

GUYS WE HOPE MAKE IT TO THE BIG LEAGUES DEPT.:

Angels prospect Nathan Haynes, who lives in Hercules, California.

Who is the only pitcher from the Dominican Republic to save at least 100 games?

Mel Rojas—126.

# # #

Why is there a big celebration every February 2 in Billy Hunter's hometown?

Because he is from Punxsutawney, Pennsylvania, the locus of Groundhog Day every year.

# # #

Who is the first Canadian to be named Most Valuable Player?

Larry Walker, Rockies, 1997. He's from Maple Ridge, British Columbia.

# # #

Name a big leaguer who was born an Olympian.

Geoff Jenkins, from Olympia, Washington.

# # #

Who is the only native Fredonian in baseball?

Woody English, from Fredonia, Ohio.

# # #

Who are the only Maoists in the major leagues?

Pedro Borbon, Sr. and Pedro Borbon, Jr., are natives of Mao, Dominican Republic. Tony Batista lives there.

# # #

Who is the only Venetian enshrined at Cooperstown?

Walter Alston, born in Venice, Ohio.

# # #

Hall of Famer Harmon Killebrew is from Payette, Idaho. During his 22–year, 8,147 at-bat career, he faced many pitchers—but only one who was also from Idaho. Who was he?

Johnny James, of Bonners Ferry, Idaho. James pitched for the Yankees in 1958 and 1960 and for both the Yankees and the Los Angeles Angels in 1961.

# # #

Name the only four Dominicans who have at least 2,000 hits.

Hint: NOT Sammy Sosa, not George Bell, and not Matty Alou.

Julio Franco–2,177, Tony Fernandez–2,240, Felipe Alou–2,101, and César Cedeño–2,087.

# # #

DEVOTED TO BASEBALL

FANS HAVE FOUND MANY WAYS to show their love of baseball. Some do it at the ballpark. As noted in a later chapter, STEP UP TO THE PLATE, some fans proclaim their devotion with vanity license plates. A number of fans, as well as players, get married at home plate or on the pitcher's mound. (See the chapter MARRIED AT HOME PLATE.) Others have found even more imaginative ways to show their devotion to the game.

# # #

On October 4, 1967, while watching the first game of the Red Sox–Cardinals World Series, 79-year-old former ambassador Joseph Kennedy had a fainting spell at Fenway Park. Luckily, he was accompanied by his sons, Senators Robert and Edward. They helped their father into his car, which took him to his home in Hyannis Port. *Then they went back to the game!*

# # #

Legendary spy/catcher Moe Berg spoke six languages, and "couldn't hit in any of them." His dying words on May 29, 1972, were: "How did the Mets do today?" (They won, beating the Cardinals 7–6.)

# # #

While he was governor of Kentucky, future Commissioner of Baseball and Hall of Famer Albert B. "Happy" Chandler was in his box seat at Crosley Field in Cincinnati, not far from from the Kentucky border, watching the Reds beat the Tigers in the final game of the World Series on October 8, 1940. Only after Paul Derringer recorded the final putout would Chandler allow himself to be taken to a hospital for an emergency appendectomy.

# # #

Pitcher Richie Lewis named his daughter, born in 1993, his first year with the expansion Marlins, McKenzie Marlina K. Lewis.

# # #

The day before the Giants clinched the 1971 National League West title, Tito Fuentes and his wife had a baby boy. They named him Clinch.

# # #

Paper money in Taiwan will soon have a picture of a generic baseball player, as well as representations of salmon, birds, and deer.

# # #

Cal Abrams, who played for the Dodgers 1949–52 and later for the Reds, Pirates, Orioles, and White Sox through 1956, left his heart in Brooklyn. Upon his death on February 25, 1997, he was buried in Ft. Lauderdale, Florida, in his Dodger uniform—#8. Does this mean that Don Zimmer is not the last Brooklyn Dodger in uniform?

# # #

When Bob Feller's mother went to Comiskey Park on Mother's Day, May 7, 1939, to see him pitch, she was hit by a foul ball off the bat of Marv Owen. The impact broke her eyeglasses. Feller checked on her, then finished the game. Mrs. Feller was hospitalized.

# # #

The ashes of baseball writer Harold Seymour were scattered near first base at Cooperstown's Doubleday Field during ceremonies in June 1995.*

*See George Grella's "Harold Seymour (1910–92)—A Cooperstown Farewell" in SABR's National Pastime, #17, 1997, p. 128.

# # #

Mary Rose Wilcox paid dearly for her devotion to baseball, particularly for her view that Maricopa County, Arizona, ought to impose a quarter of a percent (.25 percent) increase in its sales tax. Wilcox, a county supervisor, voted for the tax increase to raise the funds needed to build the Bank One Ballpark in Phoenix, home of the Diamondbacks. In fact, the tax increase raised $238 million of the $354 million cost of the stadium.

But Larry Naman, who had a history of mental illness, disapproved of her vote and shot her in the pelvis. Naman was convicted of attempted murder in the first degree. Wilcox suffered no permanent injury and returned to work in a few weeks. Just before he was sentenced, Naman was given the opportunity to apologize to Wilcox. Said Naman: "I will say I'm sorry I shot you the day you stand before the court and admit what you did was an act of violence." The judge gave Naman 15 years in prison.

# # #

Charlie Grimm's ashes were scattered over Wrigley Field, where he had played for the Cubs (1925–36) and managed them (1932–38, 1944–49, 1960).

# # #

Shortly before he was to pitch for the New York Yankees on August 17, 1937, Lefty Gomez was called aside by manager Joe McCarthy, who handed Gomez a telegram informing him of the death of his mother. Gomez composed himself, threw a three-hitter against the Senators, then left the team to return to California for his mother's funeral.

# # #

Bob Pastor, a fan from Middlesex, New Jersey, was buried in his Mets tie.

# # #

Toots Shor's, on West 52nd Street, was the original sports bar. No bats and gloves on the wall, no games on TV—it was just a place where ballplayers and other athletes, as well as writers (including sportswriters), liked to go. They knew they would be treated right, and, if they wished, left alone. It was Joe DiMaggio's favorite spot in New York. Tom Henrich tells the story of Toots (true name Bernard; his wife went by "Baby") talking with Sir Alexander Fleming, who discovered penicillin in 1928. Shor suddenly broke off his conversation with Fleming when Mel Ott walked in. "I got to go," he explained. "Somebody important just walked in."

# # #

Allen Halley, a 26-year-old pitcher for the Duluth–Superior Dukes in the independent Northern League, died in his sleep after a seizure, mistaken by his roommates for a nightmare, on March 23, 1998, in Miami. Funds were raised in the community to return his body to his native St. Maarten, Dutch Antilles, where he was buried in his Dukes uniform on May 30.

# # #

Rogers Hornsby's mother died just before the 1926 World Series. The Cardinals player-manager decided not to attend her funeral, believing that his mother would have understood. The Cardinals won the Series 4–3 over the Yankees.

# # #

MR. HORNSBY, MEET MR. SUHR:

Gus Suhr of the Pirates had a consecutive game playing streak that began on September 11, 1931, and was at 822 games when he missed a game on June 5, 1937. What happened?

He went to his mother's funeral.

# # #

Tony LaRussa was in the Cardinals dugout the day after his mother died. Why?

The date was September 5, 1998, and LaRussa wanted to see Mark Mc-Gwire hit home run number 60 of 1998. He did.

# # #

Todd Jones and Brian Moehler slept at Tiger Stadium on Monday, September 27, 1999, after the final game at Tiger Stadium. Jones slept on the couch in the manager's office, while Moehler slept on a mattress in the clubhouse. The team had been scheduled to leave Detroit for Minneapolis after the closing ceremonies, but switched to an early Tuesday flight. Jones had planned to sleep at the stadium, but Moehler had not. He had moved out of his Detroit home, and his family was not with him. Both knew they had to be at the ballpark early Tuesday to leave for the airport so they decided to spend the night at the stadium.

# # #

Sammy Sosa played for the Cubs in Philadelphia on September 29, 1999, after being informed that his wife had been hospitalized in Chicago with a reaction to a prescription medicine. He not only played, he broke out of an 0-for-9 slump and became the first player ever to hit 62 home runs in consecutive seasons.

# # #

Paul O'Neill played in Game 4 of the 1999 World Series and helped the Yankees sweep the Braves on October 27, 1999–the day his father died.

# # #

Max Patkin, the "Clown Prince of Baseball," was still handing out his baseball cards from his hospital bed on October 30, 1999–the day before he died.

# # #

New York lawyer Gregory Messer–a devout Red Sox fan–and his wife, Elinor Molbegott, planned the reception for their son Steven's 1999 bar mitzvah with baseball in mind. Instead of having just sequentially numbered tables for the guests, tables were given the numbers of his son's favorite ballplayers, including "Table 8" for Carl Yastrzemski, and "Table 9" for Ted Williams.

# # #

Jack Webb's immortal character, Sgt. Joe Friday on *Dragnet*, carried shield #714–Webb's tribute to Babe Ruth's career home run total.

# # #

When John Pastore was promoted to detective on the New Rochelle, New York, police force, he asked for shield #15, in honor of his favorite ballplayer, Thurman Munson.

# # #

Frank Graddock went too far. He killed his wife, Margaret, in Queens, New York, on July 8, 1969, because she wanted to watch the soap opera *Dark Shadows* instead of the Mets game. (The Mets defeated the Cubs 4–3 that day with 3 runs in the ninth inning.)

# # #

MARRIED
AT HOME PLATE

I N 1938 MINOR LEAGUER ROBERT LUDWICK and his wife, Dorothy, were married before a crowd of 3,500 at home plate in Nashua, New Hampshire. They spent their honeymoon at the Waldorf–Astoria in New York City.

# # #

Charlie Montoyo, who went on to play four games for the 1993 Montreal Expos, was the shortstop for the El Paso Diablos of the Texas League (Brewers, AA) when he was married at home plate to Dana Espinosa on June 19, 1990, at the Cohen Center, the team's home. Nearly 4,000 fans watched the wedding, then saw the Diablos beat Midland, 12–2, for the first-half championship in the West Division. A picture of the happy couple appears in the April 1991 issue of *National Geographic*. They met in her hometown of Stockton, California, where she managed the souvenir shop at the home of the Stockton Ports (Brewers, Class A Advanced, California League). He played there in 1988.

As Dana told us:

"The families of the bride and groom as well as the players' wives sat in chairs on the field between home plate and the backstop. Both teams lined up with hats off outside their dugouts ... Because the field was new and not yet complete, there were no showers, and the team was forced to change in a trailer and shower at home. Charlie had to report to batting practice before the game and then go to a nearby ballpark employee's house to shower and change into a tuxedo prior to the ceremony. Following the ceremony, he rushed into the trailer and changed into his uniform to start the game at shortstop. He had two singles, scored once, and drove in a run."

# # #

On October 5, 1996, Chris Coste, catcher for the Fargo–Moorhead RedHawks of the independent Northern League was married at his team's home plate (in his hometown) to Marcia Gylten. They manage the team's gift shop at the stadium–"The Nest."

Invitations to the wedding were printed to look like tickets to the game. Although Coste dressed in a tuxedo for the photographer, his bride insisted that he change into his baseball uniform for the ceremony.

# # #

In an interview with the authors behind home plate at Yankee Stadium on July 2, 1998, Don Zimmer told us that his wedding was to have been a double ceremony. His roommate, Ed Roebuck (later Zimmer's Dodger and Senator teammate), was scheduled to join Zimmer in a double ceremony at the plate but for religious reasons decided upon a church ceremony instead. The Zimmers have been married for 48 years.

# # #

Catcher John Jarvis was married at home plate in Greensboro in 1989.

# # #

Mr. Taiki Yanagisawa and Ms. Tomie Masuda, both 26, were married at home plate at Tokyo's Korakuen Stadium before a Fighters' game on March 14, 1976, to celebrate the first use of artificial turf in a Japanese ballpark. Other couples were married there on March 13, 1977, and March 21, 1978.

# # #

Patty Kuca and Arnie Braunstein were married at a home plate in their hometown of Clarkstown, New York, on March 12, 1983–the 80th anniversary of an American League franchise being awarded to New York. The cantor who performed the ceremony did so wearing a New York Yankees cap.

# # #

George "Mercury" Myatt and Georgia Smith were married at home plate in Lane Field, home of the Class AA San Diego Padres of the Pacific Coast League, in an unusual ceremony involving three teams—the Padres, the Oakland Oaks, and the National City team on August 27, 1936.

Before a crowd of 10,000, Superior Court Judge Gordon Thompson performed the ceremony, uniting Myatt with Smith, a star pitcher for the National City girls' softball team. The couple walked under crossed bats, and just before the home-plate ceremony they were serenaded by a quartet consisting of Padres Berlyn Horne, Archie "Red" Campbell, Vince DiMaggio, and Lee Cook. (One of their selections was "Those Wedding Bells Are Breaking up That Old Gang of Mine.") The best man was Myatt's teammate Bobby Doerr.

Myatt played shortstop for the Padres in the game that followed the wedding, going 2-for-4, as the Padres beat the Oaks 3–2.

The happy couple honeymooned in San Francisco, as the team owner had promised to pay for the trip if they agreed to get married at home plate.

Myatt went on to play for the Giants and Senators, 1938–39, 1943–47, and managed the Phillies 1968–69.

# # #

Ontario (California) Orioles outfielder Leandro Garcia was married at home plate to Dorothy Riggins on August 24, 1947, between games of a doubleheader in Anaheim, then in the Sunset League.

Fans passed the hat and collected $105 for the happy couple. The groom went 2-for-4 in the first game and walked twice with a single in the second game. The teams split the twin bill, with the Orioles losing the first game, 3–5, then winning the second, 12–1.

# # #

Beverly Hanson and Bob Upton of the Richmond Roses (Ohio State League) were married at home plate between games of a doubleheader on June 24, 1947, in Richmond, Upton's hometown, before a crowd of 2,000. Upton then pitched and lost the second game to the Newark Browns, 11–6.

# # #

Former Oakland A Troy Neel and his fiance, Jasmine "J. J." McGowan, were married in August 1999 at Green Stadium in Kobe, Japan, before a game between the Orix Blue Waves, for whom Neel played first base, and the Fukuoka

Daiei Hawks. The best man was Neel's Blue Wave teammate, former Met, Astro, and Red Sox Chris Donnels. Neel wore his uniform, #99.

# # #

Micah Bowie (Braves, Cubs, 1999–) and his wife, Keeley, were married on the pitcher's mound in Durham, North Carolina, in August 1995.

# # #

Benny Agbayani was married at home plate in Norfolk, Virginia, before the Pacific Coast League/International League AAA All-Star Game on July 9, 1998. Although Agbayani was designated to represent Norfolk in the game, his July 6 call-up to the Mets made him ineligible to play. But when a home-plate wedding was suggested, Agbayani and his fiancee, Niela Guigui, agreed. He wore a Hawaiian shirt, while Niela wore a matching blue dress.

Adorned with leis, they walked under crossed bats held by the All Stars, and left the field in a white stretch limousine. As Mets broadcaster Hall of Famer Ralph Kiner pointed out, the Agbayanis, both Hawaiian, became perhaps the first couple from Hawaii to spend their honeymoon in Flushing, Queens, New York.

# # #

On June 22, 1987, Jeff Nelson (Mariners, Yankees, 1992–) was married to Collette Tomkins on the pitcher's mound at Sam Lynn Ballpark in Bakersfield, California, during his minor league career.

Thanks to Judy and Bill Nelson, Jeff's parents, for this item. The authors met them at the Hall of Fame Library in Cooperstown, July 18, 1998.

# # #

In a minor league promotion worthy of the late Bill Veeck, Boudreaux and Clotile, mascots of the New Orleans Zephyrs, were "married" at home plate before a game against the Memphis Redbirds on August 15, 1998.

# # #

They met in a Cubs chat room, and on Valentine's Day 1997, Stefan Watts proposed to Kathy Sue. They were married before a Mets game at Wrigley Field on August 20, 1998, wearing "Bride" and "Groom" baseball hats.

# # #

Gene Sunnen and Diane Sauvageot were married on May 22, 1993, at home plate at Codornices Park in Berkeley, California. Sunnen was president of the Society for American Baseball Research from 1986 to 1989. He was also comptroller of three leagues and served as general manager of the Watertown Pirates in the New York–Penn League.

Relatives of the bride were on the third-base side, and the groom's were on the first-base side. Gene's father tossed the first pitch to his niece in lieu of a flower girl. The guests sang the National Anthem before the ceremony, which was performed by Judge Joe Murphy, also a SABR member. Instead of walking down the aisle, Diane was escorted around the bases. (The third-base coach, a guest, waved them home.) Gene told us that he was reduced to tears when Judge Murphy presented the newlyweds with sacred soil from Dyersville, Iowa's "Field of Dreams."

# # #

On August 7, 1999, Tim Bottorff and Kerri Elberson were married on the steps of the library of the National Baseball Hall of Fame in Cooperstown, New York. Both were interns there.

# # #

Karl Rhodes and his wife were married at Hi Corbett Field in Tucson on September 1, 1992, before a game.

# # #

WHAT'S YOUR HOBBY?

——————

THE THREE MOST POPULAR HOBBIES of major leaguers are fishing, golf, and hunting. (In the case of Larry Parrish, boar hunting.) Many players list all three. Marshall Boze of the Brewers says his hobby is "life." Jason Kendall lists his hobby as "sleeping." Other hobbies of big leaguers are listed below.

WOULD YOU LIKE TO SEE MY COLLECTION?

Guns	Dizzy Trout
Baseball cards	Alan Mills, Kirk Rueter, Tom Pagnozzi, Gary Bennett, Steve Montgomery, Jeff D'Amico, Michael Potts, Brian Edmondson, Jarvis Brown, Mike Welch
Baseball memorabilia	Joe Kerrigan
Watches	Mark Loretta
Wine	Steve Carlton, umpire Terry Tata
Indian arrowheads	Steve Rogers
Miniature model trains	Rod Carew (not surprising for a guy born on a moving train!), Mike Schmidt
Stamps	Dave Leiper
Knives	Greg McMichael
Ticket stubs	Expos broadcaster Elliott Price

# # #

Training bird dogs	Wes Gardner
Radio-controlled cars	Andruw Jones
Radio-controlled model planes	John Vander Wal, Ozzie Virgil, Galen Cisco
Model shipbuilding	John Denny
Off-roading	Jason Giambi
Backgammon	Ozzie Smith, Charlie Hudson
Motocross racing	Jeff Kent
Drag racing	Rob Deer, John Roskos
Dominoes	Charlie Hudson
Wine tasting	Mark Loretta
Biking	Ricky Jordan
WWF	Jason Giambi
Mountain biking	Rusty Greer
Cricket	Graeme Lloyd (the pride of Geelong, Australia)
Rollerblading with his Great Dane	Chris Widger
Snowmobiling	Mark Grudzielanek
Deep-sea fishing	André Dawson
Watching rodeos	Mike Lansing
Knitting	Frank Oberlin
Cleaning cars	Wayne Gomes
Watching soap operas	Mike Jorgensen
Boxing	Brian Downing, Jon Zuber
Practical jokes	Larry Andersen
Antiques	Toby Harrah, Mike Ryan
Crossword puzzles	Albert Belle, Steve Scarsone, Steve Rogers, Paul Kilgus, Mike Jorgensen, Larry Andersen
Reading about sports	Frank Cimorelli
Reading David Morrell novels	Brad Pennington
Reading Stephen King novels	Mike Mussina
Reading the Bible	Brian Harper
Studying Biblical prophecies	Umpire Durwood Merrill
Writing novels and screenplays	Shane Rawley
Woodworking	Nick Leyva, Jeff Fassero, Vern Law, Vance Law
Listening to reggae music	Randall Simon
Composing Christian music	Kent Bottenfield
Cartooning	Cal Abrams, Bob Tewksbury

Badminton	Rheal Cormier
Rock climbing	Mike Duvall
Two-way radios	Don Mattingly
Chess	Luis Andujar
Word puzzles	Ozzie Smith
Military board games	Curt Schilling
Playing the piano	Kent Bottenfield, Steve Montgomery
Playing the violin	Mark Loretta
Cooking	Dean Palmer
Being an Elvis fan	Cregg Jeffries
Karate	David Justice
Doing impressions	Mark Eichhorn (He does John Wayne, the Cowardly Lion and the Wicked Witch of the West from *The Wizard of Oz*, Julio Iglesias, Popeye, and Willie Nelson.)
Tae kwan do	Carlos Alfonso
Visiting zoos	Joel Bennett
The stock market	Steve Montgomery
Surfing	Jaret Wright
Bow hunting	Travis Fryman, Jim Eisenreich, Ryan Klesko, Mel Stottlemyre, Sr., Mel Stottlemyre, Jr., Todd Stottlemyre
Archery	Danny Patterson, Ken Forsch
Playing the drums	Jerry Spradlin, Paul O'Neill
Going to the beach	Bobby Estalella
Art	Omar Vizquel, Steve Falteisek, Andres Galarraga, Don Carman, Kevin Gross, Curt Flood, Gene Locklear
Drawing	Marquis Grissom
Arts and crafts	George Lombard
Magic	Doug Bochtler, former Red Sox coach Wendell Kim
Ice fishing	umpire Tim Tschida
Making picture frames	Jimmy Reese
Logging	Richard Rodas
Splitting wood	umpire Terry Tata
Playing street hockey	John Habyan

Accompanying police on patrol	Ryan Klesko
Cutting hair	Doug Bochtler, Billy Bean
Waterskiing	Pat Hentgen
Watching David Letterman and bungee jumping (presumably not at the same time)	Bob Scanlan
Watching reruns of *The Andy Griffith Show*	Steve Sparks, umpires Terry Craft and Chuck Meriwether
Dancing	Al Reyes, Antonio Osuna, Barry Bonds, Ben Rivera, Wayne Gomes, Derrin Ebert, Bruce Chen
Whistling show tunes	Steve Sparks
Singing	Chan Ho Park, José Lind, Lamar Johnson, Deacon Jones
Home restoration	William Vanlandingham

# # #

Although it is not a hobby, Bert Roberge (Astros, White Sox, Expos, 1979, 1980, 1982, 1984–1986) is an expert on bean and alfalfa sprouts.

We hope Chris Aguila makes it to the major leagues. The minor leaguer, who spent 1999 with the Kane County Cougars in the Marlins chain (Class A Midwest League), performs the Samoan Fire Knife Dance with knives he made himself. Aguila, who is of Filipino and Polynesian heritage, is also a member of a Polynesian dance group.

# # #

FIRST AND LAST

FIRST OF ALL

In his major league debut on Opening Day in Cincinnati, April 13, 1954, Hank Aaron went 0–5. That day marked another important first for baseball. What happened?

This was the first game in which outfielders were required to bring their gloves into the dugout between innings, rather than follow the previous baseball tradition of leaving them in the field.

\# \# \#

Who was the first man to represent four different teams in All-Star Games?

Rich Gossage. White Sox (1975), Pirates (1977), Yankees (1978), Padres (1984).

\# \# \#

Who was the first man to be traded just after he hit 50 home runs in a single season?

Greg Vaughn of the San Diego Padres. He hit exactly 50 homers in the Padres' 1998 pennant-winning season but was traded on February 2, 1999, to the Cincinnati Reds for Reggie Sanders and two minor leaguers.

# # #

Who was the first modern player to have at least 200 hits for six straight seasons?

Wade Boggs, 1983–1989.

# # #

Who was the first player to hit a home run in his first minor league at bat and in his first major league at bat?

Will Clark. On June 21, 1985, batting for the Fresno Giants against the Visalia Oaks of the Class A California League, he homered. Less than a year later, he homered in his first major league at bat as a San Francisco Giant, off Nolan Ryan of the Astros on April 8, 1986.

# # #

When was the first time in the 20th century that pitchers with identical names—first and last—faced each other?

On May 11, 1999, Bobby Jones of the Colorado Rockies beat Bobby Jones of the New York Mets in Denver, 8–5. (They are not related.) They became Mets teammates in 2000.

# # #

Who was the first Yankee to pinch-hit two grand slams in the same season?

Darryl Strawberry. On May 2, 1998, batting for Joe Girardi, Strawberry blasted one into the seats with three men aboard.

Then, on August 4, 1998, in the top of the ninth, with the Yankees down by four runs, Strawberry came to bat with the bases loaded—again batting for Joe Girardi—and homered off Oakland reliever Billy Taylor to tie the game. The Yankees went on to win, 10–5.

# # #

What year was the first with two Canadian All Stars?

The 1997 game, on July 8, at Cleveland's Jacobs Field. They were Larry Walker of the National League Colorado Rockies (a native of Maple Ridge, British Columbia) and the American League California Angels' Jason Dickson (from London, Ontario). Dickson did not get into the game.

That was also the game in which Cleveland catcher Sandy Alomar, Jr., became the first man to be named the All-Star Game's Most Valuable Player in his home park. Alomar's two-run homer in the seventh inning propelled the American League to a 3–1 win.

# # #

Who was the first black player signed by the New York Yankees?

Bob Thurman, in 1949. The first black to *play* for the Yankees was Elston Howard, who made his major league debut on April 14, 1955. Howard was a nine-time All Star and was the American League's Most Valuable Player in 1963. Thurman made the majors in 1955–59 with the Reds.

# # #

When was the first major league game broadcast in five languages?

July 5, 1994, Dodgers vs. Expos in Los Angeles. The game was broadcast on the radio in English (Rick Monday), Spanish (Broadcast Wing Hall of Famer Jaime Jarrin), French (Jacques Doucet), Korean (Richard Choi), and Mandarin (Steven Cheng).

# # #

What was the first expansion team to rise in the standings in each of its second, third, fourth, and fifth years in the major leagues?

The Florida Marlins of the National League East. They went from sixth place their first year, 1993, to fifth, fourth, third, and second in 1997, when they rode their wild card ticket all the way to the World Championship. In 1998 they were last again.

# # #

Who was the first veteran of American baseball to be elected captain of a Japanese team?

Julio Franco. After a 15-year career with the Phillies, Indians, Rangers, White Sox, and Brewers, he was named captain of the Chiba Lotte Marines in the Pacific League in 1998.

# # #

Who made the first error in an All-Star Game?

First baseman Lou Gehrig, in the fifth inning of the first All-Star Game, held in Chicago's Comiskey Park on July 6, 1933. Gehrig dropped a foul ball.

# # #

Who was the first Jewish All-Star?

Charles "Buddy" Myer, Senators, American League, 1935.

# # #

Who was the first player on a first-year expansion team to hit 20 homers and steal 20 bases?

Devon White of the 1998 Arizona Diamondbacks—22 homers, 22 stolen bases.

# # #

Who had the first certified gold record?

Hint: His number was retired.

Gene Autry, sole owner of the California Angels from their first year in 1961 until 1996, when he sold 25 percent of the team to the Disney Corporation. (Disney bought the rest from Autry's heirs on March 31, 1999.) The Anaheim Angels retired #26 for Autry.

The record was "That Silver-Haired Daddy of Mine." Autry sold over 100,000,000 records—a record for a team owner that will probably stand forever.

# # #

What was the first all "Q" battery?

On April 13, 1980, Dan Quisenberry, pitching in relief, was caught by Jamie Quirk of the Royals.

# # #

When was the first time that Latin American managers faced each other in the major leagues?

April 5, 1993, when the Cincinnati Reds, managed by Tony Peréz (born in Camaguey, Cuba), faced the Montreal Expos, managed by Felipé Alou (from Haina, Dominican Republic).

The Reds won 5–1, before a crowd of 55,456—the largest regular-season crowd at Riverfront Stadium until that time.

# # #

Who was the first White Sox player to hit 20 home runs and steal 20 bases in the same season?

Tommie Agee. In 1966 the Magnolia, Alabama, native smacked 22 homers and stole 44 bases.

# # #

Who was the first man to hit 20 home runs and steal 50 bases in consecutive seasons?

César Cedeño, Houston Astros, 1972—22 home runs, 55 stolen bases; 1973—25 homers, 56 stolen bases.

# # #

Who were the first three Jewish major league teammates?

Sandy Koufax, Larry Sherry, and his brother Norm Sherry—teammates on the Los Angeles Dodgers, 1959–62.

# # #

Who was the first player on a losing team to be named Most Valuable Player in a National League Championship Series?

Mike Scott, 1986 Astros. Although the Mets beat the Astros 4 games to 2, Scott won both of the Astros' games with an ERA of just 0.50 in 18 innings.

# # #

When was the first game in which both starting pitchers were born in the 1970s?

In Oakland on September 11, 1991, in his major league debut, Todd Van Poppel of the Oakland A's, born December 9, 1971, faced Wilson Alvarez of the White Sox, born March 24, 1970. The A's won 6–5, but neither starter got a decision.

# # #

Which was the first major league stadium with an organ?

Chicago's Wrigley Field, where Roy Nelson first played it before the April 26, 1941, game.

# # #

Who was the first man to play every inning in seven consecutive All-Star games?

Joe DiMaggio, 1936–42.

# # #

Who were the only starting brother battery in the history of the All-Star Game?

The Coopers—Mort the pitcher, and Walker, his catcher, in 1942.

# # #

What was the first date on which all big league games were played at night?

August 9, 1946.

# # #

Who was the first president of the Major League Baseball Players Association?

Bob Feller, elected December 2, 1953.

# # #

Who was the first outfielder to play a full 162-game schedule with no errors?

Rocky Colavito, Cleveland Indians, 1965—274 chances, no errors.

# # #

Which was the first team to hit more than 10,000 home runs?

The New York Yankees. Jack Clark hit number 10,001 on April 20, 1988.

# # #

On September 6, 1963, the Cleveland Indians played the Senators in Washington. Besides the fact that the Senators won, what was memorable about this game?

It was baseball's 100,000th game. Don Zimmer was the Senators third baseman.

# # #

Who was the first Colombian to play in an All-Star Game?

Edgar Renteria, Florida Marlins, 1998. On November 4, 1997, in recognition of achievements in the 1997 World Series for the Marlins, Renteria was presented with the "San Carlos Cross of the Order of the Great Knight," Colombia's highest civilian honor.

# # #

Who was the first Columbian to play in an All-Star Game?

Lou Gehrig, who attended but was not graduated from Columbia University—in the first All-Star Game, July 6, 1933.

# # #

The man who threw out the ceremonial first ball at the Astros' last home opener in the Astrodome, on April 6, 1999, also threw out one of the first balls at the Astrodome's first home opener. Who is he, and where had he been all those years?

When the Astrodome opened on April 12, 1965, 23 astronauts—who lived and trained in Houston—threw out the first pitches. Neil Armstrong, the first man on the moon, made a rare public appearance to repeat the throw at the Astrodome's last home opener. He was escorted onto the field by original Astros Jimmy Wynn ("the Toy Cannon") and Bob Aspromonte, as 70 current astronauts stood on both baselines.

# # #

Who was the first man to hit 25 home runs in a season for five different teams?

Bobby Bonds.

San Francisco Giants 1969—32, 1970—26, 1971—33, 1972—26, 1973—39
New York Yankees 1975—32
California Angels 1977—37
Texas Rangers 1978—29 (He hit two for the White Sox that year, too.)
Cleveland Indians 1979—25

# # #

This unusual display of power has since been accomplished by what two others?

Jack Clark
Giants 1978—25, 1979—26, 1982—27
Cardinals 1987—35
Yankees 1988—27
Padres 1989—26, 1990—25
Red Sox 1991—28

José Canseco
A's 1986—33, 1987—31, 1990—37, 1991—44
Rangers 1994—31
Red Sox 1996—28
Blue Jays 1998—46
Devil Rays 1999—34

# # #

Who were the first major leaguers to earn these annual salaries? Choose your answers from the names at right.

a. $1,000,000
b. $2,000,000
c. $3,000,000
d. $4,000,000
e. $5,000,000
f. $7,000,000
g. $8,000,000
h. $11,000,000
i. $12,000,000
j. $13,000,000
k. $15,000,000

1. Mike Piazza
2. Pedro Martinez
3. Nolan Ryan
4. Ken Griffey, Jr.
5. José Canseco
6. Albert Belle
7. Kevin Brown
8. Roger Clemens
9. Kirby Puckett
10. Ryne Sandberg
11. George Foster

ANSWERS: (with year contract was signed and team)

a. Nolan Ryan, 1979 Astros; b. George Foster, 1982 Mets; c. Kirby Puckett, 1989 Twins; d. José Canseco, 1990 Athletics; e. Roger Clemens, 1991 Red Sox; f. Ryne Sandberg, 1992 Cubs; g. Ken Griffey, Jr., 1996 Mariners; h. Albert Belle, 1996 White Sox; i. Pedro Martinez, 1997 Red Sox; j. Mike Piazza, 1998 Mets; k. Kevin Brown, 1998 Dodgers.

# # #

Babe Ruth was the first player to hit 50 home runs in a single season and then have a multiple home-run game in the World Series the same year. Ruth did this in 1928 when he hit 54 home runs for the New York Yankees, plus 3 homers in Game 4 of the Series, which the Yankees won 4–0 over the Cardinals. Who was the second man to accomplish this feat?

Greg Vaughn did it 70 years later for the 1998 San Diego Padres. He finished the season with exactly 50 homers and hit 2 homers in Game 1 of the World Series. No matter—the Yankees swept the Padres 4–0 in the Series.

# # #

Who was the first New York Met to start an All-Star Game?

Ron Hunt, at Shea Stadium in 1964. He was the National League's starting second baseman.

# # #

The first time Yankee teammates had 200 hits in a single season was in 1937, when Lou Gehrig had 200 and Joe DiMaggio had 215. Name the next two Yankees to have 200 hits in the same season.

Derek Jeter and Bernie Williams, 1999. Jeter finished the season with 219, Williams with 202.

# # #

Who was the first Oriole to have 100 walks and 100 RBIs in the same season?

Albert Belle, 1999—101 walks, 117 RBIs.

# # #

On September 24, 1940, four Red Sox sluggers hit home runs in one inning—a first for the American League. Three became Hall of Famers—Ted Williams, Joe Cronin, and Jimmie Foxx. Who was the fourth?

Jim Tabor.

# # #

Who was the first man honored as National League "Player of the Month" in three consecutive months?

Mark McGwire, September 1997 and April and May 1998.

LAST OF ALL

"I was the last active pitcher to have surrendered a home run to Mickey Mantle. Who am I?"

Tommy John. The last time Mantle homered off John was on May 8, 1964, when John was pitching for the White Sox.

John's excellent career (1963–89) spanned seven presidencies—John Kennedy, Lyndon Johnson, Richard Nixon, Gerald Ford, Jimmy Carter, Ronald Reagan, and George Bush.

# # #

On June 14, 1949, Ken Keltner of the Cleveland Indians did something that no major leaguer has done since in a regular season game. What did he do?

He was the last "courtesy runner" used in a regular season game. Player-manager Lou Boudreau was hit on the elbow by a pitch and had to take himself out of the game. Keltner, who had scored earlier in the inning, ran for Boudreau and scored again. Next inning, Boudreau had sufficiently recovered to go back into the game.

Thanks to David Smith and Retrosheet *for this look back.*

# # #

Who was the last surviving player of the first All-Star Game, played on July 6, 1933?

Hall of Famer Rick Ferrell. He died on July 27, 1995.

# # #

Who was the last man to bat at Ebbets Field?

Dee Fondy. His Pirates beat the Dodgers on September 24, 1957—the last major league game in Brooklyn.

# # #

This man—a nonpitcher—has not made an error since May 25, 1990, when he played left field for the Angels, although he has played every season since then. Who is he?

Theodore "Chili" Davis. Although he has played 25 games in the field since 1990, he has been primarily a designated hitter. He retired in 1999 after two consecutive World Championships with the New York Yankees.

# # #

"I started the very last game in Brooklyn Dodgers history. I also started the very first game in New York Mets history. Who am I?"

Roger Craig. On September 29, 1957, he pitched Brooklyn to a 2–1 loss to the Phillies. On April 11, 1962, he started for the Mets in their inaugural game against the Cardinals. To his right was third baseman Don Zimmer.

# # #

Who was the first player to bat on television?

Billy Werber, the Reds third baseman who led off against the Dodgers at Ebbets Field on August 26, 1939, in the first televised big league game, which was broadcast by Red Barber.

# # #

When was the first time pitchers with palindromic last names faced each other?

August 3, 1994, when Robb Nen of the Marlins faced Dave Otto of the Cubs. The Marlins won 9–8 in Chicago.

# # #

Who was the first player selected in an expansion draft?

Eli Grba, selected by the Los Angeles Angels in 1960.

# # #

Which was the last major league team to begin playing on Sunday?

The Pittsburgh Pirates, starting in 1934. (So if you asked "Did Honus Wagner ever lose a home game on a Sunday?", the answer would be "No." He retired in 1917.)

# # #

Who was the last batter to face Sandy Koufax?

Davey Johnson. Koufax's last game was October 6, 1966, Game 2 of the 1966 World Series, when his Dodgers faced Johnson's Baltimore Orioles. Baltimore swept the Series 4–0.

ONLY WHO?

———

MAJOR LEAGUE BASEBALL has been played in New York City since 1883. New York is the only city which has been home to four modern big league teams—the Giants, Dodgers, Yankees, and Mets. Thousands of major league games have been played in New York. On May 29, 2000, in a game at Yankee Stadium, Randy Velarde of the Oakland A's did something nobody had ever done before in New York. What did he do?

Second baseman Velarde—a former Yankee—turned an unassisted triple play—only the 11th in history. With no outs in the bottom of the sixth inning, Jorge Posada was on first and Tino Martinez was on second. Shane Spencer hit a liner directly to Velarde (1 out), who tagged Posada coming from first (2 outs), then stepped on second base to get Martinez (3 outs). It was the second unassisted triple play ever turned by a second baseman. (The first was turned by Mickey Morandini of the Phillies on September 20, 1992.) But the Yankees won, 4–1.

# # #

QUESTIONS TO BE READ TWICE DEPT.:

Who is the only man to make his major league debut in the uniform of a team he never played for?

Kyle Peterson. The pitcher's major league debut came on July 19, 1999, with the Brewers in Milwaukee in a game against the White Sox. That was "Turn Back the Clock Night," so he broke in wearing the Brewers' uniform of 1969—when the Brewers were the Seattle Pilots.

# # #

Who is the only man to pinch run and pinch hit in the same game?

On June 8, 1923, third baseman Homer Ezzell of the St. Louis Browns was on first base in a game against the Philadelphia A's when he needed to use the bathroom. With the permission of A's manager Connie Mack, Pat Collins pinch-ran for Ezzell as a "courtesy runner." Ezzell later returned to the game, and Collins was used as a pinch hitter for pitcher Ray Kolp. The A's won, 6–5.

# # #

Who is the only major league manager to appear on CBS's long-running news/interview program *Face the Nation?*

Frank Robinson, the first African American to manage in the major leagues, on October 13, 1974—just 10 days after the announcement that Robinson would manage the Cleveland Indians in 1975.

# # #

A number of ballplayers have played in the Little League World Series and the Major League World Series. Likewise, quite a few have appeared in the College World Series and the Major League World Series.

But only one man has played in the Little League World Series, the College World Series, and the Major League World Series. Who is he?

Ed Vosberg. In 1973 he played in the Little League World Series for Tucson of the Cactus Little League, the U.S. East team, which lost in an early round. In 1980 he was with the University of Arizona, which beat Hawaii to win the College World Series. And in 1997 he was with the World Champion Florida Marlins, who beat the Cleveland Indians 4–3 in the World Series.

# # #

Only one man has hit a home run in an All-Star Game without a single home run during the regular season of the same year. Who is he?

Mickey Owen. He homered as a pinch hitter in the eighth inning of the July 6, 1942, game at the Polo Grounds.

# # #

Who is the only man to (1) own a World Series ring and (2) be named *Billboard* magazine's "Man of the Year?"

H. Wayne Huizenga, owner of the World Champion 1997 Florida Marlins. For his contributions to the video industry, as the owner of Blockbuster Video, he was *Billboard*'s "Man of the Year" in 1990.

# # #

Who is the only major leaguer who received diplomas from two high schools?

Brian McRae. During the fall, he played football for Blue Springs, Missouri, High School. In the spring, he was off to Manatee High in Bradenton, Florida, for baseball.

# # #

Who is the only man to sing the National Anthem before a major league game, then swat two home runs in the game?

Lamar Johnson of the Chicago White Sox, at Comiskey Park on June 19, 1977, against Oakland.

# # #

Who is the only man to go from playing major league baseball for a living to playing the violin for a living?

Eddie "Fiddler" Basinski, Dodgers, Pirates, 1944–45, 1947. In 1945 Basinski's Dodger teammate Frenchy Bordagaray snatched his violin away just long enough to play "Pop Goes the Weasel." In 1948 while playing second base for the Indianapolis Indians of the American Association, Basinski was the first violinist for the Buffalo Symphony.

# # #

Many fans recall nonpitchers who pitched: Stan Musial (1952), Ted Williams (1940), and Rocky Colavito (1958 and 1968), for example. But who is the only nonpitcher to strike out the side?

Mark Whiten, who pitched for the Indians on July 31, 1998, in Oakland. He struck out three Oakland batters (although not consecutively): Mike Blowers, Miguel Tejada, and Mike Neill, but the A's won, 12–2.

# # #

Only one big leaguer had at least 3,000 hits, 600 doubles, 300 home runs, 200 stolen bases, and 100 triples. Who is he?

George Brett—3,154 hits, 665 doubles, 317 home runs, 201 stolen bases, 137 triples.

# # #

Only one Los Angeles Dodger has hit at least 30 home runs and driven in at least 100 runs in a season three years in a row. Who is he?

Eric Karros, 1995–97.

# # #

Only one major leaguer has had at least 15 home runs in a single season without at least twice as many RBIs as home runs. Who is he?

Kevin Maas of the 1990 New York Yankees. He hit 21 home runs, but drove in just 41 runs.

# # #

Rod Carew is the only player (and hence the only Hall of Famer) born on a moving train. Can you name the only future Hall of Famer born in the back seat of a 1956 Chevy?

Rickey Henderson, born December 25, 1958, in Chicago, Illinois. His father was driving his mother to the hospital. Unlike Rickey, he couldn't go any faster.

# # #

Who is the only man to win the American League batting crown without leading the league until the very last day of the season?

George Henry "Snuffy" Stirnweiss, New York Yankees, 1945. On September 30, the day after "Snuffy Stirnweiss Day" at Yankee Stadium, Stirnweiss went 3-for-5 in a 12–2 Yankee win over the Red Sox to clinch the title. Stirnweiss's average was .3085443, rounded to .309, just .000866 better than Tony Cuccinello's .3084577.

# # #

Who is the only player involved in the baseball strikes of 1972, 1981, and 1994?

Rich "Goose" Gossage. In 1972 he was with the White Sox. By 1981 he had moved on to the Yankees, and in 1994 he was a Mariner. Gossage retired after the 1994 season with 310 saves, having appeared in 1,002 games, averaging 45.5 games per season for 22 seasons.

# # #

Who is the only man to throw out the ceremonial first pitch in the very first home opener for two different teams in the same city?

Senator Henry "Scoop" Jackson (D-Wash.) He threw out the first pitch at Sicks Stadium for the first Seattle Pilots home game on April 11, 1969, and on April 6, 1977, for the Mariners' first home game at the Kingdome.

# # #

Who is the only man to hit a home run in the All-Star Game and the World Series off the same pitcher in the same year?

Frank Robinson of the Orioles homered off Dock Ellis of the Pirates in the 1971 All-Star Game in Detroit, as the American League won, 6–4. Three months later, on October 9, in Game 1 of the Series, he homered off Ellis again, as Baltimore won the game, 5–3. But the Pirates won the Series, 4–3.

# # #

Who is the only pitcher to give up a home run to Tommie Aaron, but not to Hank Aaron?

Jack Hamilton. Tommie Aaron, with the Milwaukee Braves, homered off Hamilton, then with the Phillies, on April 26, 1962—one of Tommie's 13 career home runs.

# # #

"I am the only man in history to play 20 years or more for the same major league team, and not make it to the Hall of Fame. Who am I?"

Mel Harder, Cleveland Indians, 1928–47. Although he didn't make the Hall, the Indians retired his #18.

# # #

Who is the only Caveman in the major leagues?

Shane Andrews, a graduate of Carlsbad, New Mexico, High School, whose athletic teams are called the Cavemen in honor of nearby Carlsbad Caverns.

# # #

Eleven players have homered in their first All-Star at bat, but only one is a Hall of Famer. Name him.

Johnny Bench, July 23, 1969, in Washington, D.C.

# # #

Who is the only man to be a teammate of both Mickey Mantle and Don Mattingly?

Bobby Murcer. His career with the Yankees started in 1965, and he teamed with Mantle through 1968. After stops with the Giants and Cubs, Murcer returned to the Yankees in 1979 and was Mattingly's teammate 1982–1983.

# # #

Who is the only pitcher to win 300 games but never strike out 200 batters in one season?

Warren Spahn. He won 363 games and struck out 2,583 batters, but never more than 191 in a season, a career high he reached in 1950.

# # #

Who is the only pitcher to throw no-hitters in his first two full seasons in the big leagues?

Steve Busby. The first was on April 27, 1973, for the Royals, against the Tigers. He followed it on June 19, 1974, with a victory over the Brewers. Busby finished his career with a record of 70–54.

# # #

Who is the only man to play for the original Washington Senators, the Minnesota Twins (which the original Senators became), the second Senators, and the Texas Rangers (which the second Senators became)?

Don Mincher. Senators (I) 1960; Twins 1961–66; Senators (II) 1971; Rangers 1972.

TRICK QUESTION DEPT.:

Who is the only Hall of Famer buried at Graceland?

William Hulbert, second president of the National League. He died on April 10, 1882, and was buried at Graceland Cemetery in Chicago, Illinois.

# # #

Who is the only man to get his 3,000th hit in his hometown?

Al Kaline. A Detroit Tiger throughout his career, his 3,000th hit came on September 24, 1974, in his hometown of Baltimore, off Dave McNally.

# # #

Who is the only woman married to a big leaguer who has appeared as a Hallmark Christmas ornament?

Mrs. Joseph Paul DiMaggio—Marilyn Monroe.

Ballplayers who have appeared as ornaments in Hallmark's "At the Ballpark" series are Nolan Ryan (1996), Hank Aaron (1997), and Cal Ripken, Jr. (1998). The "Baseball Heroes" series has included Babe Ruth (1994), Lou Gehrig (1995), Satchel Paige (1996), and Jackie Robinson (1997). Mark McGwire was featured in a 2000 ornament.

# # #

Who is the only man married during a 19th-century World Series named after his bride?

Hint: He's a Hall of Famer.

John Montgomery Ward. He was married to Broadway star Helen Dauvray (née Gibson) on October 12, 1887, during the World Series between the Detroit Wolverines of the National League and the St. Louis Browns of the American Association. The winner of three Series in a row would retire the Dauvray Cup.

Thanks to Dave Stevens, author of the definitive biography of Ward, Baseball's Radical for All Seasons.

# # #

The Seattle Pilots existed for only one year—1969—before moving to Milwaukee to become the Brewers. Who was the only Seattle Pilot All-Star?

Mike Hegan.

# # #

Who is the only professional ballplayer to homer for the cycle?

Tyrone Horne, an outfielder with the Arkansas Travelers, the Cardinals affiliate in the AA Texas League, hit four homers on July 27, 1998—a two-run shot in the first inning, a grand slam in the second, a solo in the fifth, and a three-run blast in the sixth. He finished the game with 10 RBIs, as his team beat the San Antonio Dodgers, 13–4.

# # #

Who is the only big leaguer to play on the Senior PGA Tour?

Hint: He's a Hall of Famer.
Johnny Bench. Ken "Hawk" Harrelson played on the PCA tour.

Thanks to Ben Lyons for this item.

# # #

In 1998, Ken Griffey, Jr., accomplished a feat that no one in baseball history ever had. What did he do?

He became the third man that season to reach the 50-home run mark. This mark was made possible by Mark McGwire's 70 and Sammy Sosa's 66 home runs. Griffey's 56 homers in 1998, like the 56 he hit the previous year, went virtually unnoticed in the avalanche of publicity for McGwire and Sosa.

# # #

Who is the only man to lead the league with the most home runs and fewest strikeouts in the same season?

Tommy Holmes, Boston Braves, 1945. He hit 28 home runs, while hitting .352, striking out only nine times. Think the depletion of the major leagues' ranks due to World War II had anything to do with his power? He hit only 88 homers during his entire career, and the only other time he had more than 10 was in 1944, when he had 13.

# # #

THIS IS THE ONLY TRIVIA QUESTION EVER TO INCLUDE THE NAME JOHNNY GORSICA.

Who is the only pitcher to give up a pinch-hit grand slam homer and to hit one too?

Hint: He's a Hall of Famer.

Early Wynn.

On May 28, 1961, when he was with the White Sox, Wynn gave up the big blast to Bob Cerv of the Yankees.

Wynn's own pinch-hit grand slam came on September 15, 1946, when he was with the Senators, off Johnny Gorsica of the Tigers.

# # #

Only one Mets pitcher had a winning record in 1962, the club's first season, when it finished with a 40–120 record, just 60½ games out of first place. Who was he?

Ken MacKenzie. He was 5–4.

# # #

"I am the only man who played in the final World Series games of both the New York Giants and the Brooklyn Dodgers. Who am I?"

Dale Mitchell.

He was with the Indians in 1954, when they lost to the Giants, and with the 1956 Dodgers, who lost to the Yankees.

# # #

Who is the only player to homer in his last regular-season at bat, and in his final World Series at bat?

Joe Rudi. On October 3, 1982, in the A's final inning of the season, he homered off Dave Frost to help the A's beat the Royals, 6–3. His final World Series at bat was against the Dodgers' Mike Marshall in the seventh inning of Game 7 on October 17, 1974, as the A's beat the Dodgers to win the Series, 4–1.

# # #

Who is the only Vice President of the United States who is a Hall of Famer?

Dan Quayle, a member of the Little League Hall of Fame in Williamsport, Pennsylvania. The glove he used in the Hoosier Little League in Huntington, Indiana, is on exhibit at the Peter J. McGovern Little League Museum's Hall of Excellence.

# # #

Only one man belongs to this 2,000 club: 2,000 hits, 2,000 walks, 2,000 RBIs, and 2,000 runs. Who is he?

Babe Ruth—2,873 hits, 2,056 walks, 2,213 RBIs, and 2,174 runs.

# # #

Who is the only man to have 200 hits in a season for three different teams?

Rogers Hornsby. He did it with the Cardinals in 1920 (218), 1921 (235), 1922 (250), 1924 (227), and 1925 (203), with the Giants in 1927 (205), and with the Cubs in 1929 (229).

# # #

On July 4, 1999, José Canseco reached a milestone that no other big leaguer had ever reached before. What did he do?

He hit his 30th homer of the season for the Tampa Bay Devil Rays. Canseco became the only player to hit 30 home runs in a single season for four different teams. The other three teams were the Oakland A's in 1986 (33), 1987 (31), 1988 (42), 1990 (37), and 1991 (44), the Texas Rangers in 1994 (31), and the Toronto Blue Jays in 1998 (46).

# # #

Who is the only man to drive in over 1,000 runs in his career while never driving in as many as 75 in a single season?

Rickey Henderson. RBI number 1,000 came on July 25, 1999. A leadoff batter for virtually his entire career, Henderson never drove in more than 74 runs, a number he reached in 1986 with the Yankees. Through 2000, Henderson has driven in 1,052 runs.

# # #

Who is the only man to score fewer than 70 runs in a season in which he had 200 hits?

George Sisler, 1929 Boston Braves—205 hits, 67 runs scored.

# # #

Who is the only man to be a teammate of both Ty Cobb and Babe Ruth in the same season?

Jack Coffey. He played with the 1909 Boston Braves, then was out of major league baseball until 1918, when he returned with the Tigers, where he teamed with Cobb, and later the Red Sox, where he and Ruth were teammates.

# # #

Who was the only Cy Young Award winner to be thrown out of a game he was not in and in which he could not have played anyway?

Jack McDowell, winner of the award in 1993, when he was with the White Sox. On May 9, 1999, home plate umpire John Shulock tossed McDowell from the game between the Angels and the Red Sox for arguing a call. McDowell was sitting on the bench in the Angels dugout. McDowell was ineligible for the game, as he was on the disabled list.

# # #

Who is the only pitcher to win an All-Star Game and a World Series game in the same stadium in the same year?

Sandy Koufax. He won the All-Star Game for the National League in Minnesota on July 13, 1965, then helped the Dodgers beat the Twins in Game 7 of the World Series.

# # #

Who is the only man to have 20 pinch hits in a season twice?

Forrest "Smokey" Burgess, of the White Sox. In 1965 he had 20 pinch hits and had 21 more the next year.

# # #

Who is the only player to have four hits in an All-Star Game and four hits in a World Series game?

Joe "Ducky Wucky" Medwick. He had four hits for the National League in the 1937 midseason classic (which the American League won, 8–3), to go with his four hits in Game 1 of the 1934 World Series for the Cardinals, who beat the Tigers 4 games to 3.

# # #

Who is the only Oscar®-winning actor to play two actual major leaguers in well-known films?

Burt Lancaster. He won the Academy Award® for best performance in a leading role for *Elmer Gantry* in 1960. In 1951 he had the title role in *Jim Thorpe, All-American*. In *Field of Dreams,* Lancaster played Moonlight Graham.

# # #

Who is the only man to hit .300 with 10 triples and 20 homers for four years in a row?

Lou Gehrig, 1927–31.

# # #

No one has yet played for all five California teams—the San Francisco Giants, Los Angeles Dodgers, Oakland A's, Anaheim Angels, and San Diego Padres. Name the one man to have played for four.

Jay Johnstone. Angels (1966–70), A's (1973), Padres (1979), and Dodgers (1981–82, 1985).

# # #

Who was the only man present when five different players hit four home runs in a single game?

Pitcher Ernie Johnson. He was with the Milwaukee Braves when Gil Hodges of the Brooklyn Dodgers hit four home runs on August 31, 1950.

Johnson was a Milwaukee Brave when teammate Joe Adcock did it on July 31, 1954.

While pitching for the Baltimore Orioles on June 10, 1959, Johnson gave up one of Rocky Colavito's four homers.

He was a public relations executive with the Milwaukee Braves when Willie Mays of the Giants blasted four home runs on April 30, 1961.

Finally, Johnson was a Braves announcer when Bob Horner connected for four round-trippers on July 6, 1986.

# # #

Who is the only man to play for both teams in one professional game?

Dale Holman. On June 30, 1986, he hit a double for the Syracuse Chiefs of the AAA International League before the game was suspended by rain. By the time the game was resumed on August 16, he was with the Richmond Braves, the opposing team.

# # #

Ouch!

Quick—which names come to mind when you hear the phrase "hit by a pitched ball"? Don Baylor and Ron Hunt, right?

Baylor holds the record for a career (267), while Hunt holds the single-season record (50) and is number two behind Baylor with 243 lifetime.

Who is the only man to be hit by a pitched ball more than 30 times in a season twice?

Jason Kendall of the Pirates, in 1997 (31) and 1998 (31).

# # #

ONLY WHAT?

Which is the only major league park below street level?

The Ballpark in Arlington, Texas, home of the Rangers.

# # #

Which is the only major league ballpark with its own microbrewery?

Coors Field.

# # #

Which is the only ballpark in professional baseball that does not serve beer?

Damaschke Field, home of the Short Season Class A Oneonta Tigers, in the New York–Penn League. The team owner likes it that way.

# # #

Which is the only big league ballpark that serves buffalo meat?

Coors Field, home of the Rockies, located just a few miles from Buffalo Bill's grave.

# # #

Name the only pro team to have its spring training in Cooperstown, New York.

The Quebec Athletics of the 1942 Class C Canadian-American League. Wartime restrictions limited the team's ability to travel to a warmer climate.

# # #

HIT RECORDS

—————

WHO HAD THE MOST HITS **in the 1990s?**
Mark Grace—1,754.

# # #

When Jeff Bagwell of the Houston Astros hit three home runs in a game on June 9, 1999, he became the 13th man to do it twice in one season. Bagwell had also hit three in one game on April 21, 1999.

But his third blast on June 9 made him the first man to do something else. What was it?

Bagwell became the first man ever to hit three home runs in a game twice in one season on the road, against different teams in the same city!

Bagwell's three homers on June 9 were at Comiskey Park, against the White Sox. His three homers on April 21 were against the Cubs at Wrigley Field.

# # #

Only one qualifying hitter led the major leagues in batting average one year without winning the batting crown. Who is he and why not?

Eddie Murray. In 1990, as a Dodger, he hit .330, leading all qualifying batters. Willie McGee won the National League batting title with a .335 average, but he finished the season with Oakland in the American League, where he hit only .274. McGee's combined batting average for 1990 was .324, 6 points below Murray's.

# # #

Who is the only man to lead both major leagues in hits?

Lance Johnson. In 1995 with the White Sox, he led the American League with 186 hits. A year later, with the Mets, he was tops in the National League with 227.

# # #

Who was the first man to hit at least 200 home runs with two different teams?

Jimmie Foxx. He hit 302 for the Philadelphia Athletics, 1925–35, then 222 with the Red Sox, 1936–42.

# # #

During his distinguished career, Andre Dawson hit 438 home runs. What was special about the one he hit on August 25, 1995?

It was the first home run he hit in his hometown of Miami. After a 19-year career with the Expos, Cubs, and Red Sox, he finished his career with the Marlins, in 1995–96.

# # #

Who hit the most career home runs as an Atlanta Brave?

Dale Murphy—371. Were you going to say Hank Aaron? Good guess, but he hit only 335 of his 755 career homers as an *Atlanta* Brave.

# # #

Who is the last batter to win the home run title with more home runs than strikeouts?

Ted Kluszewski, Cincinnati Reds, 1954: 49 home runs, 35 strikeouts.

# # #

DEPT. OF CLOSE:

Was Carl Furillo a .300 career hitter?

No, but almost. The Dodger outfielder 1946–60 hit over .300 in 1949 (.322), 1950 (.305), 1953 (a league-leading .344), 1955 (.314), and 1957 (.306). But he had a number of sub-.300 seasons too, sinking as low as .247 in 1952. In all, he had 1,910 hits in 6,378 at bats–a .2994669 average. This may be the closest anyone ever came to hitting .300 for a career without doing so. One more hit, or one fewer at bat, and his average would have been rounded off to .300. But .2994669 rounds to .299.

# # #

"I retired more than 70 years ago, yet I still hold the single-season batting average record for three different teams. Who am I?"

Rogers Hornsby. Cardinals (1924—.424), Braves (1928—.387), and Cubs (1929—.380).

# # #

Which number-one draft pick hit the most career home runs?

Reggie Jackson. He was the first draft pick of the Kansas City A's in 1966. During his career with the A's, the Orioles, the Yankees, and the Angels, 1967–87, he hit 563 homers.

# # #

Who were the first teammates to hit back-to-back, inside-the-park home runs?

Eddie Waitkus and Marv Rickert, Chicago Cubs, June 23, 1946, in the fourth inning of the first game of a doubleheader against the Giants.

# # #

Who hit the most home runs at the start of his career before hitting his first grand slam?

Sammy Sosa of the Cubs–246. Sosa's first grand slam–his second homer of the game–was career home run number 247, which he hit on July 27, 1998, in a 6–2 defeat of the Arizona Diamondbacks.

According to David Vincent, coeditor of *SABR Presents the Home Run Encyclopedia*, Sosa's record eclipsed Glenn Davis's 190, Jeff Bagwell's 187 (through 1997), Ron Kittle's 176, and Claudell Washington's 164.

# # #

When did Sosa hit his second grand slam?

July 28, 1998—the very next day.

Cal Ripken, Jr., still holds the record—266—for most consecutive home runs without a grand slam. He achieved this dubious distinction between July 13, 1984, and July 3, 1994—just 10 days short of a decade.

Al Kaline went 13 years (September 11, 1960–August 15, 1973) and 245 home runs without a grand slam.

# # #

Which foreign-born player has hit the most career home runs?

José Canseco, from Havana, Cuba. On July 26, 1998, he broke Tony Perez's record with home run number 380. Through 2000, Canseco has belted 446 homers.

# # #

Who is the youngest man to hit at least 40 homers in a season four times?

Ken Griffey, Jr., was just 28 when he reached this amazing plateau. He hit 45 homers for the Mariners in 1993, 40 in 1994, 49 in 1996, and 56 in 1997. In 1998, he hit another 56.

# # #

Only seven players have hit at least 100 home runs in two consecutive seasons. Who are they?

Mark McGwire 135 (1998–99)
Sammy Sosa 129 (1998–99)
Mark McGwire 128 (1997–98)
Babe Ruth 114 (1927–28)
Babe Ruth 113 (1920–21)
Ken Griffey, Jr., 112 (1997–98)
Mark McGwire 108 (1998–99)
Jimmie Foxx 106 (1932–33)
Ken Griffey, Jr., 104 (1998–99)
Ralph Kiner 101 (1949–50)
Roger Maris 100 (1960–61)

# # #

Who is the only man to have at least 150 walks, runs, and RBIs in the same season?

Ted Williams, 1949: 162 walks, 150 runs, 159 RBIs. Williams also led the American League in homers (43) and doubles (39).

# # #

"I hit a home run in 1987, but I did not homer again until 10 years and 1,869 at bats later. Who am I?"

Rafael Belliard. His first homer since May 5, 1987, when he was with the Pirates, was on September 26, 1997, when Belliard was playing for the Braves.

# # #

How many home runs did U. L. Washington of the Royals hit in 1979?

Two. Both came on September 21. One from the right side and one from the left.

# # #

Who had the most hits in his first 1,000 at bats?

Joe Jackson—389.

# # #

Who had the most home runs in his first 1,000 at bats?

Jim Gentile—75.

# # #

Only four players in history have hit at least 50 home runs, driven in at least 150 runs, and amassed at least 400 total bases in the same season. Who are they?

PLAYER	YEAR	TEAM	HOMERS	RBIs	TOTAL BASES
Babe Ruth	1921	Yankees	59	171	457
Babe Ruth	1927	Yankees	60	164	417
Hack Wilson	1930	Cubs	56	190	423
Jimmie Foxx	1932	Athletics	58	169	438
Sammy Sosa	1998	Cubs	66	158	416

# # #

Name the three natives of Mexico who hit more than 100 home runs in their careers.

Vinny Castilla, 209 through 2000
Jorge Orta, 130
Aurelio Rodriguez, 124

# # #

Only three men managed to hit two home runs in a single game off Sandy Koufax. One was a Hall of Famer. Who are they?

Ernie Banks, the Hall of Famer, did it on June 9, 1963. The others are George Altman and Felipe Alou.

# # #

Which Homer hit the most career homers?

Homer Summa—18.

# # #

"After my very first game in the major leagues, I was tied for career home runs with Hank Aaron. Who am I?"

Charlie White. In the same game in which Aaron hit his very first big league home run off Vic Raschi on April 23, 1954, White hit his first one, too, off Cot Deal. That one was also White's last.

# # #

Only three American Leaguers have won home run, batting, and RBI titles more than once. Who are they?

Ted Williams, Jimmie Foxx, Joe DiMaggio.

# # #

Eight players had 200 hits in a single season but batted under .300. Who are they?

Jo-Jo Moore, 1935 Giants, 201 hits, .295
Maury Wills, 1962 Dodgers, 208, .299
Lou Brock, 1967 Cardinals, 206, .299
Matty Alou, 1970 Pirates, 201, .297
Ralph Garr, 1973 Braves, 200, .299
Dave Cash, 1974 Phillies, 206, .299
Buddy Bell, 1979 Rangers, 200, .299
Bill Buckner, 1985 Red Sox, 201, .299

# # #

Which player went the longest between 100 RBI seasons?

Harold Baines. He drove in 113 runs in 1985 with the White Sox. On September 23, 1999, playing for the Indians, Baines singled in the first inning for his 100th RBI of the season, his first 100 RBI year since 1985.

# # #

One season this team boasted five batting champions—past or future—on its roster. Name the team and the batting champs.

The 1947 Brooklyn Dodgers. Their batting champions were Arky Vaughan (1935), Pete Reiser (1941), Dixie Walker (1944), Jackie Robinson (1949), and Carl Furillo (1953).

# # #

Ken Williams of the 1922 St. Louis Browns had the first 30–30 season in the majors—39 homers and 37 steals. Who are the only two Hall of Famers in the 30–30 club?

Hank Aaron, 1963 Milwaukee Braves (44 homers, 31 steals) and Willie Mays, 1956 New York Giants (36–40) and 1957 Giants (35–38).

# # #

Babe Ruth won the American League RBI title three times with fewer than 500 at bats. Only one other American Leaguer accomplished this rare feat in a full season. Who is he?

Roger Maris of the 1960 Yankees—499 at bats, 112 RBIs.

# # #

Who was the first player to lead the National League in RBIs with fewer than 500 at bats in a nonstrike season?

Darren Daulton, 1992 Phillies—485 at bats, 109 RBIs.

# # #

"I hit .300 with 30 or more home runs in a single season for four consecutive seasons, yet I am not in the Hall of Fame. Who am I?"

Ted Kluszewski.

The Hall of Famers who accomplished this powerful combination are Babe Ruth (who did it twice), Hack Wilson, Lou Gehrig, Chuck Klein, Jimmie Foxx, Joe DiMaggio, Hank Greenberg, Mickey Mantle, and Orlando Cepeda.

# # #

Only one eligible player has hit at least 40 home runs in three straight years and is not a Hall of Famer. Who is he?

Ted Kluszewski, 1953–55. The others are Hall of Famers Babe Ruth, Jimmie Foxx, Ralph Kiner, Duke Snider, Eddie Mathews, and Ernie Banks, as well as Andres Galarraga, Ken Griffey, Jr., Mark McGwire, and Sammy Sosa, and Vinny Castilla.

# # #

What did Reggie Jackson do 17 years to the day after his first big league home run?

He hit his 500th. September 17, 1984.

# # #

Who is the biggest man to win a batting title?

Frank Thomas, Chicago White Sox, 1997: 6'5", 240 pounds, .347.

# # #

Who is the only player in the history of the major leagues to have back-to-back 40-home run seasons with two different teams?

Andres Galarraga. In 1997, he hit 41 homers for the Rockies. As a free agent in the off-season, he went to Atlanta, for whom he hit 44 in 1998.

\# \# \#

Only three batters have had three consecutive seasons in which they drove in at least 140 runs. Who are they?

Hint: Two are Hall of Famers.

Babe Ruth (1926–31; 146, 164, 142, 154, 153, 163), Lou Gehrig (1930–32; 174, 184, 151) and Ken Griffey, Jr., (1996–98; 140, 147, 146).

\# \# \#

Only three switch hitters have slugged 100 or more home runs in each league. Who are they?

Eddie Murray (American League: 396, National League: 108)

Charles Theodore "Chili" Davis (American League: 249, National League: 101).

Carl "Reggie" Smith, (American League: 149, National League: 165).

\# \# \#

Frank Robinson was the first man to record 1,000 hits in each league–1,624 in the National and 1,184 in the American. Who was the second?

Dave Winfield–1,759 in the National League and 1,976 in the American.

\# \# \#

Which was the first American League team to hit at least 200 home runs three years in a row?

The Cleveland Indians, 1995–97.

\# \# \#

By hitting his first big league home run on September 13, 1997, for the Oakland A's, Ben Grieve helped the A's set a record. Which one?

Grieve's homer made the A's the first team ever to have every position player on its roster hit at least one home run during the season.

\# \# \#

Name the four sets of three teammates who wound up their careers with more than 400 home runs.

Willie Mays (660), Willie McCovey (521), and Duke Snider (407), teammates on the 1964 Giants.

Willie Mays (660), Willie McCovey (521), and Dave Kingman (442), teammates on the Giants, 1971 and 1972.

José Canseco, (446+), Mark McGwire (554+), and Dave Kingman (442), teammates on the 1986 Oakland A's.

José Canseco, (446+), Mark McGwire (554+), and Reggie Jackson (563), teammates on the 1987 Oakland A's.

# # #

"I had 63 at bats in my big league career and only one hit—a bunt. My batting average, .016, is the worst ever for players with at least one hit. Who am I?"

Hint: Yes, he was a pitcher.

Fred Gladding. Tigers, Astros, 1961–73.

# # #

Mark McGwire finished the 1998 season with a dramatic 70 home runs smashing Roger Maris's easy-to-remember 61 in '61. Also in 1998, Sammy Sosa hit an incredible 66 homers. Name all the numbers between 50 and 70 that complete this sentence: "Nobody has ever hit a total of exactly ____ home runs in a season."

53, 55, 57, 62, 64, 67, 68, 69.

# # #

Who was the first Canadian in the American League to hit 20 home runs in a season for three consecutive seasons?

The Oakland A's Matt Stairs, of St. John, New Brunswick: 1997—27; 1998—26; 1999—38. He's also the first Canadian to hit 20 homers for four consecutive seasons: He hit 21 in 2000.

# # #

Who was the first man to slug 500 home runs without ever hitting 40 in a single season?

Eddie Murray. He retired after the 1997 season with a total of 504 homers, but the most he ever hit in a single season was 33, in 1983, when he was with the Baltimore Orioles.

# # #

Only five players had at least 500 at bats in a single season while hitting below .200. Which five?

Monte Cross, 1904 A's—503 at bats, .189 batting average
Charles Moran, 1904 Senators and Browns—515, .196
Jim Levey, 1933 Browns—529, .195
Frank Crosetti, 1940 Yankees—546, .194
Tom Tresh, 1968 Yankees—507, .195

# # #

Who hit the most home runs in his first five years in the major leagues?

Ralph Kiner, 215.

# # #

Fourteen modern players have amassed 400 bases in a single season, some of them more than once. All of these sluggers have done so in seasons in which they smacked at least 30 home runs. But only one of these elite power hitters has ever had a 30 home run/400 total bases season without even one triple. Who is he?

Sammy Sosa, 1998 Chicago Cubs—416 bases, 66 home runs, 20 doubles, 112 singles, 0 triples.

# # #

On September 7, 1993, this man hit four home runs in a single game, driving in 12 runs. Others had hit four homers in a game before, and one other (Sunny Jim Bottomley) had also driven in 12 runs in a single game. But nobody had ever done both in the same game. Who is he?

Mark Whiten, Cardinals, in a 15–2 shellacking of the Cincinnati Reds.

# # #

Who was the first Yankee to lead the American League in home runs?
Wally Pipp, who smacked 12 in 1916.

# # #

Who hit the most career home runs against righthanded pitchers?
Hank Aaron—534.

# # #

Who hit the most career home runs against lefthanded pitchers?
Hank Aaron—221.

# # #

Who led his league in home runs with the fewest at bats in a single season?
Gavvy Cravath. In 1919 with the Pittsburgh Pirates, he hit 12 homers in only 214 at bats.

# # #

Who had the fewest hits in a season in which he hit at least 30 home runs?
Mark McGwire, 1995 Oakland A's. He had 39 homers but just 87 hits. The only other man to have fewer than 100 hits with at least 30 home runs is Rob Deer, who had 97 hits and 32 homers for the 1992 Tigers.

# # #

Before the 1998 assault on slugging records, who was the only National Leaguer to drive in at least 150 runs in two different seasons?
Lewis "Hack" Wilson of the Cubs—159 in 1929 and 191 in 1930.

# # #

Who is the only modern big leaguer to hit two homers and two triples in the same game?

> *Hint: He singled in the same game, giving him 15 total bases in one game.*

Willie Mays of the San Francisco Giants, on May 13, 1958, against the Dodgers at their temporary home, the Los Angeles Coliseum.

# # #

Which player went the longest between his first 20-home-run season and his second?

Devon White. In 1987 with the Angels, he hit 24 home runs. His next 20 home run season wasn't until 1998, when he hit 22 for the Arizona Diamondbacks.

# # #

Only one man who has hit at least 50 home runs in a single season exactly matched his homer output the following season. Who is he?

Ken Griffey, Jr. In 1997 he hit 56 for the Seattle Mariners—he matched it exactly in 1998.

# # #

Which American Leaguer had the most consecutive at bats without hitting a home run?

Eddie Foster—2,702, from April 20, 1916, to the end of his career in 1923. He played for the Senators, Red Sox, and Browns.

# # #

What is the only team that had two players hit 30 homers for four different teams apiece?

The 1999 Tampa Bay Devil Rays. José Canseco (Oakland, Toronto, Texas, and Tampa Bay) and Fred McGriff (San Diego, Atlanta, Toronto, and Tampa Bay).

# # #

Who was the first shortstop in American League history to hit at least 40 home runs in a single season twice?

Alex Rodriguez of the Seattle Mariners. He hit 42 in 1998 and 42 again in 1999.

# # #

Who is the only modern player to win batting titles with two different teams?

Bill Madlock—twice with the Cubs: 1975 (.354), 1976 (.339) and twice again with the Pirates: 1981 (.341) and 1983 (.323).

\# \# \#

Who is the only player to hit 40 home runs in the same season in which he had a 30-game hitting streak?

Rogers Hornsby. In 1922, while with the Cardinals, he hit 42 home runs and had a 33-game hitting streak.

\# \# \#

Who is the only man to win the RBI crown in consecutive years with different teams?

Babe Ruth. He led the American League in 1919 with 114 RBIs when he was with the Boston Red Sox. The next season, with the Yankees, he drove in 137—again topping the league.

\# \# \#

Who was the first man to have 40 homers and 40 doubles in the same season?

Babe Ruth, 1921 Yankees—59 homers, 44 doubles.

\# \# \#

Only one man in the 1980s hit at least 20 home runs six years in a row. Who was he?

Dwight Evans, Boston Red Sox, 1981—22, 1982—32, 1983—22, 1984—32, 1985—29, 1986—26, 1987—34, 1988—21, 1989—20.

\# \# \#

Why did Mark Grace once apologize for hitting a home run?

He did it on September 13, 1998, as a Chicago Cub against the Milwaukee Brewers at Wrigley Field. Grace's homer in the bottom of the ninth inning came in the game in which Sammy Sosa hit home runs number 61 and 62 of the 1998 season, temporarily tying him with Mark McGwire. Grace's homer won the game but left Sosa in the on-deck circle, deprived of a chance to hit number 63 and pull ahead of McGwire.

\# \# \#

Who had the most RBIs in a single season without a hit?

The immortal Hi Jasper, who drove in four runs for the 1914 Chicago White Sox without a hit.

# # #

Between 1929 and 1931, Al Simmons of the Philadelphia A's averaged over .360. Who was the next player to reach this impressive plateau?

Larry Walker, Colorado Rockies, 1997–99.

# # #

Who is the first major leaguer to hit .300, hit 40 homers, and 40 doubles, drive in 100 runs, score 100 runs, walk 100 times, and steal 20 bases in the same season?

Lawrence "Chipper" Jones, 1999 Atlanta Braves: .319, 45 homers, 41 doubles, 110 RBIs, 116 runs, 126 walks, 25 stolen bases.

# # #

Almost every man who hit at least .350 with at least 40 home runs and 200 hits in the same season is a Hall of Famer. Only two are not—at least not yet. Who are they?

Hint: They reached these lofty numbers in the same season.

The Hall of Famers on this list are Lou Gehrig (1927, 1930, 1934, 1936), Babe Ruth (1921, 1923, 1924), Jimmie Foxx (1932, 1933), Chuck Klein (1929, 1930), Hack Wilson (1930), and Rogers Hornsby (1922).

The non–Hall of Famers who have reached this plateau are Larry Walker and Mike Piazza—both in 1997.

# # #

Who had the most total bases in a single season while failing to hit .300?

Sammy Sosa, Chicago Cubs, 1999: 397 total bases, batting average .288.

# # #

Who hit the most solo home runs in a career?

Hank Aaron—400.

# # #

HERE'S THE PITCH

―――――

WHO IS THE ONLY MAN in the history of baseball to throw a perfect game on Thanksgiving Day?

Don Larsen. His perfect game in Game 5 of the World Series came on October 8, 1956–Thanksgiving Day in Canada.

# # #

Which pitcher lost the most games in the 20th century?

Nolan Ryan–292.

# # #

Only two pitchers in history have struck out at least 300 batters in a single season in both leagues. Who are they?

Hint: Not Nolan Ryan.

Randy Johnson and Pedro Martinez.

Johnson struck out 308 for the 1993 Seattle Mariners and 364 for the 1999 Arizona Diamondbacks.

He also struck out 329 in 1998, which he split between the Mariners (213) and the Houston Astros (116).

Pedro Martinez whiffed 305 in 1997 for the Montreal Expos and 313 for the 1999 Boston Red Sox.

# # #

What was the first team to have two pitchers with at least 40 saves per season in consecutive seasons?

The New York Yankees. In 1996 John Wetteland had 43 saves, followed by Mariano Rivera's 43 in 1997.

# # #

In 1978 Ron Guidry of the New York Yankees had one of the best seasons ever, winning 25 games while losing just 3 with an ERA of 1.74.

The three pitchers who beat him that season had the same first name. What is it?

Mike. On July 7 Guidry lost to Mike Caldwell of the Brewers in Milwaukee; on August 4 Mike Flanagan of the Orioles beat him in New York; finally, on September 20 it was Mike Willis of the Blue Jays who beat Guidry and the Yankees in Toronto.

# # #

Only five pitchers have recorded 50 or more saves in a single season. Who are they?

Hint: Two did it in the same year in the same league.

Bobby Thigpen, 1990 White Sox—57
Denis Eckersley, 1992 A's—51
Randy Myers, 1993 Cubs—53
Rod Beck, 1998 Cubs—51
Trevor Hoffman, 1998 Padres—53

# # #

Who were the only pitchers to strike out at least 200 batters in each of their first three seasons?

Dwight Gooden, Mets, 1984–86: 276, 268, 200
Hideo Nomo, Dodgers, 1995–97: 236, 234, 233

# # #

Which pitcher lost games for the most major league teams?

Mike Morgan. Between 1978 and 2000, he lost games for 12 teams: the A's, Yankees, Blue Jays, Mariners, Orioles, Dodgers, Cubs, Cardinals, Reds, Twins, Rangers, and Diamondbacks.

# # #

Which pitcher won games for the most major league teams?

The answer is, once again, Mike Morgan. He recorded wins for 11 teams: the A's, Yankees, Mariners, Orioles, Dodgers, Cubs, Cardinals, Reds, Twins, Rangers, and Diamondbacks. He was 0–3 with the Blue Jays.

# # #

Hall of Famer Warren Spahn broke into the majors in 1942 with the Boston Braves. He relieved in two games and started two more, including one complete game. Yet his record was 0–0. How did he have a complete game without a decision?

Spahn was pitching in the eighth inning on September 26, 1942, at the Polo Grounds, with the Giants trailing the Braves 5–2, when unruly fans could not be cleared from the field. Although the Braves were awarded a 9–0 forfeit (one run per inning), the rules prohibited a decision for Spahn, as his team was losing at the time the forfeit was declared.

# # #

Which pitcher went the longest between 20-win seasons?

David Cone. He won 20 games with the 1998 New York Yankees, his first 20-win season since 1988, when he won 20 for the Mets. Cone's achievement eclipsed the record of Yankee broadcaster Jim Kaat, who won 25 with the 1966 Twins and didn't win 20 again until his 21-win season with the White Sox in 1974.

# # #

A number of pitchers have notched 300 wins or 300 saves. So far, nobody has accomplished both.

But one man has over 300 saves and 100 complete games to go with his 197 wins. Who is he?

The amazing Dennis Eckersley. He recorded 197 wins in his career (including a 20-win season in 1978), 390 saves, and 100 complete games.

On September 26, 1998, Eckersley broke Hoyt Wilhelm's record for most games pitched in a career when he pitched in his 1,071st game against the Orioles.

# # #

Who was the first pitcher to be named "Pitcher of the Month" in his first month in the major leagues?

Marty Bystrom of the Phillies. In September 1980, he helped the Phillies to the National League pennant by going 5–0 with an ERA of 1.50. Bystrom's career stats: 29–26, 4.26 ERA.

# # #

Who is the only man to throw a perfect game and win the Cy Young Award in the same season?

Sandy Koufax. As a Dodger, he threw a perfect game against the Cubs on September 9, 1965. He went on to win the National League Cy Young Award that year, with a 26–8 record, 382 strikeouts and an ERA of 2.04.

# # #

Only five pitchers have struck out 300 batters in consecutive seasons. Who are they?

Rube Waddell, Philadelphia A's, 1903 (302), 1904 (349)
Sandy Koufax, Los Angeles Dodgers, 1965 (382), 1966 (317)
J. R. Richard, Houston Astros, 1978 (303), 1979 (313)
Nolan Ryan, who did it twice: California Angels, 1972 (329), 1973 (383),
    1974 (367) and 1976 (327), 1977 (341)
Curt Schilling, Philadelphia Phillies, 1997 (319), 1998 (300)

Schilling struck out Kevin Orie of the Marlins on September 26, 1998, the next-to-last day of the season, in the seventh inning of the first game of a doubleheader at Pro Player Stadium to notch number 300. Orie was Schilling's 150th strikeout on the road in 1998. He matched that with 150 strikeouts at home.

Talk about a balanced attack!

# # #

Only two pitchers have won 20 games in a season with ERAs of over 5.0. Which two?

Bobo Newsom, 1938 Cardinals—20 wins, ERA 5.08
Ray Kremer, 1930 Pirates—20 wins, ERA 5.02

# # #

Which pitchers have won six or more ERA titles?

Lefty Grove—9; Roger Clemens—6.

# # #

Which pitcher had the most career decisions without having a winning record?

Charlie Hough. He pitched for the Dodgers, Rangers, White Sox, and Marlins from 1970 to 1994, compiling a record of 216 wins and 216 losses. That's 432 decisions and a winning percentage of exactly .500.

# # #

Only one pitcher who has won the Triple Crown of pitching twice is not a Hall of Famer. Who is he?

Roger Clemens—1997, 1998. He is not a Hall of Famer because he is not yet eligible.

The six others who have accomplished this (leading the league in wins, strikeouts, and ERA) twice are Christy Mathewson (1905, 1908), Walter Johnson (1913, 1918, 1924), Grover Cleveland Alexander (1915, 1916, 1917 [three consecutive years!], 1920), Lefty Grove (1930, 1931), Lefty Gomez (1934, 1937), and Sandy Koufax (1963, 1965, 1966).

# # #

"One year, I struck out over 300 batters, yet I did not lead the league in strikeouts. I'm the only man to achieve this dubious distinction. Who am I?"

Vida Blue. In 1971 Blue struck out 301 batters for the Oakland A's, only to lose the strikeout crown to Mickey Lolich, who fanned 308 for the Tigers.

# # #

Who was the first man to be the losing pitcher in the All-Star Game two years in a row?

The Cardinals' Mort Cooper, 1942 and 1943.

# # #

Who is the only man to appear in a modern World Series after pitching in only one major league game?

Ken Brett. He made his major league debut with a two-inning stint on September 27, 1967, for the Boston Red Sox—his only big league appearance before pitching for the Sox in the 1967 Series. Brett went on to pitch in 349 games during a 14-year big-league career for the Red Sox, Brewers, Phillies, Pirates, Yankees, White Sox, Twins, Dodgers, Angels, and Royals, compiling a record of 83–85, with an ERA of 3.93.

# # #

Pitcher Joe Ausanio (Yankees, 1994–95) had seven perfect games. Explain.

None of his perfect games were achieved as a pitcher in a baseball game. He bowled them.

# # #

Was September 21, 1986, a happy day for then-Phillies pitcher Marvin Freeman?

Yes, yes. He won his first big league game, beating the Mets, 7–1, in New York and his daughter Paris was born.

# # #

Which two pitchers threw the first combined extra-inning no-hitter?

Francisco Cordova and Ricardo Rincon of the Pirates beat the Houston Astros in Pittsburgh on July 12, 1997.

# # #

Name the first teammates to notch 25 or more saves each in a single season?

Norm Charlton (26) and Rob Dibble (25)—the "Nasty Boys" of the 1992 Cincinnati Reds.

# # #

Who is the only man to lead two different teams in saves in the same season?

Jeff Shaw, 1998. He had 23 saves for the Reds and 25 for the Dodgers—tops on each club.

# # #

Only five pitchers have ever thrown 200 or more innings in a single season and given up more homers than walks. Who are they?

Hint: Three did it in 1998.

Robin Roberts, 1956 Phillies: 297⅓ innings, 46 homers, 40 walks
Gary Nolan, 1976 Reds, 239⅓ innings, 28 homers, 27 walks
Brian Anderson, 1998 Diamondbacks, 208 innings, 39 homers, 24 walks
Jose Lima, 1998 Astros, 233⅓ innings, 34 homers, 32 walks
Rick Reed, 1998 Mets, 212 innings, 30 homers, 29 walks

# # #

Only four pitchers have won 15 or more games for 11 consecutive seasons. Who are they?

Hint: Three are Hall of Famers.

Cy Young (15 consecutive seasons), Christy Mathewson (12), Warren Spahn (11), and Greg Maddux (12). Maddux is a sure Hall of Famer, but he'll have to stop pitching first.

# # #

Who is the only pitcher to beat the Boston Braves, the Milwaukee Braves, and the Atlanta Braves?

Robin Roberts.

# # #

Only two pitchers have struck out at least 10 batters in seven consecutive games. Who are they?

Nolan Ryan (1977 Angels) and Pedro Martinez (1998 Red Sox).

# # #

The Detroit Tigers won the World Series in 1945. How many saves did their top closer record that memorable year?

Four. Detroit's relief ace was Stubby Overmire. The first glove ever owned by Jim Kaat was a Stubby Overmire model.

# # #

Who are the only two pitchers to strike out their ages?

Kerry Wood. He was 20 years old on May 6, 1998, when, as a Chicago Cub, he struck out 20 Astros at Wrigley Field.

On September 13, 1936, 17-year-old Bob Feller of the Cleveland Indians struck out 17 and beat the Philadelphia A's, 5–2, on two hits.

# # #

Pitcher Clem Labine came to bat 31 times during the Dodgers' 1955 world championship season. He had only three hits. What was memorable about them?

They were all home runs.

# # #

Who was the first man to record his first 300 saves with the same team?

Jeff Montgomery of the Kansas City Royals. He recorded save number 300 on August 25, 1999.

# # #

Perfect games have been pitched by five Hall of Famers. Name them.

Cy Young, Addie Joss, Jim Bunning, Sandy Koufax, and Jim Hunter.

Too easy? Which two Hall of Fame pitchers were on the losing ends of perfect games?

Rube Waddell, who lost Cy Young's perfect game, and Ed Walsh, who lost Addie Joss's.

# # #

Only two men have won Cy Young Awards while leading their league in walks. Who are they?

Bob Turley, 1958 Yankees. Although he sported a 21–7 record with the World Champion Yankees, he managed to lead the American League with 128 walks.

The only other time this has happened was the very next year. Hall of Famer Early Wynn of the 1959 Chicago White Sox went 22–10, but he issued 119 passes.

# # #

"I am the only man ever to strike out 300 batters in a single season and still have a losing record that year. Who am I?"

Nolan Ryan, who struck out 327 but went 17–18 for the 1976 California Angels.

# # #

When was the first game in which every single batter for the losing team went exactly 0–3?

David Wells's perfect game for the New York Yankees, May 17, 1998. The Twins did not use a pinch hitter.

# # #

How many men did Scott Bailes retire on May 21, 1998, when he secured a win in the Rangers' 9–8 victory over the Mariners?

None. With two outs in the ninth inning of a tie game, Bailes, pitching in relief, threw two pitches to Rob Ducey, then picked Russ Davis off first base. When the Rangers won, so did Bailes.

# # #

Who is the only man to save more than 30 games in single season while losing 15?

Mike Marshall, 1979 Twins. He saved 32 but lost 15.

# # #

Which pitcher needed the fewest games to strike out 300 batters in a single season?

Randy Johnson of the 1999 Arizona Diamondbacks. Number 300 was Kevin Millar of the Florida Marlins—Johnson's eighth whiff of the game—on August 26, 1999, in his 29th start of 1999.

# # #

Who made the most consecutive relief appearances in the big leagues before his first start?

Mike Stanton. He appeared in 552 games—all in relief—before his first start, with the New York Yankees, on May 9, 1999, in Seattle. The Yankees won, 6–1, but Stanton did not get the win.

# # #

Who is the first pitcher to record 300 saves in a career without ever leading his league in saves in a single season?

Doug Jones, who recorded save number 300 on September 11, 1999, for the Oakland A's, in a 5–4 victory over the Tampa Bay Devil Rays.

# # #

Since 1900, only three pitchers with at least 50 innings pitched have given up more hits than innings pitched in a season with an ERA under 2.00. Who are they?

Hugh Casey, 1946 Brooklyn Dodgers—101 hits, 99 innings, 1.99 ERA
Jim Scott, 1917 Chicago White Sox—126 hits, 125 innings, 1.87 ERA
Paul Quantrill, 1997 Toronto Blue Jays—103 hits, 88 innings, 1.94 ERA

# # #

How many modern pitchers have had over 350 career starts—all with one team?

Nineteen:

Walter Johnson	666	Washington Senators
Jim Palmer	521	Baltimore Orioles
Bob Feller	484	Cleveland Indians
Ted Lyons	484	Chicago White Sox
Red Faber	483	Chicago White Sox
Bob Gibson	482	St. Louis Cardinals
Don Drysdale	465	Brooklyn and Los Angeles Dodgers
Whitey Ford	438	New York Yankees
Mel Harder	433	Cleveland Indians
Carl Hubbell	432	New York Giants
Steve Rogers	393	Montreal Expos
Paul Splittorff	392	Kansas City Royals
Hooks Dauss	388	Detroit Tigers
Tom Glavine	399	Atlanta Braves
Chuck Finley	379	Anaheim Angels
Vern Law	364	Pittsburgh Pirates
Tommy Bridges	362	Detroit Tigers
Mel Stottlemyre	356	New York Yankees
Bob Lemon	350	Cleveland Indians

# # #

Name two Dwights who pitched for the Mets.

Dwight Bernard (1978–79) and Dwight Gooden (1984–94).

Thanks to Josh Davidson for this question.

# # #

Rocky Colavito hit 374 career homers, and is one of the very few position players given the opportunity to pitch twice in the majors. Colavito pitched for the Indians on August 13, 1958, in the second game of a doubleheader. On August 25, 1968, as a Yankee, Colavito pitched again.

Which future Hall of Famer did he face in both pitching stints?

Al Kaline, Tigers right fielder.

# # #

Which pitchers have won at least 20 games in a single season for three different teams?

Just three.

TEAM	YEAR	WINS
Grover Cleveland Alexander		
Phillies	1911	28
Phillies	1913	22
Phillies	1914	27
Phillies	1915	31
Phillies	1916	33
Phillies	1917	30
Cubs	1920	27
Cubs	1923	22
Cardinals	1927	21
Carl Mays		
Red Sox	1917	22
Red Sox	1918	21
Yankees	1920	26
Yankees	1921	27
Reds	1924	20
Gaylord Perry		
Giants	1966	21
Giants	1970	23
Indians	1972	24
Indians	1974	21
Padres	1978	21

# # #

Who are the only modern pitchers to collect at least 2,500 career strikeouts without ever leading the league in that category?

Don Sutton, 3,574 strikeouts
Jerry Koosman, 2,556 strikeouts
Gaylord Perry, 3,534 strikeouts

# # #

On June 25, 1999, José Jimenez pitched a no-hitter for the St. Louis Cardinals at the Bank One Ballpark in Phoenix against the Diamondbacks. On August 17, he was sent down to the AAA Memphis Redbirds. Was Jimenez the first pitcher to be demoted to the minor leagues in the same season in which he pitched a no-hitter?

No. That dubious distinction is held by Bobo Holloman, who pitched a no-hitter in his first major league start, for the St. Louis Browns on May 6, 1953. By August he was back in the minors, never to return to the majors.

# # #

Which was the first team to clinch a division title on a no-hitter?

The 1986 Astros. Mike Scott no-hit the Giants, 2–0, on September 25, 1986, to clinch the National League title for the Astros, who went on to lose the National League pennant in the League Championship Series to the New York Mets.

# # #

Only three 20th-century pitchers won 200 games before they turned 31. Who are they?

Walter Johnson, Christy Mathewson, and Jim "Catfish" Hunter.

# # #

In 1999, Pedro Martinez struck out 313 batters. In so doing, he broke a record that Sandy Koufax set in 1963. Which record?

Fewest walks allowed in a season in which he struck out 300.

In 1963, Koufax struck out 306 while walking 58. Martinez allowed only 38 passes, including one intentional.

# # #

Name a pitcher who won games in all four Canadian major league ballparks.

John Candelaria won games at both Expos' home parks, Jarry Park and Olympic Stadium in the National League, and both Blue Jays' homes, Exhibition Stadium and SkyDome in the American League. From 1975 to 1993, he pitched for the Pirates, Angels, Mets, Yankees, Expos, Twins, Blue Jays, and Dodgers.

# # #

Which pitcher lost the most games the year before he won the Cy Young Award?

Dean Chance. In 1963 with the Angels, he lost 18 games but came back in 1964 to win the award with a league-leading 20 wins.

# # #

Which pitcher had the lowest ERA in a season in which he lost 20 games?

Ed Walsh. In 1910 for the White Sox he went 18–20 but had an ERA of only 1.27.

# # #

Only three pitchers fanned 200 batters in 10 or more seasons. Who are they?

Tom Seaver, Nolan Ryan, and Roger Clemens.

# # #

Who was the first pitcher to start on Opening Day, in the All-Star Game, Game 1 of the League Championship Series, and Game 1 of the World Series in the same year?

Dave Stewart of the 1989 Oakland A's.

# # #

Who is the only man to strike out 300 batters and win 30 games in the same season?

Walter Johnson, Washington Senators, 1912: 303 strikeouts, 33 wins.

# # #

Who is the only pitcher to make the last out in a perfect game that he lost?

Rube Waddell. On May 5, 1904, in the first modern perfect game, Waddell, of the Philadelphia A's, flied out to center field—the final out in Cy Young's gem for the Red Sox.

# # #

On September 28, 1975, Vida Blue of the Oakland A's pitched the first five innings of no-hit ball against the Angels. He left the game before the sixth inning and was followed by Glenn Abbott, Paul Lindblad, and Rollie Fingers—a combined no-hitter.

Most pitchers stay in the dugout or the clubhouse after being removed—especially in a no-hitter—to watch the rest of the game and support their teammates. Where did Blue go?

Home. The football season had started, and Blue went home to watch a football game, not realizing until later that he had pitched part of a no-hitter.

# # #

In 1920, Jim Bagby won a league-leading 31 games for the Indians. How many batters did he strike out?

Just 73. He's the only pitcher ever to win more than 30 games with fewer than 100 strikeouts in a single season. Also the only one to do it with fewer than 90 and with fewer than 80!

# # #

Who is the only pitcher in Red Sox history to record 100 wins and 100 saves?

Bob Stanley. Between 1977 and 1989, he won 115 and saved another 132.

# # #

Who pitched the most games without ever appearing in a World Series?

Lee Smith. He retired during the 1997 season, having appeared in 1,022 games.

# # #

On September 26, 1999, Tom Gordon—who had spent three months recovering from an injury—was summoned to take the mound for the Boston Red Sox against the Baltimore Orioles. But before he threw even one pitch, manager James "Jimy" Williams sent him to the shower. Why?

Sharp-eyed Red Sox general manager Dan Duquette saw Gordon on the mound and realized that he had not yet been activated off the disabled list. Had he thrown a pitch, the Red Sox would have forfeited the game. Duquette called Williams in the dugout and had Gordon yanked. The Red Sox lost anyway.

# # #

WHAT'S
THE CONNECTION?

———

JOHN GLENN, TED WILLIAMS.

When Ted Williams was recalled to serve as a United States Marine Corps pilot during the Korean War, one of his commanders was future astronaut and United States Senator John Glenn. As Senator Glenn told us, "I was assigned with Ted to Marine Fighter Squadron 311 near Pohang Dong Ni, Korea, in February 1953. At that time, I was just one of many Marine pilots—Ted was the real celebrity of our unit. His last full season with the Red Sox before fighting began in Korea—I believe Ted had a .318 batting average with 30 home runs. During our service together, Ted flew with me as my wingman on several bombing missions. We struck up a friendship in Korea, and we remain friends to this day."

Thanks to former senator Glenn for this great story.

# # #

David Cone, Red Sox broadcaster Joe Castiglione.

Cone's mother-in-law, Angela Corso, was Castiglione's ninth-grade biology teacher at Michael Whalen Junior High School in Hamden, Connecticut. Cone married her daughter Lynn. Lynn competed in dance figure skating against Castiglione's sister Hope.

Thanks to Joe Castiglione for this story.

# # #

David Cone, Norm Cash, Darryl Hamilton, Frank White, Mike Hargrove, Moises Alou, Joe Adcock, Dave McNally, Roger Maris, Jerry Spradlin, Claudell Washington, John Anderson, George Hendrick, Bill Henry, Pat Meares, Jim Hisner.

None of these major leaguers played baseball in high school—many because their schools did not have baseball teams.

# # #

Former Mariners owner Danny Kaye, Ted Williams, Thurman Munson, Buddy Lewis, Luis Pujols, Denny McLain, Don Sutton, Rick Monday, Reggie Smith, Jim Bouton, Commissioner William Eckert.

All were pilots, except Jim Bouton, who was a Pilot.

# # #

Wilbert Robinson, John McGraw, Joe Kelley.

These three Hall of Famers are all buried in New Cathedral Cemetery in Baltimore, the only cemetery to boast three Hall of Famers.

Photographs of the burial sites of a number of sports stars are at www.findagrave.com/gravesports.html.

# # #

Albert Belle, Rafael Palmeiro.

Each hit his 300th home run on the same day, July 17, 1998.

# # #

Jackie Robinson, Monty Stratton, Lou Brissie, Lou Gehrig, Babe Ruth, Jackie Jensen, Jim Thorpe, Pete Gray, Ron LeFlore.

These big leaguers have all been the subject of film or made-for-television biographies. *The Jackie Robinson Story* (starring Jackie Robinson as himself), *The Stratton Story*, *The Comeback* (a film for television starring Chuck Connors as Brissie), *Pride of the Yankees* (Gehrig), *The Babe Ruth Story*, *The Babe*, *The Jackie Jensen Story* (starring Jackie Jensen), *Jim Thorpe, All-American*, *A Winner Never Quits* (the Pete Gray story), and *One in a Million* (LeFlore).

# # #

Jeff Bagwell, Frank Thomas, Eddie Mathews.

As noted in *Out of Left Field,* Bagwell and Thomas were born the same day, May 27, 1968. On that date, Eddie Mathews, then with the Detroit Tigers, hit his final home run, number 512.

# # #

Billy Williams, Bill Mazeroski.

Both got their 2,000th hit the same day—August 17, 1971.

# # #

The first and last man listed alphabetically in *Total Baseball.*

They were both home run champions. The first man is Henry Aaron, who led the National League in home runs in 1957 (44), 1963 (44), 1966 (44), and 1961 (39).

The last man listed is Edward "Dutch" Zwilling, who was the home run champion of the Federal League in 1914 (16).

# # #

Baseball, HMS *Titanic.*

The distance from the waterline to the boat deck on the *Titanic* was 60′6″—the exact distance from the pitcher's rubber to home plate.

Thanks to Hannah Madge Lyons for this insight.

# # #

Garret Anderson, Steve Avery, Greg Hansell, Gene Kingsale, Marcus Moore, Curtis Pride, Benito Santiago, Geno Petralli, Greg Vaughn, R. J. Reynolds, Jose Guzman, Randy Ready, Gabe Molina.

They all attended high schools named for John F. Kennedy. Anderson—Granada Hills, California; Avery—Taylor, Michigan; Hansell—La Palma, California; Kingsale—Dranjestad, Aruba; Moore—Richmond, California; Pride—Silver Spring, Maryland; Santiago—Ponce, Puerto Rico; Petralli—Sacramento, California; Vaughn—Sacramento; Reynolds—Sacramento; Guzman—Santa Isabel, Puerto Rico; Ready—Fremont, California; Molina—Denver, Colorado.

# # #

Roberto Alomar, Walker Cooper, Goose Gossage, George Kell, Lee Smith.

Each has represented four different teams at the All-Star Game.

# # #

Don Drysdale, Frank Robinson, Luis Aparicio.

Each of these future Hall of Famers made his big league debut on April 17, 1956.

# # #

Nomar Garciaparra, Monica Lewinsky.

Both were born on July 23, 1973.

# # #

Jackie Robinson, Hank Greenberg.

Full-size photos of these two baseball Hall of Famers are on exhibit at the Basketball Hall of Fame in Springfield, Massachusetts, in recognition of their excellent careers in high school basketball.

# # #

Reggie Jackson, Benjamin Netanyahu.

Mr. October and the future Prime Minister of Israel ("Mr. Elul"?) attended Cheltenham High School in Wyncote, Pennsylvania. Jackson graduated in 1964 and Netanyahu in 1967.

# # #

Mickey Lolich, Jim Kaat, Juan Marichal.

Each won 25 games in a single season, yet failed to win the Cy Young Award that year.

In 1966 Kaat won 25 games for the Twins, and Marichal won 27 games for the Giants, but the Cy Young Award went to Sandy Koufax of the Dodgers, who had a record of 27–9, with an ERA of 1.73.

In 1971 Lolich won 25 games for the Tigers, but the American League Cy Young Award went to Vida Blue, who was 24–8 with an ERA of 1.82 for the Oakland A's.

# # #

Jim Kaat, Tony LaRussa, Dave Cash.

All are vegetarians.

# # #

Hall of Fame broadcaster Ernie Harwell, author Margaret Mitchell.

Harwell was Mitchell's paperboy, delivering newspapers to her home in Atlanta, Georgia. In 1937 she won the Pulitzer Prize for fiction for *Gone with the Wind,* her only published book. Harwell was given the Ford C. Frick Award at the Hall of Fame in 1981.

# # #

Jeff Torborg, Art Kusnyer, Tom Egan, Ellie Rodriguez, Alan Ashby, John Russell, Mike Stanley.

Each of these men caught one of Nolan Ryan's no-hitters.

# # #

Willie Mays, Tommy Lasorda, Lou Piniella.

Their godsons are all big leaguers.

Willie Mays–Barry Bonds; Tommy Lasorda–Mike Piazza; Lou Piniella–Dave Magadan. Indeed, Lasorda became one of the few men to manage his own godson in the major leagues, when Piazza was with the Dodgers, 1992–98.

# # #

Hall of Famers Hughie Jennings, Luke Appling, Don Sutton.

They have the same birthday–April 2 (1869, 1907, and 1945, respectively).

# # #

Cal Ripken, Jr., Doug DeCinces.

In 1972, 12-year-old Ripken was on the field during a workout of the AA Asheville Orioles, managed by his father. When shots fired by a kid in the stands landed on the field near Ripken, third baseman Doug DeCinces scooped him up and rushed him to the safety of the dugout.

Talk about the ultimate assist!

# # #

Clark Griffith, Dizzy Dean, Tony Fernandez, Sandy Koufax, Joe Torre, Mickey Mantle, Roberto Clemente, Pee Wee Reese, Ban Johnson, Casey Stengel, Willie Mays, Babe Ruth, Joe DiMaggio, Stan Musial, Connie Mack, Raul Mondesi, Cal Ripken, Jr., Frank White, Ted Williams.

They all have youth leagues or tournaments named after them. In 1985 the Casey Stengel Baseball League, in which Frank White played, was renamed the Frank White League. In 1999 the Babe Ruth League changed the name of its section for 5–12 year olds from the Bambino Division to the "Cal Ripken" Baseball Division.

# # #

Stan Musial, Carl Erskine, Phil Linz.

They all play the harmonica. Musial is quite good at it. (Musial is a member of the Society for American Baseball Research [SABR]. In the SABR directory, members list their "expertise"–i.e., the frequently obscure niches of baseball research and history they have studied. For example, minor league teams in North Carolina; 19th-century baseball in Toledo, Ohio; Negro League catchers; the Oakland Oaks of the Pacific Coast League. In a triumph of understatement, Musial lists his expertise as: "Hitting a baseball.")

Carl Erskine's playing was good enough to earn him the honor of playing the national anthem before an Expos-Dodgers game in Los Angeles in July 1992. He played the Canadian national anthem, too.

As for Phil Linz, his exploits on the mouth organ became a baseball legend. After the Yankees lost to the White Sox on August 20, 1964, Linz played the harmonica in the back of the team bus. Manager Yogi Berra, still smarting from the loss, was incensed and told him to stop playing, but Linz was sitting so far back that he couldn't discern Yogi's exact words, so he asked the guy sitting next to him, Mickey Mantle, "What did Yogi say?" Mantle told Linz that Yogi wanted him to play louder! When he did, Berra came back to Linz's seat, grabbed the harmonica out of his hand, and threw it, hitting Joe Pepitone's knee. Pepitone screamed in agony.

The publicity surrounding this unusual incident resulted in a contract for Linz with the Hohner harmonica company.

# # #

Goose Gossage, Nolan Ryan.

On July 23, 1991, Gossage recorded career save number 308 (his only save in 1991 and his only save for the Rangers) and preserved Nolan Ryan's career win number 308.

# # #

Sammy Sosa, Mark McGwire, Rafael Roque.

On September 18, 1998, Brewers pitcher Roque gave up McGwire's 64th home run in Milwaukee. In his next start, on September 23—also in Milwaukee—Roque surrendered Sosa's 64th home run.

# # #

Joe Carter, Ted Kluszewski, Benito Santiago.

They all wore uniforms with misspellings. Carter's said TOROTNO instead of TORONTO on July 14, 1994.

As a publicity stunt in 1960 Bill Veeck's White Sox intentionally misspelled Big Klu's name KLUSZEWSKI.

Santiago's Padres uniform had his name as SANTAIGO.

Dennis Eckersley is said to have received a shipment of ECKERSELY jerseys when he was with the Oakland A's.

# # #

Randy Kutcher, Scott Louks, Curt Schilling, Steve Staggs, and Tom Sullivan.

All are natives of Alaska—the only five in big league history. Kutcher, Louks, Schilling, and Staggs are from Anchorage, while Sullivan is from Nome.

# # #

Rick Dempsey, Nolan Ryan, Carlton Fisk.

These are the only three men to play in the majors in the 1960s, the 1970s, the 1980s, and the 1990s.

# # #

Jimmie Foxx and his wife, Dorothy.

Both choked to death on food.

Jimmie Foxx died on July 21, 1967, after choking on dinner at his brother's house in Miami.

His wife, Dorothy, was only 48 when she died on May 7, 1966, in Miami, when she choked on a piece of pork, according to her daughter Nanci.

# # #

Jackie Robinson, Ernie Banks, Nolan Ryan.

They have the same birthday: January 31 (1919, 1931, and 1947, respectively).

# # #

Lou Gehrig, Gates Brown.

Brown was born on May 2, 1939—the day Gehrig's consecutive game playing streak ended.

# # #

Jimmie Foxx, Mickey Cochrane, Pinky Higgins.

These Philadelphia Athletics teammates hit for the cycle within 13 days of each other in 1933. Cochrane's came on August 2 against the Yankees, Higgins did it on August 6 against the Senators, and Foxx hit for the cycle on August 14 against the Indians.

# # #

Steve Finley, Ken Caminiti, John Flaherty, Brian Johnson, Greg Vaughn.

These are the only men to hit home runs in the U.S.A., Canada, and Mexico. They played in the Padres-Mets game in Monterrey, Mexico, on August 16, 1996.

# # #

Edd J. Roush, Harry S. Truman.

Each had a middle initial but no middle name.

# # #

T. J. Mathews, Eric Ludwick, Blake Stein.

These three St. Louis Cardinals were traded to the Oakland A's on July 31, 1997, for Mark McGwire.

# # #

George Brett, Nolan Ryan.

On October 3, 1993, their glorious careers ended in the same game. Before the very last game at Arlington Stadium, the future Hall of Famers exchanged lineup cards. After the game, home plate was removed and transferred to the Rangers' new home, The Ballpark. They were inducted into the Hall of Fame in Cooperstown together on July 25, 1999.

# # #

Tony Clark, Frank Howard, Ron Jackson, Walt Bond, Bill Davis, Billy Ashley, and Desi Wilson.

They are the only position players in baseball history who stood 6'7" or more.

# # #

Tony Armas, Barry Bonds, Joe Carter, Rocky Colavito, Chili Davis, André Dawson, Doug DeCinces, Darrell Evans, Carlton Fisk, Jimmie Foxx, Andres Galarraga, Joe Gordon, Frank Howard, Reggie Jackson, Dave Kingman, Lee May, Fred McGriff, Mark McGwire, Johnny Mize, Rafael Palmeiro, Dave Parker, Larry Parrish, Frank Robinson, George Scott, Vern Stephens, and David Winfield.

Through 1999, these are the only sluggers to hit at least 100 career home runs for two different teams.

# # #

Walter Johnson, Everett Scott.

On May 2, 1923, Walter Johnson beat the New York Yankees 3–0—his 100th career shutout. One of the Yankees in that game was Everett Scott, playing his record 1,000th consecutive game.

# # #

Lou Gehrig, Rocky Graziano.

Yes, both had successful films made about their careers (*Pride of the Yankees, Somebody Up There Likes Me*), but that's not the answer.

After being forced to retire as a ballplayer because of his illness, Gehrig was given the job of New York City Commissioner of Parole. As such, he adjudicated allegations of parole violation charges against 19-year-old Rocco Barbella, who was sent to reform school. Upon his release, Barbella changed his name to Rocky Graziano, changed his life, and became middleweight champion of the world in 1946.

# # #

Jim Kaat, Tim McCarver, Willie McCovey.

These are the only three men to play in the majors in the 1950s, the 1960s, the 1970s, and the 1980s.

Coincidentally, Kaat and McCarver have both broadcast for the New York Yankees since 1999.

# # #

The New York Mets, Admiral Richard E. Byrd.

Both had exactly three ticker-tape parades in their honor up Broadway in New York City's "Canyon of Heroes."

Admiral Byrd's parades were on June 23, 1926, after his flight over the North Pole; on July 18, 1927, after he and the crew of *The America* flew across the Atlantic; and exactly three years later, on July 18, 1930, to commemorate his expedition to Antarctica. No other individual has ever been accorded three separate ticker-tape parades in New York City.

The Mets have also had three parades. The first was on April 12, 1962, to celebrate their upcoming first season; on October 20, 1969, to celebrate the "Miracle Mets" world championship; and on October 28, 1986, to commemorate the Mets' triumph over the Boston Red Sox in the World Series.

(The New York Yankees have had seven ticker-tape parades, to commemorate their World Series triumphs in 1961, 1962, 1978, 1996, 1998, 1999, and 2000.)

Thanks to Stan Newman for unearthing this one.

# # #

Carlton Fisk, Tony Perez.

Sure, they were inducted into the Hall of Fame together in 2000. And they played against each other in the 1975 World Series. They were teammates on the 1980 Red Sox. But what else?

Fisk is the oldest man in the history of the major leagues to hit a grand slam—October 3, 1991, for the White Sox. Fisk was 43 years, 9 months old.

Perez is the second oldest. His grand slam came on May 13, 1985, for the Reds, the day before his 43rd birthday.

# # #

Larry Sherry, Rollie Fingers, John Wetteland, Mariano Rivera.

These are the only relief pitchers to be named Most Valuable Player in the World Series.

Larry Sherry, Los Angeles Dodgers, 1959; Rollie Fingers, Oakland A's, 1974; John Wetteland, New York Yankees, 1996; Mariano Rivera, New York Yankees, 1999.

# # #

Jesse Orosco, Rick Ferrell, Jake Daubert, Lou Whitaker, Willie Kamm, Luis Aparicio, Rickey Henderson.

These players hold the records for most games played at one position: Orosco, pitcher—1,093 (as of May 2000); Ferrell, catcher—1,806; Jake Daubert, first base—2,002; Lou Whitaker, second base—2,308; Willie Kamm, third base—1,672; Aparicio, shortstop—2,581; and Henderson, outfield—2,856.

# # #

RAH, RAH, RAH

━━━━━━━

CHRISTY MATHEWSON MADE BASEBALL a respectable profession for young men. He was, after all, a "college man"—from Bucknell. In the past, other important players also brought the cachet of a college education (and the refinement that was thought to follow) to the big leagues: Eddie Collins (Columbia), Lou Gehrig (who attended but was not graduated from Columbia), and Eddie Grant (Harvard College, Harvard Law School), for example.

A number of modern big leaguers went to the pros right out of high school. Many ballplayers honed their skills, albeit with metal bats, in college. Some colleges are known for their baseball programs—USC, Seton Hall, Texas, and Arizona, for example. Others, while producing major leaguers, are less well known.

Here's our list of less well-known colleges attended by big leaguers.

Biola University, La Mirada, California
Cameron University, Lawton, Oklahoma
Chapman University, Orange, California
College of the Siskiyous, Weed, California
Coastal Carolina University, Conway, South Carolina
Elon College, Elon, North Carolina
Erskine College, Due West, South Carolina
Faulkner University, Montgomery, Alabama
Ferrum College, Ferrum, Virginia

Grand Valley State, Allendale, Michigan
Jackson State, Jackson, Mississippi
Lamar College, Beaumont, Texas
Lewis University, Romeoville, Illinois
Linfield College, McMinville, Oregon
Livingston University, Livingston, Alabama
Masters College, Newhall, California
McNeese State, Lake Charles, Louisiana
Otterbein College, Westerville, Ohio
St. Francis College, Brooklyn Heights, New York
St. Leo College, St. Leo, Florida
University of Montevallo, Montevallo, Alabama
Winona State University, Winona, Minnesota

# # #

BASEBALL
BY THE NUMBERS

TWO

Only two players have had 200 or more hits and 150 or more strikeouts in the same season. Who are they?

Bobby Bonds, 1970 Giants, 200 hits, 189 strikeouts.

Mo Vaughn, 1996 Red Sox, 207 hits, 154 strikeouts.

# # #

Name both players who have hit at least 20 homers and stolen at least 80 bases in the same season.

Hint: One did it twice.

In 1985 Rickey Henderson became the first man to accomplish this feat, with 24 homers and 80 stolen bases for the Yankees. Henderson did it again for the 1986 Yankees—28 homers and 87 stolen bases.

The other is Eric Davis, 1986 Reds, 27 homers, 80 stolen bases.

# # #

Only two men have hit at least 50 home runs in a season for two different teams. Who are they?

Jimmie Foxx was the first. He hit 58 for the 1932 Philadelphia A's and another 50 for the 1938 Red Sox.

Mark McGwire was the second. In 1996 he hit 52 for the Oakland A's, then went on to hit 70 for the 1998 St. Louis Cardinals.

# # #

Only two men have hit World Series home runs before they connected for regular season shots. Who were they?

The first to accomplish this unusual feat was pitcher Wilfred Patrick Dolan "Rosy" Ryan, who connected for his very first home run in New York on October 6, 1924, in Game 3 of the World Series for the Giants, against the Senators. His only regular season home run did not come until May 25, 1925.

Next was outfielder Frank Demaree, who hit a home run in Chicago for the Cubs on October 2 in Game 4 of the 1932 World Series. His first regular season home run was on June 15, 1933. Demaree hit 72 regular season homers.

Pitcher Mickey Lolich's first big league home run was in St. Louis on October 3 in 1968 in Game 2 of the World Series for the Tigers.

Although Lolich had 821 at bats during his major league career, he never hit a regular season home run.

# # #

Tris Speaker had 53 doubles and stole 52 bases for the Boston Red Sox in 1912. For 86 years, he was the only man with 50 doubles and 50 stolen bases in a single season, until this player joined Speaker, and "50–50" became a real club. Who is he?

Craig Biggio of the Houston Astros. In 1998 he had 51 doubles and 50 steals.

# # #

When baseball fans get together, talk frequently turns to the question, "Who was the greatest ever?" Ty Cobb's name is usually mentioned (4,189 hits, 892 stolen bases, 12 batting titles, .366 career batting average, even leading the American League in home runs in 1909). Despite his enormous talent as a ballplayer, Cobb was one of the most disliked men in baseball. In fact, only three players went to his funeral in Cornelia, Georgia, on July 19, 1961. Who were they?

Hall of Famers Ray Schalk and Mickey Cochrane. Hall of Fame Director Sid Keener also attended, as did former pitcher Nap Rucker.

# # #

Who are the only two players to have at least 300 career home runs without a single 30-home run season?

Al Kaline: 399 total, with a single-season high of 29 homers, in both 1962 and 1966, and Harold Baines—373 homers through 1999, with a high of 29 with the White Sox in 1984.

# # #

Only two men have hit at least 100 home runs for three different teams. Who are they?

Hint: One is a Hall of Famer.

Reggie Jackson and Darrell Evans. Jackson hit 269 with the A's, 144 for the Yankees, and 123 for the Angels.

Evans hit 131 for the Braves, 142 for the Giants, and 141 for the Tigers.

# # #

In a home game against the Tampa Bay Devil Rays (the only modern big league team with four words in its name), on September 26, 1999, Derek Jeter drove in his 100th run of the season—a double that scored Chad Curtis in the sixth inning. So? That RBI made Jeter only the second Yankee shortstop to drive in 100 runs in a single season. Who was the first?

Lyn Lary, 1931—107 RBIs.

# # #

Who are the only two managers to be fired during spring training?

Alvin Dark, March 21, 1978, by the Padres and Phil Cavarretta, by the 1954 Cubs.

# # #

Only two men played for the Mets in the 1960s, 1970s, and 1980s. One is Hall of Famer Tom Seaver (1967-77, 1983). Who is the other?

Mike Jorgensen—1968, 1970-71, 1980-83.

# # #

Name two players who played for two big league teams in the same city—twice.

Cy Young played for the Cleveland Spiders in the National League and the Cleveland Indians in the American League, and the Boston Braves (National League) and the Red Sox (American League).

Dick Tidrow played for the White Sox and Cubs, as well as for the New York Yankees and Mets. Tidrow is the only man to play for the Cubs, White Sox, Yankees, and Mets.

# # #

Name the two players who led their league in significant pitching and batting categories, 18 years apart.

Nolan Ryan—then with the Angels—led the American League in strikeouts in 1972 with 329. Eighteen years later, when he was with the Rangers, he led the league again with 232 in 1990.

Rickey Henderson led the American League in stolen bases with the Oakland A's in 1980 with 100. Eighteen years later, in 1998, Henderson, back with the A's, led the American League with 66.

Coincidentally, Henderson was Ryan's 5,000th strikeout victim.

# # #

Only two major league baseball players—both 6′6″—have been teammates in the National Basketball Association. Who are they?

Dave DeBusschere and Ron Reed on the Detroit Pistons, 1965–66, 1966–67.

# # #

Only two sets of teammates were Rookies of the Year and went on to hit more than 400 career home runs.

Who were they?

Willie Mays (National League Rookie of the Year 1951, 660 home runs) and Willie McCovey (National League Rookie of the Year 1959, 521 home runs) were teammates on the San Francisco Giants, 1959–72.

José Canseco (American League Rookie of the Year 1986, 431 home runs through 1999) and Mark McGwire (American League Rookie of the Year 1987, 522 home runs through 1999) were teammates on the Oakland A's 1986–92 and again in 1997.

# # #

Only two men have had three consecutive years with 200 hits and 100 walks. Who are they?

Lou Gehrig and Wade Boggs.

# # #

Who are the only 20th-century managers to have big league stadiums named after them?

Connie Mack and Ted Turner. In 1953 Shibe Park in Philadelphia was renamed Connie Mack Stadium, in honor of the "Tall Tactician," who managed and owned the Philadelphia A's from 1901 to 1950.

Ted Turner, the irrepressible owner of the Atlanta Braves, managed his team in uniform on May 11, 1977, before being reminded that baseball rules expressly prohibit a team owner from managing—or even from sitting in the dugout during a game.

The Braves moved into Turner Field, converted to baseball after the 1996 Olympics, in time for the 1997 season.

# # #

THREE

Name the three men who hit more than 300 career home runs and have exactly three letters in their first names and their last names.

Mel Ott (511), Ron Cey (316), and Lee May (354).

# # #

Only three major leaguers have stolen at least 20 bases in a season in which they also hit at least 50 homers. Who are they?

Willie Mays, 1955 New York Giants: 51 homers, 24 stolen bases.
Brady Anderson, 1996 Baltimore Orioles: 50 homers, 21 stolen bases.
Ken Griffey, Jr., 1998 Seattle Mariners: 56 homers, 20 stolen bases.

# # #

Only three players in history have hit 40 home runs, had 200 hits, and stolen 30 bases in a single season. Who are they?

Hank Aaron, 1963 Milwaukee Braves—44, 201, 31; Ellis Burks, 1996 Colorado Rockies—40, 211, 32; and Alex Rodriguez, 1998 Seattle Mariners—42, 213, 46.

# # #

In 1997 Nomar Garciaparra of the Boston Red Sox scored 122 runs. Only three men scored more runs in their rookie seasons. Who are they?

Joe DiMaggio, 1936 New York Yankees—132
Ted Williams, 1939 Boston Red Sox—131
Roy Johnson, 1929 Tigers—128

# # #

Who are the only three natives of Mexico to hit more than 100 career home runs?

Vinny Castilla—209 (through 2000), Aurelio Rodriguez—124, and Jorge Orta—130.

FOUR

Since the major-league amateur draft began in 1965, only four men have gone directly from high school to the big leagues. Who are they?

David Clyde, Texas Rangers, 1973
Todd Van Poppel, Oakland A's, 1990
Alex Rodriguez, Seattle Mariners, 1993
Josh Beckett, Florida Marlins, 1999

# # #

Only four men have been Rookie of the Year, Most Valuable Player, and have hit 400 career home runs. Which four?

Willie Mays, National League Rookie of the Year 1951, National League Most Valuable Player 1954 and 1965, 660 career homers.

Frank Robinson, National League Rookie of the Year 1956 (unanimously), National League Most Valuable Player 1961, American League Most Valuable Player 1966, 586 career homers.

José Canseco, American League Rookie of the Year 1986, American League Most Valuable Player 1988, 446 career homers (through 2000).

Cal Ripken, Jr. was American League Rookie of the Year in 1982, American League Most Valuable Player in 1983 and 1991, and has 417 homers through 2000.

# # #

For many years, it was thought that only three players appeared in the major leagues during the 1930s, 1940s, 1950s, and 1960s: Ted Williams, Mickey Vernon, and Early Wynn. But there is a fourth. Who is he?

Elmer Valo. In 1939 Valo appeared in the last game of the season for the Philadelphia Athletics and walked. But after the game, A's owner and manager Connie Mack asked Red Smith, the official scorer, to delete Valo's name from the official account of the game, as the A's had neglected to have Valo sign a major league contract. Smith complied.

# # #

Who are the only four players who hit 30 homers and drove in 100 runs in seven consecutive years?

Babe Ruth, Lou Gehrig, Jimmie Foxx, and Albert Belle.

# # #

Only four men have 3,000 career hits, 300 home runs, and 200 stolen bases. Which four?

	HITS	HOMERS	STOLEN BASES
George Brett	3,154	317	201
Hank Aaron	3,771	755	240
Willie Mays	3,283	660	338
Dave Winfield	3,110	465	223

# # #

Name four sets of batterymates who became major league managers.

Walter Johnson and Muddy Ruel were batterymates on the Washington Senators 1923–27. Johnson later became the manager of the Senators and Indians, while Ruel managed the Browns.

Pitcher Fred Hutchinson and his catcher Birdie Tebbetts were teammates on the Detroit Tigers 1939–40 and in 1946–60. Tebbetts went on to manage the Reds, Milwaukee Braves, and Cleveland Indians, while Hutchinson managed the Tigers, Cardinals, and Reds.

"Steady" Eddie Lopat and Yogi Berra were batterymates for the Yankees 1949–55. Lopat managed the Kansas City Athletics and Berra managed both the Yankees and the Mets.

One of Lopat's other catchers was Ralph Houk, his Yankee teammate (1948–54), who managed the Yankees, the Tigers, and the Red Sox.

# # #

Only four men have managed six different big league teams since 1900. Which four?

Jimmy Dykes—White Sox, Philadelphia A's, Orioles, Reds, Tigers, Indians
Rogers Hornsby—Cardinals, Giants, Boston Braves, Cubs, Browns, Reds
John McNamara—Oakland A's, Padres, Reds, Angels, Red Sox, Indians
Dick Williams—Red Sox, Oakland A's, Angels, Expos, Padres, Mariners

# # #

Only four Canadians have been general managers of major league teams. Who are they?

Gordon Ash (Blue Jays), Doug Melvin (Rangers), George Selkirk (Senators), and Murray Cook (Expos and Reds).

# # #

FIVE

Only five switch hitters have driven in at least 100 runs in a single season in both leagues. Who are they?

Eddie Murray, Ken Singleton, Ted Simmons, Bobby Bonilla, and J. T. Snow.

# # #

Only five men have hit at least 30 home runs in their first two full major league seasons. Who are they?

Rudy York, Detroit Tigers, 1937—35; 1938—33
Ron Kittle, Chicago White Sox, 1983—35; 1984—32
José Canseco, Oakland A's, 1986—33; 1987—31
Mark McGwire, Oakland A's, 1987—49; 1988—32
Nomar Garciaparra, Boston Red Sox, 1997—30; 1998—35

# # #

SEVEN

Only seven men (including five Hall of Famers) played in the Negro League East-West Game and a big league All-Star Game. Name them.

Jackie Robinson, Roy Campanella, Ernie Banks, Satchel Paige, Larry Doby, Minnie Minoso, and Jim Gilliam.

# # #

TEN

Name the 10 Rookies of the Year who went on to manage in the major leagues.

Hint: So far, only one is a Hall of Famer.

Mike Hargrove, Lou Piniella, Bill Virdon, Jim Lefebvre, Tommy Helms, Harvey Kuenn, Frank Howard, Pete Rose, Alvin Dark, and Hall of Famer Frank Robinson.

# # #

Only 10 big leaguers have hit 40 home runs in a season for three consecutive seasons. Which ten?

Hint: Two were teammates.

Babe Ruth, New York Yankees: 1926—47, 1927—60, 1928—54, 1929—46, 1930—49, 1931—46, 1932—46

Harmon Killebrew, Minnesota Twins: 1961—46, 1962—48, 1963—45, 1964—49

Ernie Banks, Chicago Cubs: 1957—43, 1958—47, 1959—45, 1960—41

Ted Kluszewski, Cincinnati Reds: 1953—40, 1954—49, 1955—47

Ralph Kiner, Pittsburgh Pirates: 1947—51, 1948—40, 1949—54, 1950—47, 1951—42

Duke Snider, Brooklyn Dodgers: 1953—42, 1954—40, 1955—42, 1956—43, 1957—40

Eddie Mathews, Milwaukee Braves: 1953—47, 1954—40, 1955—41

Frank Howard, Washington Senators: 1968—44, 1969—48, 1970—44

Jay Buhner, Seattle Mariners: 1995—40, 1996—44, 1997—40

Ken Griffey, Jr., Seattle Mariners: 1996—49, 1997—56, 1998—56, 1999—48

# # #

FIFTY

How many men can you name who spent more than 50 years in a big-league uniform?

Even though he spent 50 years as manager of the Philadelphia A's, Connie Mack cannot be included in this list, as he managed while wearing a business suit rather than a baseball uniform.

Among those who did spend at least 50 years in uniform are Don Zimmer, Jimmy Reese, Red Schoendienst, Frank Crosetti, and Casey Stengel.

# # #

Who was the first second baseman to turn an unassisted triple play in the regular season?

Mickey Morandini of the Philadelphia Phillies. Playing at Pittsburgh's Three Rivers Stadium on September 20, 1992, in the sixth inning, Morandini caught Jeff King's liner (1 out), stepped on second base to retire Andy Van Slyke leading off second (2 outs), then tagged Barry Bonds coming from first base (3 outs).

# # #

Which big leaguer is a part owner of the Indian Motorcycle Club of Toronto?

David Wells.

# # #

Which future Dodger was born on September 9, 1965–the day of Sandy Koufax's perfect game?

Todd Zeile.

# # #

Which Yankees had the most RBIs in their first 500 games as Yankees?

Hint: Two are Hall of Famers.

Babe Ruth–483
Joe DiMaggio–475
Tino Martinez–407

# # #

Chuck Klein drove in 100 runs, hit 40 doubles, scored 100 runs, and hit 30 homers for the Phillies in 1929, 1930, and 1932. Who was the next Phillie to reach all of these plateaus in a single season?

Scott Rolen in 1998, when he drove in 110 runs, hit 45 doubles, scored 120 runs, and hit 31 homers.

# # #

"I gave up 2 of Babe Ruth's historic 60 home runs in 1927. I also scored more points in one NFL game than anyone in history. Who am I?"

Football Hall of Famer Ernie Nevers. He went 3–8 pitching for the 1927 St. Louis Browns and surrendered homers to Ruth on May 11 in St. Louis (number 8) and on August 27 in St. Louis (number 41).

On November 28, 1929, he scored all 40 points for the Chicago Cardinals against the Chicago Bears. Nevers scored six touchdowns and kicked four points after touchdown. Final score: 40–6.

# # #

Ty Cobb holds the major league record for most runs scored in a career, with 2,246. Rickey Henderson finished 2000 with 2,178. Hank Aaron and Babe Ruth are tied for third place on this list at 2,174. Why are they tied?

Because on October 3, 1976, in the final at bat of his career, Aaron singled in the bottom of the sixth inning off Dave Roberts of the Tigers. Aaron was then lifted by manager Alex Grammas so he could be greeted by thunderous applause (or at least as thunderous as a "crowd" of 6,858 can manage) at Milwaukee County Stadium as Aaron ran off the field. Pinch runner Jim Gantner scored what would have been Aaron's 2,175th run, which would have broken his tie with Ruth and put him alone in second place on the all-time runs scored list.

Thanks, Alex.

# # #

Who is the most expensive batting-practice pitcher in history?

Dale Sveum. Hitting just .155 in 58 at bats, Sveum, a utility infielder, was cut by the Yankees July 27, 1998. No other team wanted to sign him, so the Yankees were required to continue paying his $800,000 annual salary. In order to stay around the game—perhaps in the hopes of being picked up by some other team—Sveum volunteered to pitch batting practice and to help out as a bullpen catcher and scout. But Sveum still wanted to play, and he got his chance with the 1999 Milwaukee Brewers.

# # #

HIGHS AND LOWS

———

Who has stolen bases in the most major league stadiums?

Rickey Henderson—who else? In his incredible career, Henderson played in both the American and the National Leagues. He has stolen bases in 39 different stadiums, in four countries (USA, Canada, Mexico, and Japan), and in Hawaii (when his Padres played a series there against the Cardinals).

# # #

Who is the oldest man to drive in more than 100 runs for the first time in his big league career?

Tony Gwynn. The 37-year-old Padre drove in 119 runs in 1997.

# # #

Who had the most RBIs in a single season with fewer than 200 at bats?

Smokey Joe Wood. In 1921, he drove in 60 runs for the Indians in only 194 at bats.

# # #

Who had the lowest single-season batting average for any player who hit at least 20 home runs?

Rob Deer. He batted just .179 (with 175 strikeouts) while hitting 25 homers for the 1991 Tigers—making Deer the only man ever to hit 20 homers while batting under .200. His career batting average was a solid .220.

# # #

Which players committed the most career errors?

Hint: They shared the same unusual nickname.

Germany Long—1,037 and Germany Smith—1,007.

# # #

Jim Bouton, author of *Ball Four*, went eight years between big league victories (1970–78). Who had an even longer gap in his major league playing career—22 years?

Paul Schreiber. He was a Dodger from 1922 to 1923, then was out of the majors for 22 years, working as a batting practice pitcher. But the major leagues were so depleted by players in the military service that Schreiber returned to the big leagues with the Yankees in 1945, when he was 42. His career record? 0–0.

# # #

Who has the most swelled head—literally—in the big leagues?

Padres manager Bruce "Bucket Head" Bochy, who wears a size 8″ hat—said to be the largest in the majors.

# # #

Who is the youngest player to lead his league in homers?

Juan Gonzalez. In 1992 he hit 43 homers for the Texas Rangers, at age 22.

# # #

Who has batted leadoff in the most games?

Rickey Henderson.

# # #

Who had the longest walk in baseball?

Pirates announcer and former pitcher Jim Rooker. Calling a game that the Pirates led 10–0 against the cross-state rival Phillies in Philadelphia on June 8, 1989, Rooker told his audience: "If the Pirates blow this one, I'll walk back to Pittsburgh!" When the Pirates did indeed lose (15–10), Rooker kept his word and walked the 315 miles back to Pittsburgh, raising $81,000 for charity along the way.

# # #

Who had the most career stolen bases without ever leading the league in that category?

Joe Morgan—689.

# # #

Roberto Clemente's career ended with exactly 3,000 hits. What record did he achieve after his final hit?

Although he had not planned to play on October 4, 1972, the next-to-last day of the season, Clemente was inserted by manager Bill Virdon in right field for Vic Davalillo in the late innings and broke Honus Wagner's record for most games played by a Pittsburgh Pirate, 2,433. That was Clemente's final game, as he died on December 31, 1972, in a plane that crashed while carrying relief supplies to earthquake-ravaged Managua, Nicaragua.

# # #

Which two pitchers with the same last name had the most wins in the same season?

The Deans, Dizzy and Daffy. Dizzy won 30 and his brother Daffy won 19 for the 1934 St. Louis Cardinals.

# # #

Too easy?
How about "most home runs in the same season by two men with the same last name"?

The Vaughn cousins—Mo and Greg. In 1998 Mo Vaughn hit 40 homers in his last year with the Boston Red Sox, while Greg hit 50 for the San Diego Padres, for a total of 90.

# # #

Which major league position player, with at least 2,500 at bats, had the lowest batting average?

Bill Bergen—.170. In his 3,028 at bats with the Reds and Dodgers between 1901 and 1911, he managed just 516 hits.

# # #

The concept of scoreboard-as-entertainment is said to have been originated by Bill Veeck, the greatest showman and promoter in the history of the game. In 1960 his Chicago White Sox installed the first exploding scoreboard at Comiskey Park I—fireworks went off to commemorate a home-team home run.

As of 2000, which ballpark has the largest scoreboard in the majors?

Detroit's new Comercia Park—180 feet across.

# # #

What is the lowest number of home runs to lead the league in a post–World War II nonstrike season?

Twenty-three by Ralph Kiner of the 1946 Pirates.

# # #

Who is the only man to have at least 150 walks, runs, and RBIs in the same season?

Ted Williams, 1949 Red Sox—162 walks, 150 runs, 159 RBIs.

# # #

Who had the fewest RBIs in a season in which he had at least 150 at bats?

Paul Popovich, 1967 Cubs: 159 at bats, 2 RBIs.

# # #

What was the biggest trade in baseball history?

On December 15, 1960, the Phillies traded 6′8″ Gene Conley to the Red Sox for 6′6½″ Frank Sullivan.

# # #

Which team had the most players scoring at least 100 runs in a single season?

The 1931 New York Yankees—6. Lou Gehrig (163), Babe Ruth (149), Ben Chapman (120), Earle Combs (120), Joe Sewell (102), and Lyn Lary (100).

# # #

Which team's lineup produced the most future managers?

The 1956 St. Louis Cardinals, who were managed by Fred Hutchinson. The nine future managers on the roster included Ken Boyer, Alvin Dark, Joe Frazier, Alex Grammas, Grady Hatton, Solly Hemus, Whitey Lockman, Red Schoendienst, and Bill Virdon.

# # #

ALL IN THE FAMILY

TRICK QUESTION DEPT.:

"**I am a big leaguer. My grandfather and my great grandfather are Hall of Famers. Who am I?**"

Shane Monahan, who broke in with the 1998 Mariners. His great grandfather Howie Morenz was inducted into the Hockey Hall of Fame in Toronto in 1945. Monahan's grandfather was Bernie "Boom Boom" Geoffrion, a 1972 inductee.

Geoffrion married Morenz's daughter Marlene. Their daughter Linda married Hartland Monahan, Shane's father.

# # #

Name five men who managed their sons in the major leagues.

Connie Mack managed his son Earle with the Philadelphia Athletics, 1910–11 and again in 1914; Yogi Berra managed his son Dale with the Yankees in 1985; Cal Ripken, Sr., became the first man to manage two sons simultaneously in the majors when he managed Billy and Cal, Jr., with the Baltimore Orioles, 1987–88; Hal McRae's son Brian played for him with the 1991–94 Royals; and Felipe Alou managed his son Moises with the Montreal Expos, 1992–96.

# # #

José Cruz, Sr., has three sons. They all have the same last name. What else do they have in common?

The same first name. José Javier, José Cheito, José Enrique. José Javier (who goes by José Cruz, Jr.) is a big leaguer.

# # #

Carlos Quintana has two sons named Carlos. Roberto Kelly has two sons with the same first name—Roberto.

# # #

When did a father and son first umpire in the same modern major league game?

On August 10, 1998, when veteran umpire Harry Wendelstedt, in the last year of his 33-year career, worked a Padres-Marlins game with his son Hunter. Harry umpired behind the plate, and Hunter was at second base.

# # #

When was the first time since 1900 that two brothers were in the majors at the same time—one as a player, the other as a nonplaying manager?

1998, when Glenn Hoffman was named manager of the Dodgers. His brother Trevor was the Padres' star closer.

# # #

Which father-and-son pitchers won the most games in history?

The Stottlemyres, Mel, Sr., Yankees, (1964–74) 164 wins, and Todd, (1988–) Blue Jays, A's, Cardinals, Rangers, Diamondbacks, 138 wins (through 2000). Total: 302. Mel, Jr., who pitched briefly for the Royals in 1990, did not record a win.

# # #

Name the first game in which one team started two sets of brothers?

September 27, 1998—the last day of the season—when the Reds lineup included Bret Boone (second base), Aaron Boone (third base), Barry Larkin (shortstop), and Steve Larkin (first base).

# # #

Which brothers have the most total saves in big league history?

The Worrells, Tim (5) and Todd (256) (through mid-2000). Total: 261.

# # #

Name the only Hall of Famers whose children were married to each other.

Herb Pennock and Eddie Collins.

# # #

Twins manager Tom Kelly and his wife, Sharon, have two children. What are their names?

Tom and Sharon's children are Tom and Sharon.

# # #

"I am a big league pitcher. My brother was my team's bullpen catcher. Who are we?"

The pitcher is Bobby Witt of the Texas Rangers (1992, 1995–98). His brother Doug was the Rangers' bullpen catcher starting in 1992.

# # #

What's the family connection? Vida Blue, Glenn Hoffman, José Oquendo, Dee Fondy, Orel Hershiser, John Burkett, Randy Ready, Darryl Kile, Mike Bordick, Robby Thompson, Doug Henry, Dick Howser, Otis Nixon, Eddie Perez, John Vander Wal, Johnny Damon, Buck Rodgers, Bucky Dent, Bruce Walton, Mike Gallego, John Wetteland, Denny Hocking (of the Twins), Matt Nokes, and National League umpire Jerry Meals.

Each is the father of twins.

Oquendo's daughters are Marilyn and Carolyn. Nixon's girls are Trivion and Trivain.

Luis Gonzalez, Dennis Cook, and Dave Righetti have triplets, and Doug Strange is the father of quadruplets—Joseph, Jackson, and Jake, and their sister, Logan.

# # #

Hall of Famer James "Pud" Galvin had nine children. Manny Mota is the father of eight. Dale Murphy also has eight—seven boys and a girl. Dennis Rasmussen has seven children.

Davey Johnson, Dwight Gooden, Whitey Lockman, Elrod Hendricks, Sal Bando, and Tony Cloninger each has six children.

LETTERS

Paul O'Neill's three children all have names starting with the letter *A,* as do Rickey Henderson's three daughters and Harvey Pulliam's three girls.

Walt Weiss's three sons all have names starting with *B.*

Brian Bohanan has five children, all of whose names start with the letter *B.*

Tom Foley's three kids all have names starting with *B.*

Bernie Williams's three children all have names starting with *B.*

All five of Jerry Narron's children have names starting with *C.*

Doug Jones and his wife, Debbie, have three sons, all of whose names start with *D.*

Ron Oester's wife and their four children all have names starting with *J.*

Jack Lamabe, his wife, and their two children all have the same first initial—*J.*

Pitcher Mike Flanagan's three kids have names starting with *K.*

So do Gary Allenson's three sons.

Roger Clemens's kids are Koby, Kory, Kacy, and Kody.

Pat Borders and his wife have five children—all have names starting with *L.*

The names of Jeff Reed's three children all start with *L.*

Frank Thomas's three children all have names beginning with *S.*

Sonny Seibert's four kids all have first names starting with *S.*

The names of Ron Gardenhire's three children all start with *T.*

Vern Law and his wife, VaNita, named their boys Veldon, Vance, Veryl, Vaughn, and Varlin, and their daughter VaLynda. Their dog is Victor.

# # #

As far as we can tell, the major leaguer with the most siblings is José Mesa, who has 24 siblings (15 born to his mother). Mesa has five children of his own.

Ralph Branca told us he was the 10th of 15 children.

George Harper had 19 siblings.

Elmo Plaskett is one of 16 children.

José Bautista is one of 16 children.

Jesus Sanchez has six brothers and nine sisters.

Bill Swift is one of 15.

Jeff Stone is one of 15 kids (nine boys, six girls).

Willie Upshaw has 14 brothers and sisters.
Veteran American League umpire Dale Ford is one of 13 children.
Hall of Famer Big Ed Walsh was the youngest of 13 children.
Fernando Valenzuela has five brothers and six sisters.
Happy Felsch, like Davey Lopes, has 11 siblings.
Josias Manzanillo is one of 11 children.
George Shuba was the youngest of 11 children.
Mookie Wilson is one of 11.
Frank Robinson is the youngest of 10 children.
Vladimir Guerrero is one of nine.
Manny Alexander has 10 brothers.
Bill Gullickson is one of nine children.
Estaban Yan has nine siblings.
Kirby Puckett is the youngest of nine.
Homer Bush is one of eight children, as is Harold Reynolds.

# # #

Who formed the first brother battery in the majors?

Tommy Thompson, pitcher, and Homer Thompson, catcher for the New York Highlanders—later the Yankees—on October 14, 1912. It turned out to be Homer's only game.

# # #

What's the family connection? Willie Randolph, Wayne Kirby, Jim Acker, Tim Salmon, Mark McGwire.

Each has a brother who played in the National Football League: Terry Randolph, Terry Kirby, Bill Acker, Mike Salmon, and Dan McGwire.

# # #

The Boones, the Hairstons, and the Bells are well-known as three-generation families of big leaguers. But another family has also featured three on-field generations. Who are they?

The Runges. Ed Runge was an American League umpire from 1954 to 1970. His son Paul umpired in the National League from 1973 to 1997, before becoming the National League's Supervisor of Umpires. Paul's son Brian, while a Pacific Coast League umpire, made his big league debut filling in for a vacationing umpire in a Mets-Cubs game at Wrigley Field on April 23, 1999.

# # #

"I'm a big leaguer. So is my brother. We have the same last name. We also have the same first name. Who are we?"

José Valentin. José Antonio Valentin—Brewers, White Sox 1992–. His younger brother, José Javier Valentin, plays for the Twins 1997–.

# # #

How do you call the Larry Walker family to dinner?

Larry, Gary, Cary, Barry [his brothers], Larry, and Mary [his parents].

# # #

Who were the first father and son to umpire in the modern big leagues?

Jerry Crawford, son of Henry "Shag" Crawford, who umpired in the National League, 1956–75. Jerry umpired in the National League, 1975–98.

# # #

Which brothers have hit home runs for opposing teams in the same game since 1900?

Rick and Wes Ferrell (Red Sox and Indians), July 19, 1933.
Tony and Al Cuccinello (Dodgers and Giants), July 5, 1935.
Jim and Graig Nettles (Tigers and Yankees), September 14, 1974.
Hector and José Cruz (Cubs and Astros), May 4, 1981.
Ken and Clete Boyer (Cardinals and Yankees) homered in Game 7 of the 1964 World Series.

# # #

These batterymates (including a Hall of Fame pitcher) played together for 11 years. Their sons and namesakes also became big league batterymates. Who are they?

Big Ed Walsh and his catcher Billy Sullivan were teammates for 11 years on the Chicago White Sox, 1904–14. Ed, Jr., and Billy, Jr., were teammates on the 1932 White Sox.

# # #

Which father and son have had the most combined career hits?

The Bondses: Bobby (1,886) and Barry (2,157 through 2000) have a total of 4,341 through mid-2000.

# # #

"I'm the team physician for a big league team. My son's a professional athlete, too—but not a baseball player. Who are we?"

Marlins orthopedist Dr. Daniel Kanell and his son, Danny, who was the quarterback for the NFL's New York Giants.

# # #

Who are the first father-and-son pair to be first-round draft picks?

The Grieves. Tom was the Washington Senators number 1 pick in 1966, and his son Ben was Oakland's number 1 selection in 1994. Tom played for the Senators, Rangers, Mets, and Cardinals, 1970, 1972–79, batting .249 with 65 home runs. Ben was the the American League Rookie of the Year in 1998.

# # #

Who is the only major league baseball player whose brother-in-law played in the National Basketball Association?

Darryl Strawberry. His wife's brother is Miles Simon, whose knee surgery limited him to five games for the Orlando Magic in 1998–99.

# # #

"My mother played on the LPGA tour for four years. Her brother played in the majors for four decades. I played in the majors, too. Who are we?"

Gregg Zaun is a big leaguer. His mother is Cherie Zaun, an LPGA golfer from 1972 to 1976, and later the women's golf coach at USC. Her brother, Gregg's uncle, is Rick Dempsey.

# # #

"I'm a big leaguer. My brother fought in a heavyweight championship boxing match. Who are we?"

The major leaguer was Dolph Camilli (Cubs, Phillies, Dodgers, Red Sox, 1933–43, 1945). His brother Frankie, who fought under the name Frankie Campbell, fought Max Baer in San Francisco on August 25, 1930. Camilli was hit with a punch in the fifth round that snapped his neck. He died the next day.

# # #

Who are the only father-and-son major leaguers with a palindromic last name?

Dick and Robb Nen.

# # #

"Before I played on a World Championship baseball team, I was the Junior National racquetball champion. My wife, Cindy, was a racquetball doubles champ. Who am I?"

Jeff Conine, a member of the 1997 Marlins.

# # #

JUNIORS AND SENIORS

———

WHO IS THE YOUNGEST PERSON **ever to play in a professional baseball game?**

Joe Louis Reliford. On July 19, 1952, the 12-year-old batboy was inserted into the lineup as a pinch hitter for the Fitzgerald Pioneers in a game against the Statesboro Pilots (Class D, Georgia State League). Reliford grounded to third in the top of the eighth inning and made a diving catch in right field in the bottom of the eighth, and the Pilots won 13–0.

# # #

The oldest college baseball field still in use appears to be Coleman Field, home of the Oregon State Beavers in Corvallis. It was built in 1907.

# # #

Who is the youngest man to hit 20 home runs and steal 20 bases in a single season?

Andruw Jones of the 1998 Atlanta Braves. He finished the season with 31 homers and 27 steals. He was 21.

# # #

On September 14, 1975, Robin Yount broke a record that had stood for 47 years. Which record?

Most major league games played by a teenager—242. Yount was still two days shy of his 20th birthday when he broke the old record set by Mel Ott.

# # #

Who is the youngest man to catch over 100 games in a single season?

Ivan Rodriguez. He caught 116 games for the 1992 Rangers, when he was 20. The previous year, he caught 88 games at age 19.

# # #

Who is the oldest pitcher to win an All-Star Game?

Nolan Ryan, who was 42 in 1989 when his American League team beat the National Leaguers 5–3 in Anaheim.

# # #

Name the youngest battery in major league history.

Pitcher Jim Waugh, age 19, and catcher Nick Koback, 18, teammates on the 1953 Pittsburgh Pirates, who finished in last place.

# # #

Who is the youngest American League Rookie of the Year?

Tony Kubek, 1957 Yankees. He was 20.

# # #

Only two men who turned 40 before the start of the season drove in at least 100 runs in a single season. Dave Winfield, who drove in 108 runs with the Blue Jays in 1992, was the first. Who was the second?

On September 22, 1999—six months after his 40th birthday—Harold Baines drove in his 100th run of the season for the Cleveland Indians.

# # #

Who is the youngest man to have 200 hits and 35 home runs in a single season?

Twenty-one-year-old Alex Rodriguez of the 1996 Seattle Mariners, who had 215 hits and 36 homers to go with his 141 runs and 123 RBIs. His batting average was .358.

# # #

WE'VE GOT
YOUR NUMBER

NO NUMBERS

Uniform numbers were introduced by the New York Yankees in 1929. By 1931, every big league team's uniforms had numbers. Since then, which players have appeared in major league games without uniform numbers?

Detroit's Gabe Kapler. On September 27, 1999, in the final game at Tiger Stadium, Detroit starters wore uniform numbers to honor the all-time Tiger team. Kapler wore no number in honor of Ty Cobb, who played before uniform numbers were used.

# # #

Joel Horlen made his major league debut pitching for the Chicago White Sox on September 4, 1961, in Minneapolis. The only extra road uniform they had did not have a number. Horlen later wore #20.

# # #

Lou Whitaker neglected to bring his Tiger uniform to Minnesota for his appearance in the 1985 All-Star Game on July 16, 1985. So he bought a souvenir Tigers shirt at the Metrodome and drew on his #1 with a felt-tip pen.

Thanks to James Robinson, author of the 2000 Official Major League Baseball Desk Calendar.

# # #

On May 19, 1984, Eric Davis—just recalled from the minors—pinch-hit for the Reds' Duane Walker in the fifth inning. He batted without a number.

# # #

WRONG NUMBER

The 1999 Yankees clinched the American League East championship on September 3. On October 3 they played their last game of the regular season at Tampa Bay. Joe Torre let Paul O'Neill manage the team that day, and Tino Martinez, a Tampa native, had his 10-year-old son, T. J., with him on the field. T. J. was wearing an official Yankee uniform and was the Yankees' batboy. Tino wears #24. What number did T. J. wear that day?

#2. He likes Derek Jeter.

# # #

May 29, 2000—Memorial Day. Also the day the Yankees got their 1999 world champion rings.

Roger Clemens has pitched in the majors for 16 years. But he did not win a World Series game until 1999, when he won Game 4 for the Yankees. The Yankees swept the Braves, 4–0.

But Clemens's diamond-studded ring had to be sent back. What was wrong with it?

It had the wrong uniform number. The ring given to Clemens had "#33" on it. That was David Wells's number in 1998. Clemens wore #22.

SAME NUMBER

After Edgar Renteria's hit won Game 7 and the 1997 World Series for the Florida Marlins, Little League players in his native Barranquilla, Colombia, all adopted his uniform number—6.

# # #

RETIRED NUMBERS

# # #

In 2000 the Cincinnati Reds decided to retire #10 in honor of Sparky Anderson, who managed the Reds 1970–78. Anderson was enshrined at the Hall of Fame that year. While nobody on the Detroit Tigers currently wears #11 (which Anderson wore when he managed in Detroit 1979–95) the Tigers have thus far declined to retire #11 for Anderson.

# # #

Most fans recall that the New York Yankees retired #8 in honor of their greatest catchers, Bill Dickey and Yogi Berra. Only one other team has retired one number for two different big league players. Which team, which number, and which players?

The Montreal Expos. #10. Rusty Staub (1993), and André Dawson (1997). When they were teammates in Montreal in 1979, Staub wore #6.

# # #

"I was the first and last person on my team to wear this number—the only time in major league history this has happened. Who am I?"

Lou Gehrig was the Yankees' first #4—because he batted fourth in the lineup. On Lou Gehrig Day, July 4, 1939, the day of his memorable farewell speech, his #4 became the first number ever retired. Thus, he was the only Yankee to ever wear #4.

# # #

When David Wells came to the Yankees in December 1997, he asked that Babe Ruth's #3 be unretired for him because he was such a big Babe Ruth fan. When this was rejected, Wells settled for #33.

# # #

When Bob Lemon's #21 was retired by the Cleveland Indians on June 9, 1998, manager Mike Hargrove was wearing #21. After some resistance, Hargrove agreed to change to #30, the number he wore in college, and his son's number in high school.

# # #

On April 15, 1997, the 50th anniversary of Jackie Robinson's first game in a Brooklyn Dodgers uniform, Bud Selig, then the acting commissioner of baseball, decreed that from then on, no new player in the big leagues would ever wear #42. Those players who were wearing it on that date would be permitted to continue to wear it until the end of their careers. They were Mo Vaughn (Red Sox), Butch Huskey (Mets)—both of whom wore it in Robinson's honor—Mike Jackson (Indians), José Lima (Astros), Buddy Groom (A's), Dennis Cook

(Marlins), Tom Goodwin (Royals), Mariano Rivera (Yankees), Jason Schmidt (Pirates), Lenny Webster (Orioles), Kirk Rueter (Giants), Scott Karl (Brewers), and Marc Sagmoen (Rangers). Sagmoen wore #42 only once—during his very first game for the Rangers on April 15, 1997—the very day it was retired—then switched to #37, deeming himself not worthy of wearing Robinson's number. Also on that date, Ken Griffey, Jr., switched his uniform number from #24 to #42, in tribute to Robinson.

# # #

On October 3, 1992, the Astros retired #25 in honor of José Cruz, Sr., one of their great stars from 1975 to 1987. He returned to the Astros as a coach in 1997, and his number was unretired.

# # #

Only one team has ever had players wear #0 and #99 at the same time. Which team and which players?

The 1998 New York Mets. Rey Ordoñez wore #0 and Turk Wendell had #99.

# # #

MAJOR LEAGUERS WHOSE NUMBERS
HAVE BEEN RETIRED BY A MINOR LEAGUE TEAM

Don Mattingly's uniform #18 was retired in 1999 by the AAA Nashville Sounds in the Pacific Coast League. Mattingly played there in 1981. His #23 was retired by the New York Yankees.

# # #

Larry Doby's #14 was retired in 1997 by the Burlington Indians of the Rookie Advanced Appalachian League.

# # #

On November 1, 1995, #33 was retired by the Princeton (West Virginia) Devil Rays (Rookie Advanced, Appalachian League) in honor of John Stearns. No other coach or player will ever again wear #33 in Princeton, the smallest town in America that has a professional baseball team. In 1994 Stearns, former Phillie and Met catcher, managed the Princeton Reds to their first Appalachian League title. A similar honor was bestowed on Brad Kelley, #34, who was Princeton's pitching coach.

# # #

On May 27, 1998, the Trenton Thunder (the Red Sox AA affiliate in the Eastern League) retired #5, in honor of one of its most illustrious alumni, Nomar Garciaparra. In fact, the Boston Red Sox were the visiting team that day and played the Thunder in an exhibition game.

The Thunder retired #33 on May 19, 1997, in honor of another alumnus, Tony Clark.

# # #

On May 30, 1997, the Las Vegas Stars (the Padres affiliate in the AAA Pacific Coast League) retired their first number—#15 in honor of Mike Sharperson, who had just been called up to the Padres when he was killed in a car crash on May 26, 1996.

# # #

On April 9, 1997, in ceremonies before a Tigers-Twins game at Detroit's Tiger Stadium, the Jamestown Jammers, the Tigers' affiliate in the New York–Penn Short Season "A" League, retired uniform #22 for Bubba Trammel—the first Jammer to make it to the big leagues. The Jammers gave Trammel his home, road, and practice uniforms—all framed.

# # #

MAJOR LEAGUERS WHOSE NUMBERS
HAVE BEEN RETIRED BY A COLLEGE TEAM

Two former Cougars at the University of Houston who went on to play in the major leagues have had their numbers retired: Doug Drabek, #16, and Tom Paciorek, #22.

# # #

Wright State University retired #34 in honor of Brian Anderson.

# # #

Arizona State University may have set the record for retiring uniform numbers of its players who went on to the major leagues: #0—Oddibe McDowell, #1—Bobby Winkles, #5—Bob Horner, #6—Sal Bando, #7—Alan Bannister, #14—Larry Gura, #19—Floyd Bannister, #24—Barry Bonds, #27—Rick Monday, and #44—Reggie Jackson.

# # #

The University of Minnesota has retired numbers for two of its players who went on to play in the major leagues: Paul Molitor, #11, and Dick Siebert, #24.

# # #

The University of Illinois has retired three numbers. Two were for football immortals Red Grange, #77, and Dick Butkus, #50. The third, #5, was for Lou Boudreau, who led Illinois to the 1937 Big Ten baseball championship.

# # #

The University of North Carolina Tarheels have retired numbers for two of its alumni who have played in the major leagues: #9–B. J. Surhoff, and #22–Dave Lemonds.

# # #

The first graduate of the University of Texas to have his baseball number retired was Roger Clemens–#21 in 1993.

# # #

Illinois State University retired #12 for Dave Bergman.

# # #

Florida's University of Miami has retired numbers for three Hurricanes who played in the major leagues: Orlando Gonzalez, #20, Neal Heaton, #26, and Mike Fiore, #12.

# # #

River Grove, Illinois's Triton College has retired the baseball uniform numbers of two alumni–Kirby Puckett, #29, and Lance Johnson, #1.

# # #

In 1995 Jay Buhner's number #19 was retired by his alma mater, McClennan Community College in Waco, Texas.

# # #

The University of Nevada at Las Vegas retired #5 for Matt Williams.

# # #

Tony Gwynn's #19 is sure to be retired by the San Diego Padres if he ever retires. Meanwhile, his #28 is the only number retired by San Diego State University. (See http://www.gwynnsport.com)

# # #

Cal Poly–San Luis Obispo has retired the numbers of three men who played in the major leagues: Ozzie Smith, #3, Mike Krukow, #21, and John Orton, #9.

# # #

MAJOR LEAGUERS WHOSE NUMBERS HAVE BEEN RETIRED BY A HIGH SCHOOL TEAM

# # #

Plant High School, in Tampa, Florida, has retired uniform numbers in honor of two of its alumni, Wade Boggs, #9, and John Hudek, #18.

# # #

January 29, 1999, was "Jeff Bagwell Day" in Middlesex County, Connecticut, where he grew up. His #9 was retired by his alma mater, Xavier High School.

# # #

Dave Tomlin's #37 was retired by West Union (Ohio) High School in 1998.

# # #

Tony Womack was the first graduate of Gretna (Virginia) High School to have his number, #7, retired.

# # #

Andre Dawson and Carlos Castillo had their numbers retired by Miami's Southwest High School.

# # #

Curt Schilling's #38 was retired by his school, Shadow Mountain High School in Arizona, on August 11, 1998.

# # #

WHY DOES HE WEAR THAT NUMBER?

Why did Hall of Famer George Brett wear #5?

That was his position number (third base). Also, it was the number worn by his favorite player, another legendary Hall of Fame third baseman, Brooks Robinson of the Orioles.

# # #

When Rickey Henderson got to the Seattle Mariners in May 2000, he asked for #24, which he had worn for years. The Mariners said no. Why?

Although they had not retired it for Ken Griffey, Jr., they weren't giving it to anybody else just yet. Rickey had to settle for #35, which he had worn early in his career.

# # #

Why did Davey Lopes wear #42 as a coach for the San Diego Padres?

To honor another former Dodgers second baseman, Jackie Robinson. When Robinson's number was retired by all of baseball, Lopes switched to #30.

# # #

Why did Kenny Rogers select #73 when he arrived at Shea Stadium for his first day as a Met on July 25, 1999?

Rogers had been wearing #37 with the Oakland A's before the Mets acquired him. But the Mets had retired #37 for their first manager, Casey Stengel, so Rogers reversed the digits.

# # #

Why did Cal Ripken, Jr., wear #8 with the Baltimore Orioles?

His father, Cal, Sr., had worn #7. When Cal, Jr., got to the Orioles in 1981, Mark Belanger was wearing #7. So Ripken took the closest one—#8.

# # #

Why does Edgard Clemente of the 1999 Rockies wear #12?

He reversed the digits of his uncle Roberto Clemente, who wore #21.

# # #

Trot Nixon wears #7 to honor Mickey Mantle.

# # #

Butch Huskey wears #44 to honor Hank Aaron, after switching from #42, which honored Jackie Robinson.

# # #

Jason Varitek wears #33 in honor of fellow switch hitter Eddie Murray.

# # #

Why did Roger Clemens wear #22 with the 1999 New York Yankees?

While he was with the Red Sox, (1984–96), he wore #12. When he got to the Blue Jays in 1997, he wanted to reverse the digits and wear #21. But Carlos Delgado already wore #21. In exchange for a Rolex watch from Clemens, Delgado agreed to a switch.

When Clemens went to the Yankees at the start of the 1999 season, he asked Paul O'Neill, who had worn #21 for his entire career, to relinquish it. O'Neill declined the offer of a Rolex and kept #21. So Clemens reversed the digits and tried #12 for a while. His record was so-so for the Yankees early in 1999, so he reversed the digits again and took it up one to #22.

# # #

Why did Chicago Cubs fireballer Kerry Wood select #34 for his 1998 Rookie of the Year season?

Because it was worn by one of his idols—Nolan Ryan. Wood wore #21 in high school (like Roger Clemens), but Sammy Sosa already had that number with the Cubs.

# # #

Why does Alex Rodriguez of the Seattle Mariners wear #17?

To honor his boyhood idol, Keith Hernandez of the Mets. Hernandez wore #17 with the Indians and Mets and #37 with the Cardinals.

# # #

Why did Wade Boggs wear #12 with the Tampa Bay Devil Rays?

In honor of Joe Namath, who wore it with the New York Jets.

# # #

Robert Smith of the Tampa Bay Devil Rays wears #9 in honor of his father, who died of cancer when Robert was 9, and in honor of his sister Stacy, who died of heart disease when she was 9.

# # #

When Carlton Fisk changed his sox (going from the Red Sox to the White Sox in 1981), he reversed his number from #27 to #72.

# # #

Why did Mike Schmidt wear #20?

To honor Frank Robinson, who played for the Cincinnati Reds when Schmidt was growing up in Dayton, Ohio.

# # #

Why did Carlos Garcia wear #13?

To honor his hero and fellow Venezuelan, Reds shortstop Dave Concepcion.

# # #

Why did Walt Weiss switch from uniform #7 to #22?

In honor of Eugene "Mercury" Morris of the Miami Dolphins and San Diego Chargers.

# # #

When Ken Griffey, Jr., was traded by the Seattle Mariners to the Cincinnati Reds just before the 2000 season, he switched uniform numbers. Why?

Griffey wore #24 in Seattle, but he could not wear it in Cincinnati, as the Reds were about to retire it for coach Tony Perez, who had just been elected to the Hall of Fame. So Griffey chose #30, which his father had worn as a Reds player. Ken, Sr., now wears #33 as a Reds coach.

# # #

Besides Jackie Robinson, seven men have had their numbers retired by more than one team:

> Frank Robinson's #20—Orioles and Reds
> Rod Carew's #29—Twins and Angels
> Nolan Ryan's #30—Angels, #34—Rangers and Astros
> Rollie Fingers's #34—A's and Brewers
> Casey Stengel's #37—Yankees and Mets
> Hank Aaron's #44—Braves and Brewers

# # #

Only one man besides Nolan Ryan had different numbers retired by different major league teams. Who is he?

> Carlton Fisk. Boston Red Sox—#27. Chicago White Sox—#72.

# # #

MAJOR LEAGUE RETIRED NUMBERS

#	PLAYER	TEAM
	Ty Cobb	Tigers
	Christy Mathewson	Giants
	John McGraw	Giants
		While Cobb, Mathewson, and McGraw played before uniform numbers were used, their teams honored them by mounting replicas of their uniforms, and their names, on their outfield walls.
	Walter Haas	Former Oakland A's owner. A numberless jersey with his name is on the outfield wall at Oakland-Alameda County Stadium/Network Associates Coliseum.
	Ray Kroc	Former owner of the Padres. A jersey in his honor hangs in Qualcomm Stadium.

	Jerry Coleman	San Diego Padres broadcaster and former manager. A jersey in his honor hangs in Qualcomm Stadium.
1	Bill Klem	National League umpire
1	Ozzie Smith	Cardinals
1	Billy Meyer	Pirates
1	Pee Wee Reese	Dodgers
1	Richie Ashburn	Phillies
1	Billy Martin	Yankees
1	Fred Hutchinson	Reds
1	Bobby Doerr	Red Sox
2	Tommy Lasorda	Dodgers
2	Red Schoendienst	Cardinals
2	Jocko Conlon	National League umpire
2	Charlie Gehringer	Tigers
2	Nellie Fox	White Sox
2	Nick Bremigan	American League umpire
3	Dale Murphy	Braves
3	Al Barlick	National League umpire
3	Bill Terry	Giants
3	Harmon Killebrew	Twins
3	Harold Baines	White Sox
3	Earl Averill, Sr.	Indians
3	Babe Ruth	Yankees
4	Mel Ott	Giants
4	Ralph Kiner	Pirates
4	Lou Gehrig	Yankees
4	Earl Weaver	Orioles
4	Duke Snider	Dodgers
4	Joe Cronin	Red Sox
4	Luke Appling	White Sox
4	Paul Molitor	Brewers
5	George Brett	Royals
5	Johnny Bench	Reds
5	Carl Barger	Marlins (former owner)
5	Hank Greenberg	Tigers
5	Brooks Robinson	Orioles
5	Lou Boudreau	Indians
5	Joe DiMaggio	Yankees
6	Steve Garvey	Padres
6	Stan Musial	Cardinals

6	Tony Oliva	Twins
6	Al Kaline	Tigers
7	Mickey Mantle	Yankees
8	Carl Yastrzemski	Red Sox
8	Gary Carter	Expos
8	Joe Morgan	Reds
8	Willie Stargell	Pirates
8	Bill Dickey	Yankees
8	Yogi Berra	Yankees
9	Bill Mazeroski	Pirates
9	Minnie Minoso	White Sox
9	Bill Kunkel	American League umpire
9	Enos Slaughter	Cardinals
9	Ted Williams	Red Sox
9	Roger Maris	Yankees
10	Rusty Staub	Expos
10	Andre Dawson	Expos
10	Phil Rizzuto	Yankees
10	Dick Howser	Royals
10	Sparky Anderson	Reds
11	Jim Fregosi	Angels
11	Carl Hubbell	Giants
11	Luis Aparicio	White Sox
12	Wade Boggs	Devil Rays
14	Kent Hrbek	Twins
14	Larry Doby	Indians
14	Gil Hodges	Mets
14	Ernie Banks	Cubs
14	Ken Boyer	Cardinals
15	Thurman Munson	Yankees
16	Hal Newhouser	Tigers
16	Ted Lyons	White Sox
16	Lou DiMuro	American League umpire
16	Whitey Ford	Yankees
17	Dizzy Dean	Cardinals
18	Ted Kluszewski	Reds
18	Mel Harder	Indians
19	Robin Yount	Brewers
19	Billy Pierce	White Sox
19	Jim Gilliam	Dodgers
19	Bob Feller	Indians
20	Don Sutton	Dodgers

20	Lou Brock	Cardinals
20	Pie Traynor	Pirates
20	Mike Schmidt	Phillies
20	Frank White	Royals
20	Frank Robinson	Orioles, Reds
21	Warren Spahn	Braves
21	Bob Lemon	Indians
21	Roberto Clemente	Pirates
22	Jim Palmer	Orioles
23	Willie Horton	Tigers
23	Don Mattingly	Yankees
24	Willie Mays	Giants
24	Walter Alston	Dodgers
24	Tony Perez	Reds
25	José Cruz, Sr.	Astros
26	Billy Williams	Cubs
26	Gene Autry	Angels owner
27	Juan Marichal	Giants
27	Jim "Catfish" Hunter	A's
27	Carlton Fisk	Red Sox
29	Rod Carew	Twins, Angels
30	Orlando Cepeda	Giants
30	Nolan Ryan	Angels
31	Dave Winfield	Padres
32	Sandy Koufax	Dodgers
32	Steve Carlton	Phillies
32	Jim Umbricht	Astros
32	Elston Howard	Yankees
33	Mike Scott	Astros
33	Honus Wagner	Pirates (worn as a coach, 1933–51)
33	Eddie Murray	Orioles
34	Nolan Ryan	Rangers, Astros
34	Rollie Fingers	A's, Brewers
34	Kirby Puckett	Twins
35	Phil Niekro	Braves
35	Randy Johnson	Padres
36	Robin Roberts	Phillies
37	Casey Stengel	Yankees, Mets
39	Roy Campanella	Dodgers
40	Danny Murtaugh	Pirates
40	Don Wilson	Astros

41	Tom Seaver	Mets
41	Eddie Mathews	Braves
42	Jackie Robinson	Dodgers (and every other team)
44	Willie McCovey	Giants
44	Hank Aaron	Braves, Brewers
44	Reggie Jackson	Yankees
45	Bob Gibson	Cardinals
50	Jimmy Reese	Angels
53	Don Drysdale	Dodgers
72	Carlton Fisk	White Sox
85	August Busch, Jr.	Cardinals owner

# # #

WHAT'S IN A NAME?

———

ONE OF THE NOTORIOUS BLACK SOX PITCHERS was Eddie Cicotte. He pitched a no-hitter on April 14, 1917, but was later banned
for life by Commissioner Kenesaw Mountain Landis for his participa-
tion in the gambling scheme. His last name has been pronounced in numerous
ways, but the July 1, 1920, *Sporting News* offered this guide to the "correct"
pronunciation in a column by John B. Sheridan:

IT'S JUST PLAIN CICOTTE
One old fan all bent and rickety,
said the name was Eddie Cicotte;
The second said this was rot,
the proper way was Eddie Cicotte;
The third one called the others dotty
and called the pitcher just Cicotte;
The fourth fan said, "Now, boys I note
that those who know call him Cicotte."
I was the fifth and advised "Don't fight.
We'll ask the S.E. to set us right."
[The "S.E." was presumably the sports editor.]
REPRINTED WITH PERMISSION OF *SPORTING NEWS*.

# # #

Name the most monstrous outfield ever.

The team fielded by the Reds on June 21, 1998, which featured Dmitri Young, Mike Frank, and Chris Stynes. Together, they were Young, Frank, and Stynes.

# # #

This name was shared by two big leaguers, not related to each other. One pitched a no-hitter. The other hit more than 50 home runs in a single season. Who are they?

George Foster and George Foster.

George "Rube" Foster pitched a no-hitter for the Red Sox on June 21, 1916, in 91 minutes, over the Yankees in Boston.

The other George Foster hit 52 home runs for the 1977 Cincinnati Reds.

# # #

Who are the only major leaguers whose last names contain all five vowels?

Jesus, Bien, and Ed Figueroa, Dee Cousineau, Ralph Mauriello, Gene Rounsaville, and Dave Wainhouse.

# # #

Name three major leaguers whose first names contain all five vowels.

Aurelio Rodriguez, Aurelio Monteagudo, and Aurelio Lopez.

# # #

Name all five major leaguers whose first names start with the letter Q.

Hint: No two have the same first name.

Quenton Lowery, Quilvio Veras, Quincy Trouppe, Quinn Mack, and Quinton McCracken.

# # #

Who is the only big leaguer whose last name contains exactly the same letters as his first name?

Gary Gray.

# # #

BALLPLAYERS NAMED AFTER PRESIDENTS
AND OTHER HISTORICAL VIPs

Andrew Jackson Bednar
Abraham Lincoln Bailey
William McKinley "Max" Venable
Franklin Pierce Harter
Franklin Pierce "Monty" Stratton
Gair Roosevelt Allie
Franklin Delano Roosevelt "Ted" Wieand
Roosevelt Lawayne Brown
Martin Van Buren Walker
George Washington Baumgardner
George Washington Bradley
George Washington Case
George Washington Harper
George Washington Simmons
George Washington Stanton
George Washington Zabel
George Washington Grant, owner of the Boston Braves
Woodrow Wilson Williams
Cesar Octavio "Tavo" Alvarez
Ethan Allen Blackaby
Victor Hugo Vernal
Charles Dickens Bold
(Perhaps these last two would like to meet Paul O'Neill, a direct descen-
    dant of Mark Twain, or Todd Zeile, a direct descendant of John Adams
    and John Quincy Adams.)
Harry Lee Biemiller
Stephen Douglas Brady
Benjamin Franklin Callahan
Benjamin Franklin Dyer
Benjamin Franklin Huffman
Mark Anthony Dalesandro
Mark Anthony Eichhorn
Mark Anthony Thurmond
Mark Anthony Whiten
Julio Cesar Franco
Ulises Candy Sierra
Lafayette Napoleon Cross

# # #

Name three players whose names have double "i"s.

Larry Biittner, Torii Hunter, and Masato Yoshii.

# # #

In 1977 and 1978 the Cincinnati Reds had five guys named George in uniform. Who were they?

Hall of Famer, manager George "Sparky" Anderson
George "Ken" Griffey, Sr.
George "Tom" Seaver
George Foster
Coach George Scherger

# # #

How did "Pistol" Pete Reiser get his nickname?

From a movie serial called *Two Gun Pete*.

# # #

When the Jacobs family bought the Cleveland Indians and built a new park in Cleveland, they named it Jacobs Field. Similarly, Wrigley Field, Turner Field, Connie Mack Stadium, Ebbets Field, Briggs Stadium, both Comiskey Parks and others were named for the team owners. Too bad Phil Ball, former owner of the Browns, didn't name a park after himself.

# # #

INTRODUCTIONS WE'D LIKE TO HAVE MADE DEPT.:

Ugueth Urtain Urbina, this is Jermane Jay Johnson.
Urban Shocker, meet Country Slaughter.
Mitchell Williams, meet William Mitchell.
Wilbur Wood, meet Wilbur Good.
Alex Kellner, meet Ellis Kinder.
Tim Teufel, say hello to Jim Gott. Their names are, respectively, the German words for Devil and God.
Lee Thomas, meet Thomas Lee.
Gorman Thomas, please say hello to Thomas Gorman.
Bob Hasty, Horace Speed, Hal Quick, say hi to Slow Jack Doyle and Bob Walk.

Catcher Joe Early, meet pitcher Early Wynn. (Teammates, Senators 1939–43, 1946.)

Addie Joss, this is Eddie Joost.

Pat Corrales, who lives in Big Canoe, Georgia, meet Ralph Terry, a native of Big Cabin, Oklahoma.

Kevin McGehee, meet Mel McGaha.

# # #

DREAM TEAMS

Are You Sure That's How You Spell That?

Liubiemithz Rodriguez, A. J. Pierzynski.

The Smallest Team in Baseball

Lil Stoner, Lloyd "Little Poison" Waner, Peanuts Lowrey, Dave Short, Wee Willie Keeler, Mark Small, Don Liddle, Tot Presnell, Tiny Bonham, Bill Short, Andy Pettitte, Jeff Little, Minnie Minoso.

The All-Verb Team

Ken Sears, Bruce Fields, Harry Dooms, Tom Seats, Dick Mills, Matt Butts, Dick Burns, Ray Shook, Davey Lopes, Harry Betts (don't introduce him to Pete Rose), Pat Borders, Dave Drew, Hubie Brooks, Earle Combs, Eddie Files, Charlie Spikes, Virgil Trucks, Charlie Sands, Rollie Fingers, Golan Putts, Ernie Banks. Larry See, Heinie Crow, Charlie Chant, Phil Garner, Mel Held, Tom Hurt, Herman Franks, Cliff Chambers.

Thanks to Tim Wiles, Director of Research at the Baseball Hall of Fame, for his contributions to this list.

# # #

Minor leaguers we hope make it to the majors: Alex Andreopoulos, Mike Zywica, Errick Williams, Darren Blood, Cewar Izturis, Chance Sanford, Joe Victery, Apostol Garcia, E. J. t'Hoen, of the Cedar Rapids Kernels (Angels affiliate of the Midwest A League). A native of the Netherlands, he played on the 1996 Dutch Olympic team.

We're also rooting for Kelley Gulledge, drafted by the Texas Rangers, just so we can hear ballpark public address announcer Chuck Morgan announce "Now batting, my son, Kelley Gulledge." And finally, Eric Stuckenschneider.

# # #

WHY DIDN'T
I THINK OF THAT?

———

BASEBALL PLAYERS ARE A CRAFTY LOT. Many fans know that the weighted donut that slips over a bat to add weight during on-deck swings was invented by Elston Howard. We have discovered a number of other devices invented by ballplayers.

SABR member Bob Timmerman writes: "A few thoughts on this subject [baseball inventions] from someone who used to work in a patent depository library . . . I can state that baseball-related inventions were always popular among 'backyard' inventors who would come into the library to do patent searches. The two most popular topics seemed to be toilets, followed by golf aids, but baseball items were pretty popular. Most people went home when they realized that their idea wasn't new."

\# \# \#

Ever see an umbrella that fits on your head? It's a Brockabrella, invented by Hall of Famer Lou Brock.

\# \# \#

Outfielder Dave Gallagher (1987–95, Indians, White Sox, Orioles, Angels, Mets, Braves, Phillies) invented the Stride Tutor, a plastic chain that, when attached to both ankles like leg shackles, prevents overstriding at the plate.

# # #

The rubber home plate is said to have been invented and patented by former player Ed Keating.

# # #

Although he did not invent the tarp, now used at every outdoor stadium, Hall of Famer Fred Clarke designed and patented a tarpaulin that could easily be rolled out and then rolled up (Patent #983,857). Clarke set his brother up to market the invention in an office called Clarke's Cover Company, housed in the same building as the Pittsburgh Pirates offices.

# # #

Clarke is also credited with inventing flip-down sunglasses, first used by the 1916 Pirates.

# # #

The goalie-style catcher's mask was invented by Charlie O'Brien and is one of the newest pieces of equipment approved for use in major league games.

# # #

Cleveland shortstop Omar Vizquel has started marketing his own brand of salsa in mild, medium, and hot. The purchaser of bottle number 100,000 was rewarded with tickets to a Cleveland home game, a meeting with Vizquel, and a signed jersey.

# # #

While Abner Doubleday's connection to baseball is apocryphal, he will long be remembered for suggesting and chartering the nation's first cable-car street railway system in San Francisco. The cable cars are the only moving National Landmark.

# # #

Mary Elizabeth "Toots" Barger, "Queen of Duckpins," died in 1998. A major sport in and around Baltimore, duckpin bowling uses a five-inch diameter, three-pound ball, and pins that are just nine inches tall. Duckpins was once seriously proposed as the official state sport of Maryland. It was said to have been invented in 1900 in a bowling alley atop a Baltimore tavern owned by John McGraw and Wilbert Robinson.

# # #

Former pitcher Bob Patterson invented "Dr. Glove," a conditioning oil for baseball gloves.

# # #

PRIZE GUYS

WHICH NON–HALL OF FAMER **has been on the most All-Star teams?**

Elston Howard—9.

# # #

In 1998 Bernie Williams of the Yankees did something no other ballplayer had ever done. What was it?

He won the American League batting title (.339), won a Gold Glove for his fine defense in center field, and helped his team win the World Series. Nobody else had ever done all three in the same season.

# # #

Each year since 1957, Rawlings has awarded 18 Gold Gloves—one each to the best fielder at each position in both leagues. Except for 1995. That year, for the only time in history, 19 Gold Gloves were awarded. The extra award went to Michael Springer.

Who is Michael Springer?

Hint: Michael Springer is not a baseball player.

On October 7, 1995, in South Philadelphia, Springer saw a baby hanging from a third-story ledge. The child's parents and brothers were home, but none had kept a close eye on the child. When the baby lost his grip, Springer caught him. The child, just 17 months old, was unharmed. Philadelphia Mayor Edward Rendell's office contacted Rawlings, and suggested a special award go to Springer for his lifesaving catch.

# # #

Who are the only father and son to be named Most Valuable Player in the All-Star Game?

Ken Griffey, Sr., 1980, and Jr., 1992.

# # #

Who was the first player to be named "Comeback Player of the Year" twice?

Dick Ellsworth, 1963 and 1968, both with the Cubs.

# # #

Who is the only pitcher to be an All-Star as a starter and a reliever in consecutive years?

Goose Gossage, 1976—White Sox, 1977—Pirates.

# # #

TRICK QUESTION DEPT.:

Name seven Most Valuable Players who were managed by Most Valuable Players.

In 1926, George Burns of the Indians was the American League's MVP. His manager was the 1912 winner in the American League, Tris Speaker of the Boston Red Sox.

Joe Medwick, the National League Triple Crown winner and MVP in 1937 with the Cardinals, was managed by Sunny Jim Bottomley, the National League MVP with the 1928 Cardinals.

Keith Hernandez, the National League's co-MVP (with Willie Stargell) in 1979 with the Cardinals, was managed by Ken Boyer, the National League's MVP with the Cardinals in 1964.

Dale Murphy, National League MVP (1982, 1983) with the Braves, was managed by Joe Torre, the National League's MVP with the Cardinals in 1971.

Don Mattingly, American League MVP with the Yankees in 1985, was managed for part of 1985 by Yogi Berra, American League MVP in 1951, 1954, and 1955.

Larry Walker, National League MVP, 1997 Colorado Rockies, managed by Don Baylor, American League MVP, with the 1979 Angels.

Finally, Mickey Cochrane, the 1934 MVP in the American League (Tigers) was managed by 1928 MVP player-manager Mickey Cochrane (A's).

# # #

In 1998, the National League Rookie of the Year was Kerry Wood of the Chicago Cubs. The American League Rookie of the Year was Ben Grieve. How far apart were they born?

Wood was born in Irving, Texas, just 16½ miles from Grieve's hometown of Arlington.

# # #

"In 1988 I played only one game at second base. Yet I was voted the American League's starting second baseman in the All-Star Game. Who am I?"

Paul Molitor, Milwaukee Brewers.

# # #

Who is the only man to play more than 10 years in the major leagues and be an All Star every year in his career?

Joe DiMaggio. He was an All Star every season he played in the big leagues—1936–51, with time out for military service 1943–45.

# # #

Which was the first All-Star Game to feature three Jewish All Stars?

The 1999 game at Boston's Fenway Park. Mike Lieberthal (Phillies), Shawn Green (Blue Jays), and Brad Ausmus (Tigers).

# # #

Who was the first Australian-born All Star?

Dave Nilsson, 1998, Brewers, the pride of Brisbane.

# # #

Who was the oldest rookie to make his major league debut for a defending world championship team?

Luke Easter. He was 34 years old when he broke in with the 1949 Cleveland Indians. Easter went on to a six-year career, in which he batted .274 with 93 home runs.

# # #

Name the first team to feature five players who had been named Rookies of the Year.

The 1962 Giants: Willie Mays (1951), Harvey Kuehn (1953), Jack Sanford (1957), Orlando Cepeda (1958), and Willie McCovey (1959).

# # #

"I was named Most Valuable Player in a year in which I hit only six home runs and drove in only 48 runs. I am not a pitcher. Who am I?"

Maury Wills. In 1962 with the Los Angeles Dodgers, Wills hit .299 with 208 hits and stole 104 bases—a record at the time—and won a Gold Glove as shortstop.

# # #

Who was the first man to be Rookie of the Year and play in an All-Star Game in his home park in the same year?

Mark McGwire, Oakland A's, 1987.

# # #

Who was the first pitcher who did not pitch for a pennant winner to win the Cy Young Award?

Don Drysdale, of the 1962 Los Angeles Dodgers. He went 25–9, in 314⅓ innings, striking out 232 (all league-leading statistics), but the Dodgers lost the pennant to their rival, the San Francisco Giants, in a three-game playoff.

# # #

Who is the only man to win back-to-back MVP Awards with two different teams?

Barry Bonds. After winning the National League MVP Award with the Pittsburgh Pirates in 1990 and 1992, he won it with the San Francisco Giants in 1993.

# # #

Who is the only man to be named Most Valuable Player of the League Championship Series in both leagues?

Orel Hershiser: 1988 Los Angeles Dodgers and 1995 Cleveland Indians.

# # #

"I was an All-Star pitcher, even though at the All-Star break I had a record of 0–1 and finished the season 0–2. Who am I and what was I doing on the All-Star team?"

John Hudek, 1994 Astros. Starting in 1970, each team was required to have at least one representative on the All-Star team. That year, Hudek was chosen as the Astros' representative. While his pitching did not help the Astros very much that year, he did help the National League win 8–7 in Pittsburgh.

# # #

THE WORLD SERIES

WHO IS THE ONLY HALL OF FAMER to hit safely in each of the 14 World Series games in which he played?

Roberto Clemente: 1960—7 games, 9 hits; 1971—7 games, 12 hits.

# # #

Who played in the most World Series without ever being on a winning team?

Fred Merkle—5. He was with the 1911, 1912, and 1913 Giants, the 1916 Robins (Dodgers), and the 1918 Cubs.

# # #

Only six players have hit World Series home runs for American and National League teams. Which six?

Enos Slaughter, Cardinals—1942, 1946; Yankees—1956
Bill Skowron, Yankees—1955, 1956, 1958, 1960; Dodgers—1963
Roger Maris, Yankees—1960, 1961, 1962, 1964; Cardinals—1967
Frank Robinson, Reds—1961; Orioles—1966, 1969, 1970, 1971
Reggie Smith, Red Sox—1967; Dodgers—1977, 1978
Kirk Gibson, Tigers—1984; Dodgers—1988

# # #

"I lost 20 games one season and still pitched in the World Series. Who am I?"

George Mullin. He went 20–20 for the 1907 Tigers during the regular season, then lost two games to the Cubs in the Series, which the Cubs won, 4–0 with a tie.

# # #

GO FIGURE DEPT.:

Prior to 2000, the Mets had been in the World Series three times—in 1969, 1973, and 1986. The first Met to bat in Game 3 of each of those Series homered. Who were they?

Tommie Agee led off on October 14, 1969, at Shea Stadium. He homered off Jim Palmer of the Orioles.

On October 16, 1973, Wayne Garrett homered in the bottom of the first inning at home off Jim "Catfish" Hunter of the Oakland A's.

On October 21, 1986, at Boston's Fenway Park, Lenny Dykstra led off by homering off Dennis "Oil Can" Boyd.

Thanks to Chris Granozio of the New York Mets for this amazing coincidence.

# # #

Which modern player had the highest career batting average without ever appearing in a World Series?

Harry Heilmann. During his 17-year career with the Tigers and the Reds (1914, 1916–30, 1932) he compiled a .342 average—good enough for the Hall of Fame.

# # #

Only five men have hit 50 home runs and played in the World Series in the same season. Who are they?

> Babe Ruth, 1921 Yankees—59 home runs
>> Yankees lost to the Giants, 5–3, in a best-of-nine Series
> Babe Ruth, 1927 Yankees—60 home runs
>> Yankees swept the Pirates, 4–0
> Babe Ruth, 1928 Yankees—54 home runs
>> Yankees swept the Cardinals, 4–0
> Mickey Mantle, 1956 Yankees—52 home runs
>> Yankees beat the Dodgers, 4–3
> Mickey Mantle, 1961 Yankees—54 home runs
>> Yankees beat the Reds, 4–1
> Roger Maris, 1961 Yankees—61 home runs
>> Yankees beat the Reds, 4–1
> Albert Belle, 1995 Indians—50 home runs
>> Indians lost to the Braves, 4–2
> Greg Vaughn, 1997 San Diego Padres—50 home runs
>> Padres lost to the Yankees, 4–0

Greg Vaughn, Babe Ruth, and Albert Belle are the only men to hit at least 50 home runs in a season and lose a World Series.

# # #

Only one man has played in the World Series following the season in which he got his 3,000th hit. Who is he?

Eddie Murray, 1995 Cleveland Indians. They lost, 4–2, to the Atlanta Braves.

# # #

Only one player on the 1999 World Champion New York Yankees was a native of New York City. Who is he?

Pitcher Allen Watson, from Queens.

# # #

HALLS OF FAME

THE PINNACLE OF THE CAREER of any baseball player, umpire, manager, coach, or executive is enshrinement in the National Baseball Hall of Fame in Cooperstown, New York. To most people, "The Hall of Fame" *is* Cooperstown, but the Baseball Hall of Fame in Cooperstown is not the only hall of fame.

Many big leaguers have been inducted into halls of fame besides Cooperstown in recognition of their achievements in college or in the minors, or in other fields. Others are enshrined because of their ethnicity or the accident of their birthplace. ("The first man from Maine to play in the big leagues!") So when you wonder why Sibby Sisti, Stump Merrill, Art Shamsky, Del Bissonette, or Kirt Manwaring are "Hall of Famers," when you finish this chapter you'll know.

# # #

TRICK QUESTION DEPT.:

After signing a seven-year, $100 million dollar contract with the Los Angeles Dodgers on December 12, 1998, Kevin Brown bought a home in Beverly Hills for $3.8 million. He bought it from a Hall of Famer. Who is he?

John Fogerty. As a member of Creedence Clearwater Revival and as a solo performer, Fogerty was inducted into the **Rock and Roll Hall of Fame** in 1993.

# # #

Ted Williams is a member of the **National Fresh Water Fishing Hall of Fame** in Hayward, Wisconsin, and the **International Game Fish Association's Hall of Fame** in Fort Lauderdale, Florida.

# # #

Who is the only former leader of the free world who is an honorary member of the American Sportscasters Association Hall of Fame?

Ronald Reagan, former sportscaster, inducted in 1984.

# # #

TEAM HALLS OF FAME

A number of teams—major league, minor league, even defunct—have created their own Halls of Fame to honor players, managers, and coaches for outstanding achievements and for long and dedicated service.

# # #

The **Anaheim Angels Hall of Fame:** Bobby Grich, Jim Fregosi, Don Baylor, Rod Carew, Nolan Ryan, and Jimmy Reese.

# # #

The Atlanta Braves have their own Hall of Fame—the **Ivan Allen, Jr., Braves Museum and Hall of Fame,** honoring greats from the team's stays in Boston, Milwaukee, and Atlanta. Allen was the mayor of Atlanta and was instrumental in bringing the team to Atlanta. Members are Hank Aaron, Phil Niekro, Warren Spahn, and Eddie Mathews.

# # #

The **Baltimore Orioles Hall of Fame,** at the Babe Ruth Birthplace Museum in Baltimore: Mike Flanagan, Brooks Robinson, Frank Robinson, Dave McNally, Boog Powell, Gus Triandos, Luis Aparicio, Mike Cuellar, Mark Belanger, Earl Weaver, Paul Blair, Milt Pappas, Jim Palmer, Ken Singleton, Al Bumbry, Steve Barber, Jim Gentile, Stu Miller, Dick Hall, Hank Bauer, Scott McGregor, Hal Brown, Gene Woodling, Don Buford, Eddie Murray, and executives Frank Cashen and Paul Richards.

# # #

Former owner Lou Perini was inducted into the **Boston Braves Hall of Fame,** created by the Boston Braves Historical Society.

# # #

The Boston Red Sox Hall of Fame: Johnny Pesky, Ted Williams, owner Jean Yawkey, Smoky Joe Wood, Carl Yastrzemski, Frank Malzone, Jim Rice, Babe Ruth, Luis Tiant, Cy Young, Jimmie Foxx, executive Dick O'Connell, Mel Parnell, Tony Conigliaro, Harry Hooper, Dom DiMaggio, Bobby Doerr, Joe Cronin, Rico Petrocelli, Dick Radatz, Jackie Jensen, and Carlton Fisk.

# # #

Just because the Brooklyn Dodgers no longer exist doesn't mean that there is no **Brooklyn Dodgers Hall of Fame.** There is. Members include Dodgers and outstanding opponents, such as Carl Erskine, Gil Hodges, Dolph Camilli, Babe Herman, Johnny Podres, Ralph Branca, Clem Labine, Carl Furillo, Don Newcombe, Preacher Roe, Ralph Kiner, Whitlow Wyatt, Cal Abrams, Tommy Henrich, Gene Hermanski, Tommy Holmes, Cookie Lavagetto, Eddie Miksis, Mickey Owen, George Shuba, Bobby Thomson (!), Rex Barney, Joe Hatten, Clyde King, Jake Pitler, Eddie Stanky, Jake Daubert, Buddy Hassett, Billy Loes, Stan Musial, Al Walker, Tommy Brown, Leo Durocher, Luis Olmo, Johnny Vander Meer, Sandy Amoros, Andy Pafko, Joe Pignatano, Robin Roberts, Al Gionfriddo, Vic Lombardi, Babe Phelps, Meyer Robinson, Barney Stein, Warren Spahn, Johnny Sain, Bobby Bragan, Bobby Morgan, Russ Meyer, the poet Marianne Moore, Joe Black, Frenchy Bordagaray, Al Campanis, organist Gladys Gooding, Kirby Higbe, Don Hoak, Paul Minner, Pete Reiser, Eddie Basinski, Rocky Bridges, Pete Coscarart, Johnny Frederick, Randy Jackson, Spider Jorgensen, Alta Cohen, Curt Simmons, Tim Thompson, Johnny Kucks, Gene Mauch, Mike Sandlock, Elmer Valo, Dick Williams, Yogi Berra, Don Thompson, Jim Hughes, Roger Craig, Don Demeter, and Angelo Ambrosio.

# # #

The Chicago White Sox Hall of Fame, on the main concourse level behind home plate at Comiskey Park, includes Nellie Fox, Harold Baines, Luke Appling, Minnie Minoso, Luis Aparicio, Ted Lyons, Billy Pierce, and Carlton Fisk.

# # #

The Cincinnati Reds Hall of Fame includes Gus Bell, Johnny Bench, Jack Billingham, Ewell Blackwell, Rube Bressler, Smoky Burgess, Leo Cardenas, Clay Carroll, Gordy Coleman, Harry Craft, Sam Crawford, Hughie Critz, Jake Daubert, Paul Derringer, Pete Donahue, Lonny Frey, Warren Giles, Ival Goodman, Wayne Granger, Heinie Groh, Noodles Hahn (surely the only person in any hall of fame anywhere named "Noodles"), Bubbles Hargrave (see previous comment), Tommy Helms, Fred Hutchinson, Dave Concepcion, Ted Kluszewski, Larry Kopf, Brooks Lawrence, Ernie Lombardi, Red Lucas, Dolf Luque, Jerry Lynch, Jim Maloney, Frank McCormick, Mike McCormick, Bill McKechnie, Roy McMillan, Joe Morgan, Billy Myers, Gary Nolan, Joe Nuxhall, Jim O'-Toole, Tony Perez, Vada Pinson, Wally Post, Bob Purkey, Eppa Rixey, Frank Robinson, Edd Roush, Ed Seymour, Johnny Temple, Johnny Vander Meer, Bucky Walters, Sparky Anderson, and Billy Werber.

# # #

The **Hall of Fame of the Class A Lake Elsinore Storm:** Bill Simas.

# # #

Kansas City Royals Hall of Fame: Amos Otis, Steve Busby, Paul Splittorff, Cookie Rojas, Dick Howser, Dennis Leonard, Hal McRae, Fred Patek, Larry Gura, Frank White, John Mayberry, Dan Quisenberry, George Brett, Whitey Herzog, Willie Wilson, executive Joe Burke, former owner Ewing Kauffman as well as his widow, Muriel Kauffman.
(See http://www.kcroyals.com/history/hall_of_fame.html)

# # #

The Minnesota Twins established their own **Hall of Fame** by inducting its first six members on August 12, 2000 before a home game at the Metrodome. The six were Harmon Killebrew, Rod Carew, Tony Oliva, Kent Hrbek, Kirby Puckett, and Calvin Griffith. The Twins Hall of Fame, created to coincide with the 40th anniversary of the team's founding in Minnesota, recognizes only those who toiled for the team in Minnesota—not men associated exclusively with the franchise's previous incarnation as the original Washington Senators.

# # #

The Montreal Expos Hall of Fame was created in 1993, the team's 25th anniversary: owner Charles Bronfman, Gary Carter, Rusty Staub, former manager Gene Mauch, French language television analyst Claude Raymond, Steve Rogers, Woodie Fryman, Jean-Pierre Roy, Bill Stoneman, Warren Cromartie, executive John McHale, Tim Burke, Ron Hassey, Ron Hunt, Larry Parrish, Andre Dawson, Bill Gullickson, Jeff Reardon, Chris Speier, and Tim Wallach are all members.

# # #

The New York Mets Hall of Fame: Casey Stengel, Keith Hernandez, former owner Joan Whitney Payson, Gil Hodges, executives George Weiss and Bill Shea, Johnny Murphy, broadcasters Lindsey Nelson, Bob Murphy, and Ralph Kiner, Bud Harrelson, Rusty Staub, Tom Seaver, Jerry Koosman, Ed Kranepool, Cleon Jones, Jerry Grote, Tug McGraw, Keith Hernandez, and William "Mookie" Wilson.

# # #

The Philadelphia Hall of Fame includes men who played for the Phillies and the Philadelphia Athletics. Members include Connie Mack, Jimmie Foxx, Robin Roberts, Elmer Valo, Mike Schmidt, Richie Ashburn, Lefty Grove, Chuck Klein, Chief Bender, Larry Bowa, Al Simmons, Grover Cleveland Alexander, Jack Coombs, Chris Short, Frank "Home Run" Baker, Jimmy Dykes, Mickey Cochrane, Del Ennis, Jim Bunning, Eddie Plank, Big Ed Delahanty, Bobby Shantz, Dick Allen, Curt Simmons, Eddie Joost, Willie Jones, Ed Rommel, Sam Thompson, Ferris Fain, Johnny Callison, Bing Miller, Greg Luzinski, Bob Johnson, Steve Carlton, Wally Moses, Paul Owens, Eddie Collins, Granny Hamner, Rube Waddell, and Cy Williams.

# # #

The San Diego Padres Hall of Fame includes Randy Jones, Nate Colbert, Dave Winfield, and former owner Ray Kroc.

# # #

The Seattle Mariners Hall of Fame, created in 1997, moved from the Kingdome to Safeco Field in 1999. Alvin Davis is its first member.

# # #

The St. Louis Cardinals Hall of Fame and Museum recognizes St. Louis major league players and managers who have been inducted at Cooperstown— those who played for the St. Louis Browns in the American Association (1882–91), the current Cardinals (1892–), the American League Browns (1902–53), and the National Negro League St. Louis Giants (1910–21) and Stars (1922–31). Only two Cooperstown Hall of Famers who played in St. Louis are not included—Walter Alston, who played in his only major league game as a Cardinal on September 27, 1936, but earned his spot in Cooperstown as the Dodgers manager (1954–76); and Vic Willis, who played just 33 games for the Cardinals in 1910. His place in Cooperstown was secured by his performance with Boston and Pittsburgh, 1898–1909. Plaques are also on display for those who have been inducted into the St. Louis Browns Historical Society Hall of Fame. They are Harlond Clift, Urban Shocker, George McQuinn, George Sisler, Ken Williams, Ned Garver, Roy Sievers, John Tobin, Satchel Paige, Baby Doll Jacobson, Luke Sewell, Bobby Wallace, Rick Ferrell, Nels Potter, Don Gutteridge, Bobo Newsom, Mark Christman, Vern Stephens, Robert Dillinger, George Stone, Chet Laabs, Roy Bell, Bob Muncrief, Hank Severeid, Denny Galehouse, Johnny Berardino, Jack Kramer, Marty McManus, Elden Auker, and Al Zarilla.

# # #

The Toronto Blue Jays Level of Excellence, on the third level at Skydome, honors former manager Cito Gaston, George Bell, and Dave Steib.

# # #

COUNTRY HALLS OF FAME

The Canadian Baseball Hall of Fame in St. Marys, Ontario, lists its members, with some brief biographies, on a Web site: http://www.baseballhof.ca/ Inductees/inductees.html. Members include Ferguson Jenkins (one of a very few pitchers to defeat 24 different teams), Oscar Judd, Frank Colman, Bobby Mattick, Rocky Nelson, Bill Phillips, Tip O'Neill, George "Moonie" Gibson—the last Canadian-born manager in the big leagues (Pirates, Cubs, 1920–22, 1925, 1932–34), Phil Marchildon, George Selkirk, Jack Graney (the first man to bat against Babe Ruth, the first Canadian pinch hitter in a World Series, and in 1916, the first player to bat wearing a uniform number. Graney was also the first former big leaguer to move into the broadcast booth; he announced Cleveland Indians games from 1932 to 1953.) Pete Ward, Claude Raymond (the first Canadian to play for a Canadian team—the Expos, whom he joined in 1969, their first year), Dick Fowler (the first Canadian to throw a no-hitter, a feat he accomplished on September 9, 1945, for the Philadelphia A's over the Browns at Shibe Park), Francis James "Blackie" O'Rourke, Terry Puhl, John Hiller, Ron Taylor, Reggie Cleveland (from Swift Current, Saskatchewan), Russ Ford, Reno Bertoia (a native of St. Vito Udine, Italy, who grew up in Windsor, Ontario), executives John McHale and Pat Gillick, and honorary inductees Jackie Robinson (whose career in the minor leagues began in Montreal) and former Prime Minister Lester B. Pearson—an amateur player and winner of the 1957 Nobel Peace Prize.

# # #

The former manager of the Seattle Kingdome is a Hall of Famer. Why?

E. O. "Ted" Bowsfield pitched for the Red Sox, Indians, Angels, and Kansas City A's, compiling a 37–39 record from 1958 to 1964. When his playing days were over, he became the director of operations for the Angels stadium in Anaheim. In 1994 he became the Director of Stadium Administration for the Kingdome. A native of Vernon, British Columbia, he was inducted into the **British Columbia Sports Hall of Fame** in 1980.

# # #

Umpire Jim McKean is a member of the **Canadian Football Hall of Fame** in Hamilton, Ontario.

# # #

Terry Puhl, a native of Melville, is the sole major leaguer in the **Saskatchewan Sports Hall of Fame and Museum** in Regina. This is one of the few halls of fame to include baton twirlers, blind athletes, lawn bowlers, judo masters, badminton players, tenpin bowlers, water-skiers, curlers, and synchronized swimmers.

# # #

Billy Harris, Paul Hodgson, and John "Chewing Gum" O'Brien are members of the **New Brunswick Sports Hall of Fame.**
(See http://www.nbshf.fundy.ca/)

# # #

The Caribbean Baseball Hall of Fame: Ted Lyons, Nolan Ryan, Rico Carty, Camilo Pascual, Willard Brown.

# # #

The Cuban Baseball Hall of Fame includes Rube Foster, Martin Dihigo, Pop Lloyd, Oscar Charleston, Judy Johnson, Mike Fornieles, Preston Gomez, Mike Cuellar, Zoilo Versalles, Tony Taylor, Cookie Rojas, Camilo Pascual, Minnie Minoso, Leo Cardenas, Bob Estalella, and Tony Oliva.

# # #

The Dominican Republic Sports Hall of Fame boasts a number of ballplayers who appeared in the American big leagues, including Pedro Borbon, Sr., Nino Espinosa, Rico Carty, Julian Javier, Diomedes Olivo, Cesar Geronimo, Winston Llenas, Juan Marichal, Teddy Martinez, Manny Mota, Chi Chi Olivo, Ozzie Virgil, Sr., Felipe Alou, Jesus Alou, and Matty Alou.

# # #

The revealing and entertaining Web site of the **Japanese Baseball Hall of Fame,** in Tokyo, is in English at http://www.baseball-museum.or.jp/museum_e/index_e.htm.

# # #

The Mexican Baseball Hall of Fame in Monterrey includes Roy Campanella, Minnie Minoso, Jorge Orta, Aurelio Rodriguez, Dolph Luque, Aurelio Lopez, and Martin Dihigo. The MBHOF provides a unique perk to its members: a life insurance policy provided by the Cuauhtémoc Moctezuma Brewery.

# # #

Venezuela's Sports Hall of Fame includes Cesar Tovar, Bo Diaz, Alfonso Carrasquel, Alejandro Carrasquel, Luis Aparicio, Ramon Monzant, and Chucho Ramos.

# # #

STATES & CITIES HALLS OF FAME

ALABAMA

Alabama's Sports Hall of Fame in Birmingham includes Willie Mays, Satchel Paige, Hank Aaron, and Bo Jackson.

# # #

ARKANSAS

The Arkansas State Hall of Fame honors individuals who have contributed to sports in Arkansas. Members include Bill Dickey, Travis Jackson, Schoolboy Rowe, Carey Sclph, George Kell, Lon Warneke, manager Hugo Bezdek, Johnny Sain, Preacher Roe, Wally Moon, manager Mel McGaha, George Harper, Sherm Lollar, Bobby Winkles, Willis Hudlin, Brooks Robinson, Ellis Kinder, Arky Vaughn, Don Kessinger, Dizzy Dean, Paul Dean, and Lee Rogers.

# # #

CALIFORNIA

Dusty Baker has been enshrined in the **Sacramento Sports Hall of Fame** and the **California Black Sports Hall of Fame.**

# # #

Bill Buckner is a member of the **Northern California Hall of Fame.**

# # #

The Orange County Sports Hall of Fame, although closed to the public, is part of Edison Field in Anaheim. Among its members honored with plaques are Bob Boone and Dan Quisenberry.

# # #

The Fresno Athletic Hall of Fame has inducted Rex Hudler.

# # #

The Breitbard Hall of Fame at the San Diego Hall of Champions honors big leaguers with a San Diego connection, as players, coaches, managers, executives, or natives. They include Ted Williams, Graig Nettles, Earle Brucker, Don Larsen, Bob Elliott, Ray Boone, Bob Boone (a rare father/son hall-of-fame combo), Bob Skinner, Deron Johnson, Randy Jones, Dave Winfield, Alan Trammell, John Moores, and executive Buzzie Bavasi.

# # #

The San Diego Baseball Hall of Fame, created when the Padres were still a Pacific Coast League team, included Dom Dallessandro, Luke Easter, Jim Chaplin, Bobby Doerr, Rupert Thompson, Minnie Minoso, Steve Mesner, Ted Williams, Jack Graham, and Max West.

# # #

The **San Francisco Prep Hall of Fame** includes Charlie Silvera, Gino Cimoli, and Bob DiPietro.

# # #

Members of the **San Francisco Bay Area Sports Hall of Fame** (http://www.bashof.org/halloffamers.htm) have their plaques at a number of locations. Inductees from baseball are listed by the location of their plaques:

Pacific Bell Park: Orlando Cepeda, Harry Heilman, Juan Marichal, Willie Mays, Willie McCovey, Lefty O'Doul.

The University of California at Berkeley: Sam Chapman.

Stanford University: Ernie Nevers (as a football player).

San Francisco International Airport: Dolph Camilli, Gate 78; Dom DiMaggio, Gate 80; Joe DiMaggio, Gate 86; Lefty Gomez, Gate 90; Eddie Joost, Gate 83; Tony Lazzeri, Gate 82; Vada Pinson, Gate 84; Bill Rigney, Gate 82.

The Oakland/Network Associates Coliseum: Dick Bartell, Vida Blue, Rollie Fingers, Curt Flood, Jim "Catfish" Hunter, Joe Morgan, Reggie Jackson, Ernie Lombardi, Billy Martin, Frank Robinson, and Willie Stargell.

Sacred Heart Prep: Joe Cronin. (It's his alma mater.)

# # #

COLORADO

The Colorado Sports Hall of Fame started inducting members in 1965. Big leaguers include Smokey Joe Wood, Goose Gossage, Carroll Hardy, John Stearns, former Padres manager Greg Riddoch, coach Sam Suplizio, and Cobe Jones.

# # #

CONNECTICUT

The Connecticut Sports Museum and Hall of Fame is at the Civic Center in Hartford. Former commissioner Fay Vincent has been enshrined there, along with Walt Dropo.

# # #

DELAWARE

Delaware's Sports Hall of Fame includes John Wockenfuss, executive Ruly Carpenter, Dallas Green, Dave May, Alexander Cartwright, Huck Betts, Chris Short, Vic Willis, umpire Bill McGowan, Judy Johnson, Spook Jacobs, Eddie Cihocki, Jack Crimian, George Estock, Harry Anderson, Renie Martin, and Costen Shockley.

# # #

WASHINGTON, D.C.

The Hall of Stars at Washington, D.C.'s RFK Stadium honors Frank Howard, Harmon Killebrew, Walter Johnson, George Selkirk, Josh Gibson, Eddie Yost, Gil Hodges, and Roy Sievers.

# # #

FLORIDA

The Florida Sports Hall of Fame and Museum of Florida Sports History, in Lake City, includes Rick Rhoden, broadcasters Curt Gowdy, Red Barber, and Bob Murphy, Herb Score, Mike Menosky, Hal McRae, Buck O'Neil, Robin Roberts, Lew Burdette, Steve Carlton, Gary Carter, André Dawson, Rip Sewell, Steve Garvey, Lou Piniella, Deacon Jones, Al Lang, Don Sutton, Paul Waner, Ted Williams, Early Wynn, Zack Taylor, Pop Lloyd, Al Lopez, Boog Powell, Ron Pruitt, Dave Hoskins, Dick Howser, Fred Hutchinson, Tim Raines, Al Rosen, Davey Johnson, and owners H. Wayne Huizenga and George Steinbrenner.

# # #

Daytona Beach Sports Hall of Fame—Carlos Alfonso.

# # #

GEORGIA

The Georgia Sports Hall of Fame in Macon includes Braves owner Ted Turner, Luke Appling, Jackie Robinson, Sherry Smith, Ty Cobb, and Hank Aaron.

# # #

Hank Aaron is enshrined on the **Atlanta Celebrity Walk.**

# # #

HAWAII

Information about the **Hawai'i Sports Hall of Fame and Cybermuseum** is available in English, Japanese, or, at the click of a mouse, in Hawaiian, at http://www.alohafame.com/hallfame.htm.

# # #

ILLINOIS

The Chicagoland Sports Hall of Fame (formerly the Chicago Sports Hall of Fame), located at Maryville Academy in Des Plaines, has inducted White Sox owner Jerry Reinsdorf, Gabby Hartnett, Phil Cavarretta, Andy Pafko, Ed Farmer, Billy Williams, Ernie Banks, Minnie Minoso, Billy Pierce, Luke Appling, Ted Lyons, Luis Aparicio, and Nellie Fox.

# # #

White Sox broadcaster and former big league pitcher Ed Farmer was also inducted into the **Chicago Catholic League Hall of Fame.**

# # #

INDIANA

The Indiana Baseball Hall of Fame (http://www.indbaseballhalloffame.org), sponsored by the Indiana High School Baseball Coaches Association, is at the Ruxer Student Center on the campus of Vincennes University in Jasper. Among those inducted are Charles Finley, Mordecai Brown, Max Carey, Billy Herman, Sam Rice, Bob Coleman, Ron Reed, Pete Fox, Edd Roush, Dizzy Trout, Oscar Charleston, Chuck Klein, Tom Underwood, Ford Frick, Kenesaw Mountain Landis, Art Nehf, Chuck Harmon, Amos Rusie, Donie Bush, Carl Erskine, Fred Fitzsimmons, Glen Rosenbaum (White Sox coach and traveling secretary), Tommy John, Bob Friend, Gil Hodges, Everett Scott, Al Pilarcik, and Steve Hamilton.

# # #

KANSAS

The Kansas Sports Hall of Fame in Topeka: Elden Auker, Fred Clarke, Ralph Houk, Walter Johnson, and Bill Russell, a native of Pittsburg, Kansas. The KSHOF's informative and illustrated Web site is http://www.kshof.org/.

# # #

LOUISIANA

Louisiana's Sports Hall of Fame in Natchitoches includes Joe Adcock, Vida Blue, Zeke Bonura, Lou Brock, Al Dark, Bill Dickey, Atley Donald, Eddie Dyer, Ralph Garr, Ron Guidry, Ed Head, Bill Lee, Ted Lyons, Mel Ott, Mel Parnell, Howie Pollet, J. R. Richard, Connie Ryan, Rusty Staub, Earl "Moose" Wilson, and Negro Leaguer Oliver Marcelle.

# # #

The Shreveport, Louisiana, Sports Museum of Champions, honoring Shreveport and Bossier City star athletes from various sports including duck calling (to the extent that duck calling is a sport), handball, weightlifting, power lifting, body building, marksmanship, kick boxing, bridge, and badminton. Major leaguers include Matt Alexander, Homer Peel, Willard Brown, Dick Hughes, Walter Stephenson, and umpire Cal Hubbard.

# # #

MAINE

Members of **Maine's Sports Hall of Fame** in Portland include Bill Swift, former Yankee manager Carl "Stump" Merrill, Bill Carrigan, "Colby" Jack Coombs, Dan MacFayden, Don Brennan, Clyde Sukeforth, Louis Sockalexis, Freddy Parent, Del Bissonette, Danny Coombs, and attorney Bob Woolf—Carl Yastrzemski's agent.

# # #

MARYLAND

The Hall of Fame of the Eastern Shore Baseball Foundation honors those who have played for, managed, coached, or umpired in the Central Shore, Interstate, Mar-Va, Eastern Shore, Mar-Del, Chesapeake, Bi-County, and professional leagues. Included are Lewis "Buttercup" Dickerson, Judy Johnson, Huck Betts, Home "Run" Baker, Jimmie Foxx, Bill "Swish" Nicholson, and Forrest "Spook" Jacobs.

# # #

MICHIGAN

Is Herb Washington, the Oakland A's "designated runner" 1974–75, a Hall of Famer?

Yes. Before being signed as an innovative publicity stunt by the A's owner Charlie Finley, Washington was a world-class sprinter. His lack of baseball experience—he had not played since high school—made it virtually impossible for any manager to give him an at bat during his 105 games with Oakland. But he did what he was hired to do—steal bases and score runs. He scored 33 runs while stealing 31 bases for Oakland.

For his achievements in track, Washington was enshrined in the **Greater Flint Area Sports Hall of Fame.** Also honored are Mike Menosky, Dave Hoskins, Steve Boros, and Ron Pruitt.

# # #

Editorial note on baseball research: On August 14, 1999, during our presentation and trivia quiz at the Baseball Hall of Fame in Cooperstown, we mentioned our interest in ballplayers, umpires, and executives who were in other halls of fame. Three days later, we received an e-mail from Paul Howland of East Grand Rapids, Michigan, who undertook his own research to assist us. An edited version of his account follows: "I set about to discover the **Lansing, Michigan, Hall of Fame.** It didn't exist in the white pages or the yellow pages, so I telephoned the Greater Lansing Visitors and Convention Bureau, where I talked with Melissa. She said that it was located in Lansing Community College's Dart Auditorium. I walked to the auditorium, only to discover that the Hall of Fame was for distinguished Lansing area citizens. Baffled, I went to the information desk, where I was told that the **Sports Hall of Fame** was located on the third floor of the Gannon Vocational Education Building. After a short walk, I wandered about the Gannon Building but was unable to find the hall, so I went to the Athletic Office. Becky came to my aid and walked me to the hall, which really was a **Wall of Fame.** Inaugurated in 1976 as part of the Bicentennial, the hall took up a considerable length of the wall. Becky then took me to the fourth-floor office of the athletic director, Richard Mull, one of the three founders of the **Greater Lansing Area Sports Hall of Fame** and its executive director. He showed me the list of Lansing area major league baseball players. The list includes Dave Campbell (now an ESPN sports announcer), Charlie Gehringer, Luke Hamlin, John Smoltz, Jim Stump, and Vic Saier.

"Finally, I thought that since Michigan State University is located in East Lansing, the Michigan State sports information people should have a list of Spartan major league baseball players. My tax dollars have not been wasted, as they faxed me a two-page document (legal size) filled with MSU baseball players. Thirty-eight "Major League Spartans" have played the game, including Chuck Baker, Steve Garvey, Kirk Gibson, Jack Kralick, Dean Look (a Lansing Hall of Famer), Al Luplow, Mike Marshall, Ron Perranoski, Dick Radatz, Robin Roberts, and Herb Washington. I feel like the Dutch boy at the dike. Your quest for information has opened the floodgates of information. The president of the **Grand Rapids Sports Hall of Fame** has sent me this year's induction program. Major league baseball players include Wally Pipp (his son still lives in Grand Rapids), Benny McCoy, Frank "Stubby" Overmire, Phil Regan, James Command, Mickey Stanley, Jim Kaat, and Rick Miller."

# # #

The Michigan Sports Hall of Fame, at the Cobo Center in Farmington Hills, honors Denny McLain (surely one of the few Hall of Famers prevented from attending future induction ceremonies because of immurement), Willie Horton, Sparky Anderson, Tommy Bridges, Harry Heilmann, Hughie Jennings, former Tigers owners Frank Navin, John Fetzer, Mike Ilitch and his wife, Marian, Walter Briggs, Sr., Jim Bunning, Norm Cash, Al Kaline, George Kell, James Campbell, Mickey Lolich, Ty Cobb, Heinie Manush, George Mullin, Mickey Cochrane, Sam Crawford, Hal Newhouser, Wish Egan, Billy Rogell, Schoolboy Rowe, Bill Freehan, Charlie Gehringer, Virgil Trucks, Goose Goslin, Vic Wertz, Rudy York, Dick McAuliffe, Harvey Kuenn, Don Lund, John Hiller, Bob Miller, Charlie Maxwell, Ray Fisher, George Sisler, Kirk Gibson, Barney McCosky, Mickey Stanley, Robin Roberts, Hank Greenberg, and broadcasters Dick Enberg, Van Patrick, Ty Tyson, Ray Lane, and Ernie Harwell.

# # #

The **Midland County Sports Hall of Fame** recently inducted Jim Kern.

# # #

The Muskegon Area Sports Hall of Fame includes former Tiger manager Jack Tighe, Frank Secory, Ira Flagstead, Jim Johnson, and Howard Bailey.

# # #

The **Alpena Sports Hall of Fame** includes Dan Rohn.

# # #

The Bay County Hall of Fame, in the lobby of the Community Center along the River Walk in Bay City, includes athletes from other sports (e.g., ice boating) as well as baseball. Major leaguers include Keith Miller, Kiki Cuyler, and Gerald Lynch.

# # #

MISSISSIPPI

The **Mississippi Sports Hall of Fame and Museum** in Jackson includes James "Cool Papa" Bell, Don Blasingame, Guy Bush, Harry Craft, Hughie Critz, Jim Davenport, Dizzy Dean, Jim Edwards, Boo Ferriss, Joe Gibbon, Jake Gibbs, Paul Gregory, Don Kessinger, Hal Lee, Sam Leslie, Eric McNair, Willie Mitchell, Buddy Myer, Claude Passeau, Hugh Pepper, Bubba Phillips, Del Unser, Sam Vick, Fred Walters, and Skeeter Webb.

# # #

MISSOURI

Stan Musial, Bill Virdon, Frank White, Whitey Herzog, Vida Blue, Jerry Lumpe, Buck O'Neil, and Royals executive Joseph T. McGuff—who is also in the "Writers' Wing" at Cooperstown—are all members of the **Missouri Sports Hall of Fame,** in Springfield. A street nearby was named Stan Musial Drive after the first member who was not born in Missouri. Musial, a star with the St. Louis Cardinals from 1941 to 1963, was born in Donora, Pennsylvania.

The Missouri Sports Hall of Fame's Web site, (http://www.mosportshallof-fame.com.baseball.htm) features separate articles about George Brett, former Cardinals owner August A. Busch, Jr., Bob Gibson, Whitey Herzog, Red Schoendienst, former Royals owner Ewing Kauffman, Jerry Lumpe, Stan Musial, Buck O'Neil, Dan Quisenberry, Ozzie Smith, Bill Virdon, and Frank White.

# # #

The St. Louis Walk of Fame (http://www.stlouiswalkoffame.org) is on the sidewalk of Delmar Boulevard in the Loop district of University City. In addition to the baseball stars Lou Brock, Stan Musial, Yogi Berra, Dizzy Dean, Cool Papa Bell, Bob Gibson, Red Schoendienst, and Branch Rickey, it honors celebrities from other fields, such as Maya Angelou, T. S. Eliot, Tennessee Williams, Grace Bumbry, Miles Davis, Phyllis Diller, Charles Eames, Al Hirschfeld, William Inge, William Masters and Virginia Johnson, poet and baseball fan Marianne Moore, Tina Turner, Redd Foxx, Charles Lindbergh, and Dred Scott, plus broadcasters Bob Costas, Joe Garagiola, and Harry Caray.

# # #

NEW JERSEY

The Sports Hall of Fame of New Jersey, part of the Continental Arena at the Meadowlands Sports Complex, includes former National League president Leonard Coleman, Leon Day, Larry Doby, Goose Goslin, Pop Lloyd, Joe Medwick, Monte Irvin, Ray Dandridge, Phil Rizzuto, and Yogi Berra. The SHO-FONJ is unique, as far as we know, for it has inducted a number of teams in their entirety, including the 1937 Newark Bears, and the 1946 Newark Eagles, champions of the Negro League.

# # #

NEW YORK

Bobby Wine is a 1993 inductee into the **Suffolk County Sports Hall of Fame.**

# # #

The New York Sports Hall of Fame, which still doesn't have a permanent building, includes Joe DiMaggio, Johnny Mize, Willie Mays, Mickey Mantle, Yogi Berra, Babe Ruth, Lou Gehrig, Jackie Robinson, Casey Stengel, Carl Hubbell, Tommy Henrich, Lefty Gomez, John McGraw, Roy Campanella, Joe McCarthy, Carl Furillo, Willie Mays, Christy Mathewson, Don Newcombe, Mel Ott, Dave DeBusschere (as a basketball player), Bill Dickey, Carl Hubbell, Miller Huggins, Reggie Jackson, Phil Rizzuto, Tim Keefe, Sal Maglie, Mickey Mantle, Tony Lazzeri, Duke Snider, Casey Stengel, Bill Terry, Babe Ruth, Leo Durocher, Tommy Henrich, Gil Hodges, Whitey Ford, Frankie Frisch, Alexander Cartwright, Tom Seaver, organists Gladys Goodding and Eddie Layton, broadcasters Mel Allen, Red Barber, Lindsey Nelson, Clem McCarthy, and Russ Hodges, sportswriters Dave Anderson, Arthur Daley, Dan Daniel, Heywood Broun, Red Smith, Bob Considine, Jimmy Cannon, Dick Young, Damon Runyon, Grantland Rice, Bill Gallo, Frank Graham, Jimmy Powers, executives Bill Cox, Branch Rickey, Jacob Ruppert, Larry MacPhail, Bob Fishel, Irving Rudd, Red Patterson, Lon Keller (who created the logos for both the Yankees and the Mets), Yankee Stadium public-address announcer Bob Sheppard, and concessionaire Harry M. Stevens.

# # #

The Buffalo Baseball Hall of Fame at Pilot Field, home of the Bisons (the Cleveland Indians affiliate in the AAA International League) includes Dan Brouthers, Pud Galvin, Luke Easter, Fred Hutchinson, Warren Spahn, Jimmy Collins, Del Bissonette, George Stallings, Deacon White, Frank Carswell, Ollie Tucker, Joe Brown, Major Kerby Farrell, Frank Gilhooley, Coaker Triplett, Sibby Sisti, Jimmy Walsh, Ray Schalk, Frank "Beauty" McGowan, Dorn Taylor, Mayo Smith, Warren "Buddy" Rosar, Babe Birrer, Rick Lancellotti, Bill Harris, Sal Maglie, Al Moore, Hal White, Terry Collins, Joe Desa, Johnny Groth, James O'Rourke, Buck Crouse, Greg Mulleavy, Jake Gettman, Steve Farr, Frank Pytlak, and Cy Williams.

# # #

The Westchester Sports Hall of Fame displays plaques for its members at the County Center in White Plains. Members include Ken Singleton, Ralph Branca, Dell Alston, Ford Frick, Frankie Frisch, Lou Gehrig, Sal Yvars, and broadcaster Bob Wolff.

Thanks to Ken Singleton.

# # #

NORTH CAROLINA

Rick Ferrell, Catfish Hunter, Hoyt Wilhelm, Buck Leonard, Enos Slaughter, and Gaylord Perry are members of the **North Carolina Sports Hall of Fame** in Raleigh. Although he was born in High Point, N.C., Baseball Hall of Famer Luke Appling has not been so honored, as he moved to Georgia at a young age.

# # #

Salem-Roanoke Baseball Hall of Fame—coach Eddie Popowski.

# # #

Members of the **Kinston Baseball Hall of Fame** include Charlie Keller, George Suggs, Stan Spence, Sam Narron, Jesse Barfield, Mike Hargrove, Leo Mazzone, Cecil Fielder, Jim Price, Steve Blass, Bobby Bragan, Clyde King, and executives Harding Peterson and Lou Gorman.

# # #

NORTH DAKOTA

The North Dakota Sports Hall of Fame in Jamestown includes Roger Maris. Although he is a native of Hibbing, Minnesota, he grew up in Fargo and always considered it his hometown.

# # #

OREGON

The Oregon Sports Hall of Fame in Portland includes Johnny Pesky, Earl Averill, Jr., Bobby Doerr, Mickey Lolich, Ad Liska, Pete Ward, Rick Wise, Artie Wilson, Dale Murphy, Carson "Skeeter" Bigbee (from Waterloo), Dave Roberts (Lebanon), Larry Jansen (Verboort), and Ken Williams.

# # #

PENNSYLVANIA

The Pennsylvania Sports Hall of Fame makes the names and brief biographies of its inductees available online at http://207.44.18.5/wbforms/sportshall/sport/htf?vsport=Baseball. Its members include John Quinn, Eddie Sawyer, Al Brancato (also in the South Philadelphia High School Hall of Fame), Dick Allen (out of Wampum High School), umpires Russ Goetz and Nestor Chylak, Stan Lopata, Art Mahaffey, Sparky Lyle, Sparky Adams, Steve Blass, former Marlins owner Carl F. Barger, Nellie Briles, Ed Ott, Manny Sanguillen, Pirates broadcaster Lanny Frattare, and Tommy Herr.

# # #

The Delaware County Athletes Hall of Fame in Brookhaven includes Mickey Vernon, Danny Murtaugh, Lew Krausse, Jr., and umpire Shag Crawford.

# # #

The Reading Baseball Hall of Fame (http://www.readingphillies.com/hof.htm) honors those major leaguers who have played for the Reading Phillies, the Reading Indians, or the Reading Red Sox, and former coaches and managers. Inductees include Kevin Gross, Tommy Barrett, Willie Hernandez, Jim Perry, Rico Petrocelli, Max Patkin, Randy Lerch, Jim Essian, Ken Reynolds, Darren Daulton, Mike Schmidt, Joe Buzas, Greg Luzinski, Jeff Stone, Lee Elia, Denny Doyle, Jerry Martin, Randy Gumpert, Bob Walk, Vic Wertz, Joe Altobelli, Carl Furillo ("The Reading Rifle"), Andy Seminick, Dick Gernert, Ozzie Virgil, Roger Maris, Whitey Kurowski, Bob Quinn, Keith Moreland, Bob Terlecki, Rocky Colavito, Julio Franco, Jim Olander, Charlie Wagner, Herb Score, Bob Wellman, Ryne Sandberg, Dallas Green, Paul Owens, Andre Thornton, Howie Bedell, Bob Boone, Mark Davis, Frank Lucchesi, Larry Bowa, and former Phillies owner Ruly Carpenter.

# # #

TENNESSEE

The Tennessee Sports Hall of Fame, soon to have a permanent home near Nashville, includes Johnny Beazley, Kerby Farrell, Todd Helton, Charlie Lea, Jim Hickman, Jim Gilliam, Tommy Bridges, Johnny Antonelli, John Gooch, Jim Turner, Hillis Layne, Fred Toney, Marv Throneberry, Larry Gilbert, Bill Terry, and broadcaster Lindsey Nelson, Walter Stewart, Harry Anderson, Lou "Farmer" Johnson, Johnny Butler, Billy Anderson, Jimmy Smyth, John Ward, Jimmy Moore, John Merritt, A. W. Davis, Gene Thompson, and Ken Burkhart.

# # #

TEXAS

The Texas Hall of Fame in Waco actually encompasses both the **Texas Baseball Hall of Fame** and the **Texas Sports Hall of Fame.** Baseball figures in the Texas Sports Hall of Fame are: Jake Atz, umpire Lee Ballanfant, Ernie Banks, Don Baylor, Roger Clemens, Snipe Conley, Larry Dierker, Eddie Dyer, Bibb Falk, Rube Foster, Bill Foster, Pinky Higgins, Rogers Hornsby, Tex Hughson, Ernie Koy Sr., Clarence "Big Boy" Kraft, Ted Lyons, Gus Mancuso, Firpo Marberry, John McCloskey, Joe Morgan, Carl "Bubba" Reynolds, Paul Richards, Pete Runnels, Nolan Ryan, Tris Speaker, Monty Stratton, and Ross Youngs.

# # #

Members of the **Texas Baseball Hall of Fame** are Jimmy Adair, Sparky Anderson, Jay Avrea, Ernie Banks, Dutch Becker, Jodie Beeler, Buddy Bell, coach Carroll Beringer, Edward Borom, Bobby Bragan, Dr. Bobby Brown, Jeff Burroughs, Dick Butler, Buster Chatham, Roger Clemens, Cecil Cooper, Harry Craft, Danny Darwin, Dizzy Dean, Larry Dierker, Bob Finley, Chet Fowler, Cito Gaston, Sal Gliatto, Jerry Goff, Lonnie Goldstein, Hank Greenberg, Tom Grieve, Jerry Grote, Buddy Hancken, Mike Hargrove, Toby Harrah, Grady Hatton, Jr., Solly Hemus, Whitey Herzog, Frank Howard, and Astros owner Drayton McLane.

# # #

VIRGINIA

Major leaguers in the **Virginia Sports Hall of Fame and Museum** in Portsmouth include Jim Coates, Clyde McCullough, Granny Hamner, Art Jones, Jim Lemon, George McQuinn, Ace Parker, Vic Raschi, Bud Metheny, Eppa Rixey, Deacon Phillippe, Mel Roach, Cy Young, Cy Twombly, Porter Vaughan, and executive Syd Thrift.

# # #

WASHINGTON

Ron Cey is a member of **Washington's State Hall of Fame.**

# # #

PUERTO RICO

The Puerto Rico Professional Baseball Hall of Fame—Roberto Clemente, Roberto Alomar, Sandy Alomar, Sr., Sandy Alomar, Jr., Hi Bithorn, Luis Arroyo, Carlos Bernier, Leon Day, Saturnino "Nino" Escalera, Rúben Gómez, Artie Wilson, Bob Thurman, José Santiago, Vic Power, Tony Pérez, Luis Olmo, José Cruz, Sr., Juan Gonzalez, Orlando Cepeda.

# # #

The Puerto Rico Sports Hall of Fame: Sandy Alomar, Sr., Luis "Tite" Arroyo, Hiram Bithorn, Roberto Clemente, Vic Power, Felix Mantilla, Orlando Cepeda, Ed Figueroa, José Cruz, Juan Beniquez, Felix Millan, Tony Perez, Luis Olmo, Luis Marquez, José Pagan, Ruben Gomez, Jose G. Santiago, Jose R. "Palillo" Santiago, Guillermo Montanez, Jerry Morales, Eddie Olivares, Saturnino "Nino" Escalera, and Juan Pizarro.

\# \# \#

OTHER HALLS OF FAME

Paul Gregory has been enshrined in the **Amateur Baseball Coaches Association Hall of Fame.**

\# \# \#

P & C Stadium in Syracuse, home of the Skychiefs, the Blue Jays affiliate in the AAA International League, boasts a **Wall of Fame.** Honorees include Dave Giusti, Hank Sauer, Grover Cleveland Alexander, Mack Jones, Bill Dinneen, Red Barrett, Dutch Mele, Jim Bottomley, Frank Verdi, Rob Gardner, Bill Kelly, and Jimmy Outlaw.

\# \# \#

Bob Uecker is in the **Wisconsin Performing Artists Hall of Fame,** the **Wisconsin Sports Hall of Fame,** and the **Wisconsin Broadcasters Association Hall of Fame.** "Mr. Baseball," although a member of the World Champion 1964 St. Louis Cardinals, is not yet a member of the **Baseball Hall of Fame.**

\# \# \#

Gregg Olson's father, Bill, is a member of the **American Baseball Coaches Association Hall of Fame,** as is Ethan Allen.

\# \# \#

Max Patkin, the "Clown Prince of Baseball," was inducted into the **Philadelphia Jewish Sports Hall of Fame,** the **Reading (Pennsylvania) Baseball Hall of Fame,** and the **Clown Hall of Fame and Research Center** in Delavan, Wisconsin.

\# \# \#

The National Association of Intercollegiate Athletics (NAIA) Hall of Fame, in Tulsa, Oklahoma, includes Lloyd and Paul Waner, Danny Litwhiler, Norm Cash, Norm Seibern, Jerry Lumpe, Mike Hargrove, Jimmy Gleeson, Ray Washburn, Pete Ward, Donn Clendenon, Wayne Causey, Ernie Shore, Jim Northrup, Clyde Wright, Wes Parker, Ed Spiezio, Marty Pattin, Dan Quisenberry, Dave Gumpert, Brett Butler, Paul Assenmacher, Tim Leslie, Butch Stinson, Ray Burris, Rusty Greer, Chuck Hiller, Paul Splittorff, Preacher Roe, and a number of coaches and managers (some of whom were big league players): Jack Russell, Mike Metheny, Carl Erskine, Joe Niekro, and Bobby Winkles.

# # #

The Little League Hall of Excellence (http://www.littleleague.org/museum/hallex.htm) includes Nolan Ryan, Jim Palmer, Mike Schmidt, and Tom Seaver, as well as a few others who did not play in the big leagues—Tom Selleck, Dan Quayle, Bill Bradley, Kareem Abdul-Jabbar, and George Will (whose book *Bunts* points out that there are no nonpitchers in the Baseball Hall of Fame named "Bob.")

# # #

The **Babe Ruth League** has its own **Hall of Fame,** too, although at present it exists only in cyberspace: (http://www.baberuthleague.org/museum.html). The Babe Ruth League Hall of Fame and Museum will be built at historic Camden Station in Baltimore. Inductees include Vada Pinson, Ford Frick, Mickey Lolich, and Lefty Gomez.

# # #

The World Sports Humanitarian Hall of Fame (www.sportshumanitarian.com) in Boise, Idaho, has inducted three baseball players: Roberto Clemente, Dale Murphy, and Tony Gwynn.

# # #

Former Angels owner Gene Autry is in the **Country Music Hall of Fame,** the **National Association of Broadcasters Hall of Fame,** and the **Nashville Songwriters Hall of Fame.**

# # #

Dodger broadcaster Vin Scully is a member of the **American Sportscasters Hall of Fame** and the **Southern California Sports Broadcasters Association Hall of Fame.**

# # #

The **South Western Athletic Conference Hall of Fame** includes Matthew Alexander from Grambling State University.

# # #

Tigers broadcaster Ernie Harwell has been enshrined in the **Radio Hall of Fame,** the **National Sportscasters Hall of Fame,** and the **Michigan Sports Hall of Fame.**

# # #

Brooks Robinson and Jim Kaat have been honored by the **Rawlings Gold Glove Hall of Fame.** Each won a record 16 Gold Gloves.

# # #

COLLECES AND UNIVERSITIES

Sunshine Srare Conference Hall of Fame—Tino Martinez, Bob Tewksbury, and Tim Wakefield.

# # #

The only NCAA Division I athletic conference with its own hall of fame is the **Mid-American Athletic Conference,** established in 1987. Big leaguers who have been inducted include Thurman Munson, Bob Welch, Bob Owchinko, Charlie Maher, and Bill Lajoie.

# # #

Galen Cisco is in the **Ohio State University Sports Hall of Fame.**

# # #

The **University of California at Berkeley**—more precisely, its Golden Bears—have sent a number of players to the big leagues. Members of the **California Athletic Hall of Fame** include Lance Blankenship, Sam Chapman, Taylor Douthit, Jackie Jensen, Andy Messersmith, Orval Overall, and Earl Robinson.

# # #

Nicholls State University ("Baseball on the Bayou," in Thibodaux, Louisiana), home of the Colonels, has selected Darryl Hamilton for its **Hall of Fame.**

# # #

The University of Toledo's Rockets Hall of Fame includes A. J. Sager, Stan Clarke, and Len Matuszek.

# # #

The Boilermakers of Purdue University have honored Bernie Allen in their **Athletic Hall of Fame.**

# # #

The Aggies of **North Carolina A & T** have inducted just one big leaguer—Al Holland.

# # #

The members of the **Louisiana State University**—the Tigers—**Athletic Hall of Fame** include Joe Adcock, Alvin Dark, Buddy Blair, and Roland Howell.

# # #

The University of Vermont (the Catamounts) has inducted Bert Abbey, Erasmus Arlington Pond, Larry Gardner, Ray Collins, Elmari Bowman, Rusty Yarnell, Ralph LaPointe, Jack Lamabe, and Kirk McCaskill into its **Athletic Hall of Fame** in Burlington.

# # #

Matt Williams was inducted into the **Athletic Hall of Fame of the University of Nevada at Las Vegas,** the Rebels.

# # #

The Hall of Fame at Brigham Young University—the Cougars—in Salt Lake City includes Danny Ainge, Doug Howard, Dane Iorg, and Scott Nielsen. See the Cougars' Web site at http://www.byucougars.com.

# # #

The Oregon State University Hall of Fame in Corvallis—home of the Beavers—has inducted Howard Maple, Glenn Elliott, Ken Forsch, and Wes Schulmerich.

# # #

There is only one major leaguer in the **Hall of Fame** of the **Xavier** Musketeers—but what a player: Jim Bunning. In his freshman year he pitched three one-hitters, then went right to the majors, to play for the Tigers.

# # #

Duquesne University's Sports Hall of Fame has only one major leaguer—Dave Ricketts.

# # #

In 1978 **Austin Peay State University in Clarksville,** Tennessee—home of the Governors—inducted Jimmy Stewart into its **Hall of Fame.**

# # #

The Hall of Fame of Southwest Missouri State University in Springfield—the Bears—has just one major leaguer—Mark Bailey.

# # #

The Raiders of **Wright State University** in Dayton, Ohio, have inducted Brian Anderson into their **Hall of Fame.**

# # #

The Hall of Fame of the Manhattan College Jaspers (surprisingly not in Manhattan, but in the Bronx) includes John "Buddy" Hassett, Chuck Schilling, and Bob Chlupsa.

# # #

Tom Paciorek is the only major leaguer enshrined in the **Hall of Fame of the University of Houston**—the Cougars.

# # #

Kip Young, Larry Owen, Doug Blair, Orel Hershiser, John Knox, Larry Arndt, and Roger McDowell are all members of the **Bowling Green State University Hall of Fame.**

# # #

Northwestern University's Hall of Fame has just one big leaguer—Joe Girardi.

# # #

James Madison University in Harrisonburg, Virginia, home of the Dukes, has enshrined Billy Sample into its **Hall of Fame.**

# # #

Dave Dravecky is the only major leaguer in the **Hall of Fame of the Youngstown (Ohio) State University**—the Penguins.

# # #

Former American League president Dr. Bobby Brown heads the list of major leaguers who have been enshrined in the **Stanford University Cardinals Hall of Fame** in Palo Alto, California. Other Cardinals so honored include Jeff Ballard, Lloyd Merriman, Jack Shepard, Zeb Terry, Jim Lonborg, Sandy Vance, Chuck Essegian, Bob Boone, Steve Dunning, Frank Duffy, Steve Davis, and Jim Hibbs.

# # #

The Sports Hall of Fame of Coastal Carolina University—the Chanticleers—has enshrined Kirt Manwaring.

# # #

St. Leo College has inducted Brian Dayett into its **Hall of Fame.**

# # #

The Hall of Fame at **Central Michigan University** in Mt. Pleasant—the Chippewas—includes Tom Tresh, Curt Young, Kevin Tapani, and broadcaster Dick Enberg.

# # #

The **C.W. Post** campus of **Long Island University** in Brookville, New York, home of the Pioneers, includes Richie Scheinblum and John Frascatore in its **Baseball Hall of Fame.**

# # #

Jack Coombs is in the **Duke University Sports Hall of Fame,** home of the Blue Devils.

# # #

Pepperdine University—the Waves—includes Gail Hopkins, Rob Picciolo, Mike Scott, and Mark Lee in its **Hall of Fame.**

# # #

Members of the **University of Arkansas Razorbacks Hall of Honor** include Kevin McReynolds, manager Mel McGaha, Johnny Ray, and Tim Lollar.

# # #

Bill Spiers and Billy O'Dell have been enshrined in the **Hall of Fame of Clemson University**—the Tigers.

# # #

Is former baseball commissioner Peter Ueberroth a Hall of Famer?

Yes. In November 1999 he was inducted into the San Jose State University's Hall of Fame in recognition of his accomplishments as captain of the school's water polo team and as a member of the freshman swimming team. Spartan big leaguers in the **San Jose State University Baseball Hall of Fame** are Jeff Ball, Ken Caminiti, Atlanta Braves infielder Randy Johnson, Mark Langston, Hal Kolstad, and John Oldham.

# # #

Tony and Chris Gwynn are both members of the **Hall of Fame** of their alma mater, **San Diego State University**—the Aztecs. So are Bud Black and Graig Nettles.

# # #

Tom Kramer is in the **Logan, Illinois, Junior College** (the Tigers) **Hall of Fame.**

# # #

Three major leaguers have been enshrined in the **Hall of Fame of the University of Portland** (Oregon)—the Pilots: Ken Dayley, Bill Krueger, and Billy Sullivan.

# # #

Southern Illinois University has enshrined three big leaguers in its **Hall of Fame:** Dave Stieb, Sean Bergman, and Steve Finley. Head baseball coach Dan Callahan informed us that the Salukis have retired #1 in honor of their long-time baseball coach, Itchy Jones. While Jones has no major league experience, he has one of the best nicknames in this book.

# # #

Former Cubs manager Jim Riggleman is a member of the **Frostburg State College Hall of Fame.**

# # #

Mark Dewey—**Grand Valley State University Hall of Fame** in Allendale, Michigan.

# # #

Jeff Reboulet and Lance Johnson are members of the **Triton Junior College Hall of Fame.**

# # #

Lance Johnson is also in the **Hall of Fame of the University of South Alabama**—the Jaguars—as are Eddie Stanky, Glenn Borgmann, Dave Stapleton, and Luis Gonzalez.

# # #

The **University of Cincinnati's Athletic Hall of Fame** includes Bearcats Miller Huggins and Ethan Allen.

# # #

The **Hall of Fame of Fordham University**—the Rams—includes Frankie Frisch ("The Fordham Flash"), Hank Borowy, John Murphy, Howie Carter, Dick Rudolph, Steve "Flip" Filipowicz (baseball and football), Babe Young, Dodger broadcaster Vin Scully, Charles Sheerin, Tony DePhillips, John Tobin, Joseph Zapustas, Ray Montgomery, and Pete Harnisch.

# # #

John Flaherty is a member of the **Athletic Hall of Fame of George Washington University**—the Colonials.

# # #

Wallace Johnson—**Indiana State University**—the Sycamores—**Hall of Fame.**

# # #

Coach Sam Suplizio is in the **DuBois, Pennsylvania, Sports Hall of Fame,** the **Central Pennsylvania Sports Hall of Fame,** the **National Junior College Hall of Fame,** the **University of New Mexico** (Lobos) **Hall of Fame,** and the **Colorado Sports Hall of Fame.**

# # #

The **Hall of Fame of the University of Northern Iowa**—the Panthers—in Cedar Falls includes two big leaguers: Duane Josephson and Ed Watt.

# # #

The **Hall of Fame of Alabama's Troy State University** Trojans includes Danny Cox and Mike Perez.

# # #

Virginia Tech's Sports Hall of Fame in Blacksburg, home of the Hokies, includes Johnny Oates, Leo Burke, Franklin Stubbs, and Paul "Buddy" Dear.

# # #

Kevin Seitzer and Marty Pattin—the **Hall of Fame of Eastern Illinois University** in Charleston—the Panthers.

# # #

The **University of Southern California**—the Trojans—has sent many players to the big leagues, but it has inducted only four into its **Hall of Fame:** Fred Lynn, Tom Seaver, Ron Fairly, and Mark McGwire.

# # #

The **Sports Hall of Fame** of Tempe's **Arizona State University**—the Sun Devils—includes such big leaguers as Gary Gentry, Rick Monday, Chris Bando, Larry Gura, Bob Horner, Lerrin LaGrow, Sal Bando, Alvin Davis, Lenny Randle, Sterling Slaughter, Craig Swan, Duffy Dyer, Jerry Maddox, Oddibe McDowell, Reggie Jackson, Paul Ray Powell, Hubie Brooks, Alan Bannister, and Floyd Bannister. Former coach Bobby Winkles is a member of the school's Hall of Distinction.

# # #

University of Hartford Alumni Athletic Hall of Fame (the Hawks)—includes Jeff Bagwell and Mets scouting director Gary LaRocque.

# # #

The National Junior College Hall of Fame—Pittsburgh Pirates general manager Cam Bonifay.

# # #

Only two big leaguers have been inducted into the **Hall of Fame of the University of New Orleans** (the Privateers): Randy Bush and Eric Rasmussen.

# # #

Steve Boros—**University of Michigan** (Wolverines) **Hall of Honor.**

# # #

Mike Hargrove is in the **Northwestern Oklahoma State Hall of Fame.**

# # #

The Thundering Herd of **Marshall University,** in Huntington, West Virginia, has inducted Rick Reed and Jeff Montgomery into its **Athletic Hall of Fame.**

# # #

Ball State University in Muncie, Indiana, home of the Cardinals, has two major leaguers in its **Hall of Fame:** Thomas Howard and Merv Rettenmund.

# # #

Two big leaguers are in the **Athletic Hall of Fame at Bucknell University**—the Bisons—in Lewisburg, Pennsylvania: Christy Mathewson and Joe Buzas.

# # #

Major leaguers in the **Hall of Fame at Florida's University of Miami**—the Hurricanes—are Orlando Gonzalez, Neal Heaton, and Wayne Krenchicki.

# # #

The University of Detroit Mercy—the Titans—has just one major leaguer in its **Hall of Fame**—Bob Miller, who compiled a 42–42 record pitching for the Phillies 1949–58. For 35 years, he has been the head baseball coach for the Titans.

# # #

The University of Florida Athletic Hall of Fame—the Gators—includes Doug Corbett, Dale Willis, George Steinbrenner, and Haywood Sullivan.

# # #

The Athletics Hall of Fame of the University of South Carolina—the Gamecocks—includes Mookie Wilson, Fritz Von Kolnitz, and Hank Small. Although Small still holds a number of USC baseball pitching records and was the Most Valuable Player in the AAA International League in 1978, his major league career spanned just one game (a loss) with the Braves, on September 27, 1978.

# # #

The University of Richmond—the Spiders—has inducted C. Porter Vaughan into its **Athletic Hall of Fame.** (See http://www.richmond.edu/~athletic/halloffame/.)

# # #

Creighton University, home of the Blue Jays, has inducted two major leaguers into its **Athletic Hall of Fame** in Omaha—Dennis Rasmussen and Bob Gibson—the latter primarily for his prowess as a basketball player.

# # #

Terry Collins, former manager of the Angles, was inducted into the **Athletic Hall of Fame** of his alma mater, **Eastern Michigan University**—the Eagles.

# # #

Cal Poly at San Luis Obispo (the Mustangs) inducted Ozzie Smith and Mike Krukow into its **Hall of Fame.**

# # #

The Rutgers University Olympic Sports Hall of Fame (http://www.athletics.rutgers.edu/history/hof.htm) includes Jeff Torborg, who set the Scarlet Knights' single season record by batting .540 in 1963.

# # #

Pete Schourek is a member of the **George C. Marshall University Athletic Hall of Fame.**

# # #

Only one big leaguer is in the **Hall of Fame of Philadelphia's LaSalle University**—the Explorers: Frank "Lefty" Hoerst.

# # #

The Hall of Fame of Texas Christian University—the Horned Frogs—includes Jeff Newman.

# # #

The **UCLA Bruins Athletic Hall of Fame** in Los Angeles includes Jackie Robinson, Dr. Bobby Brown, Mike Gallego, Tim Leary, Torey Lovullo, and Eric Karros.

# # #

Seton Hall University's Athletic Hall of Fame, home of the Pirates, includes Rick Cerone, John Valentin, Mo Vaughn, Craig Biggio, Charlie Puleo, Ted Lepcio, Ed Madjeski, and Pat Pacillo.

# # #

The University of Texas Longhorns Baseball Hall of Fame features Roger Clemens, J. Walter Morris, Pete Laydon, Tom Hughes, Murray Wall, Frank Howard, Burt Hooton, and Grady Hatton.

# # #

Clyde Sukeforth is in the **Athletic Hall of Fame** of his alma mater, **Georgetown University,** the Hoyas.

# # #

The Sports Hall of Fame of Norfolk, Virginia's **Old Dominion University**—the Monarchs—includes Kevin Bearse, Mark Wasinger, Yankee executive Mark Newman, and Bud Metheny, a former Yankee who coached for the school's baseball team from 1948 to 1980. The school named its baseball complex after Metheny. In 1984 in honor of his career with the Yankees, Old Dominion changed its home uniforms to white with blue pinstripes. Metheny has also been enshrined in the Virginia Sports Hall of Fame, the Tidewater Baseball Hall of Fame, and the Hall of Fame of the College of William and Mary.

# # #

The **University of Tennessee**—the Volunteers—have enshrined Sam Ewing, Phil Garner, and Rick Honeycutt into the school's **Baseball Hall of Fame.**

# # #

Wichita State (Shockers) **Hall of Fame**—Charlie O'Brien, Joe Carter, and Kennie Steenstra.

# # #

The only big leaguer in the **Murray** (Kentucky) **State University Athletic Hall of Fame**—home of the Thoroughbreds—is Jack Perconte.

# # #

Lehigh University's Hall of Fame in Bethlehem, Pennsylvania, home of the Mountain Hawks, includes Paul Hartzell.

# # #

The Georgia Tech Yellow Jackets Hall of Fame includes Tom Angley, Ray "Buddy" Blemker, executive Cam Bonifay, Kevin Brown, Scott Jordan, Riccardo Ingram, Jim Poole, and Bobby Reeves.

# # #

Western Michigan University's Hall of Fame in Kalamazoo includes these Broncos: Frank Quilici, Frank Secory, Frank "Stubby" Overmire, Albert Johnson, Ron Jackson, Bill Lajoie, Wayne Terwilliger, Jim Johnson, Jeff Kaiser, and Mike Squires.

# # #

The **Missouri University Athletic Hall of Fame** includes Phil Bradley and Hub Pruett.

# # #

The University of Arizona in Tucson has inducted 13 Wildcats who played or worked in the big leagues into its **Sports Hall of Fame:** Scott Erickson, Terry Francona, Chip Hale, Ron Hassey, Gil Heredia, Don Lee, Craig Lefferts, Hank Leiber, Eddie Leon, Kenny Lofton, Charlie Shoemaker, David Stegman, and Joe Magrane.

# # #

Long Beach State University—the 49ers—has inducted two players in its **Athletic Hall of Fame:** Rod Gaspar and Randy Moffitt.

# # #

Rider University has inducted Jeff Kunkel and Ed Whited into the **Broncos Hall of Fame.**

# # #

Jason Thompson was elected to the **Sports Hall of Fame of California State University** at Northridge—the Matadors.

# # #

The Sports Hall of Fame of Mississippi State University, home of the Bull-dogs, includes Hughie Critz, Boo Ferriss, Buddy Myer, Alex Grammas, Paul Gregory, Del Unser, Ken Tatum, and Jack Lazorko.

# # #

Bill Stoneman was inducted into the **University of Idaho Alumni Hall of Fame.**

# # #

The University of Iowa in Iowa City—the Hawkeyes—has inducted only one big leaguer into its **National Iowa Varsity Club Athletic Hall of Fame.** (NIVCA-HOF): Jack Dittmer.

# # #

Michigan State University's Hall of Fame includes Kirk Gibson and Robin Roberts, who played there, and former coach Danny Litwhiler.

# # #

EXECUTIVES AND OTHERS

Arizona Diamondbacks Executive Vice President Roland A. Hemond was in-ducted into the **Hall of Fame** of his native **Central Falls, Rhode Island.**

# # #

Texas Rangers general manager Doug Melvin is a member of the **Chatham (Ontario) Kent Secondary School Athletic Hall of Fame,** for his athletic prowess.

# # #

Dodgers Vice President Tommy Hawkins is in the **California Black Sports Hall of Fame** and the **Chicagoland Sports Hall of Fame.** Hawkins also has a star on the San Pedro, California, Walk of Fame.

# # #

H. P. Hunnicutt, after whom Hunnicutt Field (home of the Princeton, West Virginia, Devil Rays) is named, is a member of the **Soft Drink Bottlers' Hall of Fame.**

# # #

H. Wayne Huizenga, former owner of the Florida Marlins, and founder of the Blockbuster chain of video rental stores, is a member of the **Video Hall of Fame.**

# # #

Marlins team physician Daniel Kanell is a member of the **University of Pittsburgh Hall of Fame.**

# # #

Royals broadcaster Bob Davis is a member of the **Fort Hays State College Athletic Hall of Fame.**

# # #

Bob Wolfe, Senior Vice President of Administration for the Atlanta Braves, was inducted into the **Athletic Hall of Fame** of his alma mater, **Oglethorpe University,** in 1989.

# # #

John Schuerholz, Executive Vice President and General Manager of the Braves, was inducted into the **Hall of Fame** of his alma mater, **Towson State University** in Maryland in 1973, in recognition of his accomplishments as an athlete (baseball and soccer).

# # #

Glenn Sherlock, a coach for the Arizona Diamondbacks, is a member of the **Rollins College Hall of Fame.**

# # #

The **Lamar Cardinals** have inducted Jerald Clark and former Phillies coach Al Vincent into its **Hall of Fame.**

# # #

Kevin Malone, Dodgers General Manager, and Fred Koster are in the **University of Louisville Athletic Hall of Fame**—home of the Cardinals.

# # #

The **Hall of Fame of Illinois State University** in Normal—the Redbirds—includes Lee "Buzz" Capra.

# # #

Keli S. McGregor, an Executive Vice President of the Rockies, is a member of the **Colorado Sports Hall of Fame** for his accomplishments as a football player.

# # #

Pat Daugherty, Vice President for Scouting for the Colorado Rockies, has been enshrined in the **American Baseball Coaches Association's Hall of Fame**, the **Simpson College Hall of Fame**, the **Iowa Coaches Hall of Fame**, and the **National Junior College Hall of Fame**.

# # #

Padres CEO Larry Lucchino is a member of **Junior Achievement's San Diego Business Hall of Fame**.

# # #

ETHNIC HALLS OF FAME

Roberto Clemente is the only baseball player in the **Hispanic Hall of Fame**, http://www.unbeatables.com/HHeroes.html.

# # #

Netanya, Israel, is the site of the **International Jewish Sports Hall of Fame** (http://jewishsports.net). Inductees from baseball include broadcasters Mel Allen and Marty Glickman, owner Barney Dreyfuss (one of the few men born in Freiberg, Germany, to be inducted into ANY baseball-related hall of fame), Hank Greenberg, Sandy Koufax, Ken Holtzman, Buddy Myer, Lip Pike, and Al

Rosen. Moe Berg, Jimmy Reese, and sportswriters Dan Daniel and Shirley Povich received the Hall's "Pillar of Achievement" award.

# # #

Joe DiMaggio, Vince DiMaggio, Dom DiMaggio, Frank Crosetti, Tony Cuccinello, Ping Bodie, Roy Campanella, Joe Garagiola, Carl Furillo, Billy Martin, Dolph Camilli, Zeke Bonura, umpire Babe Pinelli, Yogi Berra, Ron Santo, Joe Torre, Rico Petrocelli, Gus Mancuso, Tony Lazzeri, Ernie Lombardi, and Rocky Colavito are members of the **National Italian American Sports Hall of Fame.** Originally located in Arlington Heights, Illinois, it recently moved to Chicago's Little Italy neighborhood. Piazza DiMaggio, with a restored statue of the Yankee Clipper, is directly across the street from the building.

# # #

Commack is the home of the **New York Jewish Sports Hall of Fame.** Its members include broadcaster Mel Allen, Moe Berg, Al Rosen, Ken Holtzman, Saul Rogovin, Sandy Koufax, Hank Greenberg, Art Shamsky, and WCBS-TV broadcaster Warner Wolf.

# # #

The National Polish-American Sports Hall of Fame, at St. Mary's College in Orchard Lake, Michigan, has inducted Stan Coveleski, Moe Drabowsky, Steve Gromek, Ted Kluszewski, Carl Yastrzemski, Whitey Kurowski, Tony Kubek, Eddie Lopat, Stan Lopata, Greg Luzinski, Bill Mazeroski, Barney McCosky, Stan Musial (the first inductee), Phil Niekro, Joe Niekro, Tom Paciorek, Jenny Romatowski (of the All-American Girls Baseball League), Al Simmons, Bill Skowron, Frank Tanana, and Alan Trammell. Vic Janowicz was inducted primarily on the basis of his football accomplishments, although he did play briefly for the Pittsburgh Pirates.

# # #

The Athletic Hellenic Hall of Fame, in Washington, D.C., has inducted Harry Agganis, Milt Pappas, Alex Kampouris, Alex Grammas, Gus Triandos, Billy Loes, umpire Chris Pelekoudas, Joe Collins, Al Campanis, John Tsitouris, and sportscaster Bob Costas.

# # #

The AHEPA Hellenic Athletic Hall of Fame in Marlboro, Massachusetts, includes Alex Grammas, Harry Agganis ("the Golden Greek"), Milt Pappas, Alex Kampouris, Gus Triandos, Billy Loes, Gus Niarhos, umpire Chris Pelekoudas, George "The Stork" Theodore, and sportscaster Bob Costas.

# # #

The American Sportscasters Association Hall of Fame, in Washington, D.C., includes Red Barber, Graham McNamee, Mel Allen, Jack Brickhouse, Curt Gowdy, Harry Caray, Jack Buck, Ernie Harwell, Keith Jackson, and, as mentioned above, Vin Scully.

# # #

Sportscaster Jack Buck may have been inducted into more halls of fame than anyone else. In 1987 he was given the Ford C. Frick Award by the **Baseball Hall of Fame** at Cooperstown. He is also a member of the **Broadcasters Hall of Fame,** the **Radio Hall of Fame,** the **Missouri Sports Hall of Fame,** the **Football Hall of Fame** twice—in different categories—and the **St. Louis Cardinals Hall of Fame.**

Major league broadcasters in the **Radio Hall of Fame** besides Jack Buck are Mel Allen, Red Barber, Jack Brickhouse, Harry Caray, Ernie Harwell, and Vin Scully.

# # #

The National Baseball Congress Hall of Fame in Wichita, Kansas, includes Ralph Houk, Whitey Herzog, Don Sutton, Rick Monday, Bob Boone, Ron Guidry, Tom Seaver, Roger Clemens, Graig Nettles, Daryl Spencer, Jug Thesenga, Harry Walker, Bobby Boyd, Bobby Bragan, Al LaMacchia, Joe Carter, Billy Martin, Allie Reynolds, Dave Winfield, Chris Chambliss, Ozzie Smith, sportswriter Bob Broeg, and Satchel Paige.

# # #

Umpire Cal Hubbard is in the **Baseball Hall of Fame,** the **Football Hall of Fame,** the **College Football Hall of Fame,** and the **Shreveport-Bossier City Sports Museum of Champions.**

# # #

White Sox owner Jerry Reinsdorf is in the **Chicago Jewish Sporting Hall of Fame,** the **National Jewish Sporting Hall of Fame,** and the **Chicago Sports Hall of Fame.**

# # #

Diamondbacks executive Sandy Johnson joined Duke Snider, Eddie Murray, Tommy Lasorda, and Ozzie Smith in the **Hall of Fame of RBI—Reviving Baseball in Innercities.**

# # #

Frank Howard is a member of the **Texas Baseball Hall of Fame,** the **Ohio State Sports Hall of Fame,** and the **Washington, D.C., Hall of Stars Hall of Fame.**

# # #

OTHER HALLS OF FAME

What's the connection: Johnny Bench, Danny Ainge, Dick Groat, Don Kessinger, Jackie Robinson, Don Sutton, and Supreme Court Justice Byron R. "Whizzer" White?

All have been inducted into the **National High School Sports Hall of Fame** in Kansas City.

# # #

Rich "Goose" Gossage is a member of the **Wasson High School Hall of Fame** in Colorado Springs.

# # #

Reggie Jackson is a member of the **Cheltenham High School Hall of Fame** in Wyncote, Pennsylvania.

# # #

El Tappe, Mel Tappe, and Scott Melvin are all in Illinois's **Quincy High School Blue Devils Hall of Fame.**

# # #

Bret Boone was among the first athletes inducted into the **Hall of Fame** of Los Angeles's El Dorado High School.

# # #

The Stephen T. Badin High School in Hamilton, Ohio, has inducted Jim Tracy into its **Hall of Fame.**

# # #

Brad Brink, whose major league career spanned 14 games (Phillies, Giants, 1992–93, 0–4) was elected to the **Downey, California, High School Hall of Fame.**

# # #

Kevin Appier was inducted into the **Hall of Fame** of his alma mater, Antelope Valley High School in Lancaster, California.

# # #

The **National Junior College Athletic Association Baseball Hall of Fame** includes Kirby Puckett.

# # #

"I played in the World Series. My aunt is in the Softball Hall of Fame. Who am I?"

Jim Thome, who played with the Indians in the 1995 World Series. His father's sister, the late Carolyn Thome Hart, was a 1970 inductee into the **National Softball Hall of Fame** in Oklahoma City. During her 15-year career, she played on 10 national championship teams and was named an All-American in 1950, 1951, 1952, and 1959. In 1950, 1951, 1952, and 1958 she was on the All World tournament team. She is also a member of the Greater Peoria Sports Hall of Fame.

# # #

The International League's Hall of Fame (which no longer inducts players) includes a number of ballplayers who went on to the major leagues: George "Specs" Toporcer, Frank McGowan, Dixie Walker, Ben Sankey, Charlie Keller,

Billy Southworth, Frank Shaughnessy, Steve O'Neill, Herb Pennock, Dick Rudolph, Leo R. "Tommy" Thomas, Ed Holly, Billy Meyer, Jack Dunn, Jewel Ens, Dan Howley, Ed Onslow, Rip Collins, Al Mamaux, Jack Ogden, George "Hooks" Wiltse, Estel Crabtree, Fred Merkle, Joe Boley, Fred Hutchinson, Bill Kelly, Glenn "Rocky" Nelson, Jackie Robinson, Jack Berly, Luke Hamlin, Merwin Jacobson, George Earnshaw, Joe McCarthy, Jimmy Ripple, Bruno Betzel, Ike Boone, Rube Parnham, Jack Bentley, George Selkirk, Jimmy Walsh, Fritz Maisel, Harry Smythe, George Stallings, Howard Moss, Joe Brown, and Dick Porter.

# # #

A **Minor League Hall of Fame** is planned for Memphis, Tennessee, part of the new home for the Memphis Redbirds of the AAA Pacific Coast League.

# # #

Dave DeBusschere, a rare two-sport standout, is in the **Basketball Hall of Fame.**

# # #

The **College Football Hall of Fame** includes a number of players from major league baseball: Harry Agganis, Bo Jackson, Jim Thorpe, umpire Cal Hubbard, and manager Hugo Bezdek.

# # #

The Pro Football Hall of Fame in Canton, Ohio, includes these men who also played major league baseball—Clarence McKay, "Ace" Parker, Red Badgro, Ernie Nevers, Greasy Neale, George Halas, Paddy Driscoll, umpire Cal Hubbard, and Jim Thorpe. Thorpe is also a member of the **American Indian Hall of Fame** in Anadarko, Oklahoma.

# # #

STEP UP TO THE PLATE

———

MANY STATES RAISE REVENUE by issuing license plates bearing team logos. For an extra annual fee of $39.50, for example, New York issues license plates with logos of every major league baseball team. Also available on New York's plates are the logos of every team in the National Basketball Association, the Buffalo Bills, Jets, and Giants in the NFL, and the Buffalo Sabres, New York Islanders, and New York Rangers in the NHL. New Yorkers can even get the logos of two minor league teams (the Buffalo Bisons and the Rochester Red Wings), the beloved Brooklyn Dodgers, and plates with the logos of pro soccer and lacrosse teams.

New Yorkers may also purchase a plate with the proclamation BIRTHPLACE OF BASEBALL, circled around a baseball.

# # #

Ontario has a wide selection of license plates adorned with team logos, including hockey, football, lacrosse teams, and the Blue Jays logo. If those earthly teams are not enough to satisfy one's craving for a personal statement, a *Star Trek*® plate is also available.

# # #

Vanity plates have been around since 1937, when Connecticut issued the first. They were called "initial plates," issued to motorists with good driving records, with the owners' initials.

# # #

Many people—fans, players, owners, umpires, executives—display their love of baseball for all to see on their license plates. The sampling of baseball license plates below not only shows the creativity of the owners in eight letters (frequently fewer), but also displays a proclamation of identity.

# # #

Two license plates are on exhibit at the Hall of Fame. Cy Young's 1954 Ohio plate, which says C511Y, and Lou Gehrig's 1 LG. Oddly, the latter is a 1942 New York plate. (Gehrig died in 1941.)

Other plates in the Hall of Fame's collection include PAL (owned by Joe Cronin, presumably when he was the president of the American League), RYAN34 (Nolan Ryan), BAG270 (Burleigh A. Grimes, who won 270 games), HF (Joe Cronin), and 41757 (Christy Mathewson).

# # #

To mark the debut of the Tampa Bay Devil Rays, Florida issued a new plate in 1997 with the team's logo.

Members of the team took it one step further, obtaining plates that said TBDR1, TBDR2, etc.

# # #

Jack Lang, former Secretary-Treasurer of the Baseball Writers Association of America (BBWAA), and a member of the Writers Wing at Cooperstown, told us that he has had his BBWAA plate for over 22 years.

# # #

A number of major league umpires provided us with information about their license plates:

Drew Coble's North Carolina plate says what he frequently says: U R-OUT.

Al Clark's two Virginia plates show his uniform number: XX4 and AL-XXIV.

Don Denkinger, American League umpire #11, has two Iowa plates: UMP and UMP 11.

Rick Reed's wife, Cindy, told us about his Michigan plate with his uniform number: AL 23.

Rocky Roe's Florida plate: YER OUT.

Tim McClelland's Iowa plate showed his umpire number, too: UMP 36.

Ken Kaiser's New York plate was UMP 21.

# # #

A National League umpire has a California plate that says NL UMP.

# # #

A sandlot umpire has this plate on his pickup: U-OUT.

# # #

Gene Michael—STICK.

# # #

Rich Grabowski has an extensive collection of Carl Yastrzemski memorabilia. Grabowski's Connecticut license plate: YAZ 2.

# # #

Former New York Yankee Dave Pavlas's New York plate said PAVBL—probably one of the few baseball-related license plates owned by a major leaguer from Frankfurt, West Germany.

# # #

John Lewis's Ohio license plate honors his favorite player: CLMENTE.

# # #

Andy Weiss's California plate shows his true loyalty—FENWAY 9. He told us that Ted Williams (#9) autographed it for him.

# # #

The plate 24 NATS—commemorating the Senators' only world championship—is owned by Washington, D.C., resident Jim Casey.

# # #

If you saw Willie Mays's plate (at one time on his pink Cadillac convertible), you'd have no doubt who was driving: SAY HEY. Mays also owned SAY HEY-24. The guy with MAYS-24 is just a fan.

# # #

Lefty Gomez's California plate was simple: LEFTY. Robert "Lefty" Grove's 1930 Pennsylvania license plate, in Barry Halper's legendary collection, was RG.

# # #

Ted Williams once had a Massachusetts plate that said what he did: HIT. Now, another Bay Stater has a plate that says BOSOX-9.

# # #

Why does J. Von Bushberger's Maryland license plate say CHRERFS?
    The letters are the initials of his favorite players on the Brooklyn Dodgers: Campanella, Hodges, Robinson, Erskine, Reese, Furillo, and Snider.

# # #

The Ohio Village Muffins—a vintage team that re-creates games of "base ball" as it was played (and spelled) in the 19th century, reports the following Ohio plates: OVMFNS (Ohio Village Muffins) and BIG BAT, both owned by Muffin Don Anderson. The team's umpire is Richard "Always Right" Shuricht. His plate is ALWSRT. Chip "Deerfoot" Moore's plate reflects his nickname—DEERFT. A member of another vintage team, the Sylvania Great Black Swamp Frogs Base Ball Club, has a plate that says FROG9.

# # #

Ken Griffey, Jr.'s plate on his Mercedes-Benz in WICKID 1. His other plate says SWINGMAN. His father's plate says GRIFF.

# # #

Devoted baseball fan Mark D. Pankin's Virginia plate lets everyone know where he stands: NO DH.

# # #

Roy Campanella's New York plate had his Brooklyn Dodger number: ROY 39.

# # #

Mike Cummings, Director of Public Relations for the Scranton/Wilkes-Barre Red Barons, the Phillies affiliate in the AAA International League, has a plate that promotes his team: **RED BRNS**.

# # #

Don Sutton: **300 WINS**.

# # #

Bob Feller (yes, *that* Bob Feller) called us to say that Hank Greenberg's Michigan license plate was **HG 5**.

# # #

Legendary baseball memorabilia collector Barry Halper, part-owner of the New York Yankees, reports the following plates: **YANKS 5** (Halper's own plate), Lefty Gomez's **GOOF**, Johnny Mize's **BIG CAT**, **LASORDA**, and George M. Steinbrenner III's **NYY**.

// // //

Bob Bogart, a Phillies fan, announces his allegiance with his Maryland plate: **PHILS**. He told us that once, leaving a Phillies game at the Vet (yes, he stayed for the entire game), he found a note on his car's windshield from the owners of the **PHILS** plate from New Jersey.

# # #

C. J. Knudsen, assistant general manager of the Vermont Expos (Short Season Class A, New York–Penn League) reports seeing **TURN 2** and **60FT6IN**.

# # #

Dick Stuart, known for his error-filled defense: **E-3**.

# # #

Brian Lepley's plate commemorates the Reds' championship years: **757690**. He knows of a Mets fan whose plate is **697386**.

# # #

We're still trying to verify that a Red Sox hater (or diehard lover) had a plate that read **86WSG6E3**.

# # #

Pete Rose: **PR 14** and **PETE**.

# # #

On September 11, 1985, when Rose broke Ty Cobb's record for most hits in a career by smacking a single off Eric Show of the Padres at home, Reds owner Marge Schott gave Rose a red Corvette with Ohio license plate **PR 4192**.

# # #

Larry Bowa: **BOWA 10** (when he was a Phillies coach).

# # #

Tom Dunton, pitching coach at Stanford: **STRIKES**.

# # #

Little League umpire: **YERR OUT**.

# # #

Stanford University and later Oriole/Pirate pitcher Jeff Ballard: **3UP 3 DWN**.

# # #

When Stan Musial smacked his 3,000th hit on May 13, 1958, Missouri governor James Blair presented him with a Missouri license plate specially made for the occasion: **3,000**. Also on hand were Tris Speaker (3,514 hits) and Paul Waner (3,152 hits).

# # #

Dave Atkins's 1994 California plate honors Christy Mathewson: **BIGSIX**.

# # #

Dock Ellis—**DOCK**.

# # #

Joe DiMaggio's lawyer drives a van with a Florida plate that says **DIMAG 5**.

# # #

A Florida fan's allegiance to Ted Williams is displayed as **TEDNO9**.

# # #

Devoted fans (and members of the Society for American Baseball Research) Cliff and Phyllis Otto have Virginia plate **SABRX2**.

# # #

A New Yorker's plate says **SABR 96**. Another has **NY METS**. A Floridian is driving around with a plate that says **RED SOX4**.

# # #

The license plate of Tex Simone, general manager of the Syracuse Skychiefs, is **SKYCHIEFS**.

# # #

Employees of the Lansing Lugnuts (the Royals' affiliate in the Class A Midwest League) sport these plates: **GO NUTS**, **LUGNUTS**, and **NUTHEAD**.

# # #

Mark Belanger: **GLOVE 7**.

# # #

Paul Andresen's Oregon plate: **RBI**.

# # #

When he was the ticket manager of the San Jose Giants (California League, Class A Advanced), Assistant General Manager Steve Fields received this plate from his wife: **WK4BBTX**. (Work for baseball tickets.)

# # #

Mickey Mantle's Oklahoma plate: MM 77.

# # #

Well-known baseball writer Marty Appel had two different New York "Birthplace of Baseball" plates—56 and 61, both great years if you were a Yankee fan.

# # #

Another renowned baseball writer, Dan Schlossberg, drives with a New Jersey plate proclaiming his loyalty: BRAVES 1.

# # #

Boosters of the Rancho Cucamonga Quakes (Padres, Class A Advanced, California League) have plates that say QUAKES and RCQUAKES.

# # #

SABR member Steve Elsberry's Iowa plate leaves no doubt as to his favorite team: SFGIANT.

# # #

Dennis Burbank, who pitched at Oklahoma State and in the Yankee system, had a plate that read O2UPNIN. His friends had plates that read: 3UP3DWN, SITDOWN, and (for Linda Ronstadt 2NV) BLUBYU.

# # #

You don't have to be from Illinois to be a Chicago White Sox fan—a Michigan plate says W SOX.

# # #

A fan at Shea Stadium on October 16, 1999, for Game 4 of the NLCS between the Mets and the Braves held up her Nebraska license plate: PIAZA-FN. Another Met fan's plate: 31 PIAZZA.

# # #

A Jeff Kent fan had this plate: 12 KENT.

# # #

The plate owned by Jim Trdinich, director of media relations for the Pittsburgh Pirates, makes sense only if you see it in your rear-view mirror or read it backwards: **SCUB OG.**

# # #

New York fan Andy Strassberg's plate: **BEISBOL.** Another New Yorker owns **69 METS.**

# # #

Orv Kelly of Fargo commemorated his friend Roger Maris's accomplishment with his North Dakota plate: **61 IN 61.**

# # #

One of the honors given to Mark McGwire when he broke Roger Maris's record of 61 home runs in a season was a Cardinal red 1962 Corvette, presented to him at Busch Stadium, complete with Missouri license plate **62.**

# # #

In recognition of his great season, on September 20, 1998, the Cubs gave Sammy Sosa a maroon Plymouth Prowler convertible with an Illinois license plate that said **SAMMY 98.**

# # #

The general manager of the Ogden Raptors (Brewers affiliate, Rookie Advanced Pioneer League) owns a Utah plate that says **CRVBALL.**

# # #

One college player noted his position on his plate: **2ND BASE.**

# # #

STATE BY STATE

Colorado's license plates include BBALL and SAFE.

One of Florida's best plates is BAS BALL.

Illinois has issued plates that say UROUT, SAFE, CUB, CUBS, SOX, and WSOX. But for those of a different opinion, there's always I BOO SOX. (That might also be the plate of an anti-Boston fan.)

Kansas plates include a number of baseball-related texts: 643, 643DPJO, BBALL, BBALLNE1SG, OUT.

Maryland: O'S FAN—one of the few plates with an apostrophe.

Minnesota plates include SAINTS (in honor of the St. Paul team in the independent Northern League), SAFE, CATCHER, TBAL, TWINS, GOTWINS, MNTWINS, YANKS, CUBSFAN, BOSOX, and REDSOX.

Nebraska has issued plates with such baseball slogans as NYYANKS, GOYANKS, YANKEES, CCHICUBS, CUBFANZ, ROYALS, and CATCHR.

Nevada: PITCHR, BBALL, SAFE, and OUT.

North Carolina has issued 643, SAFE, and BBALL plates.

Ohio: BSBL FAN.

Pennsylvania has issued a number of clever plates, including BASBAL, BASBALL, SAFE, OUT, FLYBALL, ERROR, ERRORS, HOMERUN, DOUBLE, TRIPLE, SINGLE, WALK, UMPIRE, PITCHER, CATCHER, STRIKE, SHORTSP, 3 BASEMN, PHILEEZ, PIRATES, and YANKEES.

South Carolina, with no major league team, has issued more baseball-related plates than many other states. Its plates include B BALL, BASBALL, GRNDSLM, HOMERUN, BRAVES, DODGERS, CUBS, PIRATES, FASTBAL, PITCHER, ORIOLES, CINREDS, MARLINS, STRIKE3, RUNNER, U R OUT, SWING, YANKEES, NYYANKS, CUBSFAN, REDS, REDSFAN, and REDSOX.

Texas vanity plates include SAFE, 643, 643DPJO, BASEBL, BBALLSA, BBALLSD, BBALLSG, BBNE1SG, and OUT. For some reason, nobody in Texas has yet obtained a plate that says ASTROS.

Vermont and Indiana have issued BBALL and SAFE plates.

Wyoming, which has a four-letter limit on its vanity plates, has issued these abbreviated baseball plates: SAFE, BALL, UMP, OUT, HOMR, MIT, BSBL, RED, MASK, and BBAL.

# # #

Guam's two baseball license plates are BEISBOL and CUBSFAN—not to be confused with another fan's FO D CUBS. Talk about far-flung! According to the National Geographic Society, Guam is approximately 7,372 miles from Wrigley Field in Chicago.

# # #

Linda McCarthy, curator of the museum at the CIA, was a great admirer of Moe Berg, who was a better spy than ballplayer. Her devotion is displayed on her license plate: **MOE BERG.**

# # #

Jim Thome's license plate says **25 DBTH**—his uniform number plus "Don't Believe The Hype."

# # #

The best baseball-related license plate we've ever seen was a New York plate proudly owned for years by the authors' oldest brother, George M. Lyons: **BASEBALL.**

# # #

THE HALL OF FAME

—————

NAME TWO MAJOR LEAGUE players who died in Cooperstown?

Vernon Sprague "Whitey" Wilshere. He pitched for the Philadelphia A's 1934–36, compiling a 10–12 record in 41 games. A native of Poplar Ridge, New York, he moved to Cooperstown and coached high school baseball there. He died in Cooperstown on May 23, 1985.

"Prince" Hal Schumacher. A native of Hinkley, New York, near Cooperstown, Schumacher pitched for the New York Giants 1931–42, and 1946, compiling a record of 158–121, with an ERA of 3.36. When he retired, Schumacher went to work for the Adirondack Bat Company, in Dolgeville, New York, just 38 miles from Cooperstown. Schumacher had lived in Dolgeville virtually all his life. He died at the age of 82, on April 21, 1993, at the Bassett Hospital in Cooperstown.

# # #

What did the number 21 mean to Hall of Famer Ted Lyons?

Lyons pitched for the White Sox for 21 years. He once pitched a 21-inning game. The lowest ERA in his career was his 1942 league-leading 2.10. In 1939 he appeared in 21 games and started them all. He walked 1,121 batters. In his first three years in the majors, his won-lost record was 2-1, 12-11, 21-11. In 1936 and 1937 he gave up the most home runs in his career—21 each year.

In 1928, 1929, and 1934, he pitched 21 complete games.

# # #

Who is the only man associated with the 1969 Seattle Pilots to be enshrined in Cooperstown?

Broadcaster Jimmy Dudley. Prior to being the voice of the Pilots in 1969, Dudley broadcast for the Cleveland Indians, 1948–67. He was given the Ford C. Frick Award—the highest award for a baseball broadcaster—at the Hall of Fame on August 3, 1997.

# # #

Who is the only future Hall of Famer to be on the Opening Day roster for an expansion team?

Richie Ashburn, who spent his final season with the new 1962 New York Mets. He led the woeful Mets in batting that year with a .306 average, 66 points higher than the team's average.

# # #

Who is the only Hall of Famer with a twin brother?

Big Edd Roush. His twin brother was Fred. (Richie Ashburn had a twin sister.)

# # #

Who hit the most career home runs off one pitcher?

Hint: They're both Hall of Famers.

Duke Snider hit 19 of his 407 off Robin Roberts. This seems appropriate because, when he retired in 1966, Roberts had given up 505 home runs, more than any other pitcher.

# # #

"During my career, I was managed by Casey Stengel, Walter Alston, and Lou Boudreau. My teammates included Duke Snider, Frank Robinson, Pee Wee Reese, Ernie Banks, Richie Ashburn, Lou Brock, Roy Campanella, Billy Williams, Sandy Koufax, Don Drysdale, Jackie Robinson, and Tommy Lasorda.

I managed (or coached) Carl Yastrzemski, Dave Winfield, Dennis Eckersley, Greg Maddux, Andre Dawson, Goose Gossage, and Ryne Sandberg. I am not a Hall of Famer. Who am I?"

Don Zimmer. He managed Yastrzemski and Eckersley with the Red Sox, Winfield with the Padres, Maddux, Dawson, Gossage, and Sandberg with the Cubs.

# # #

There are two "Lefty"s in the Hall of Fame—Robert Moses Grove and Vernon Louis Gomez. While Steve Carlton was called Lefty, he was not usually referred to as "Lefty Carlton." But another nickname—"Red"—is shared by three Hall of Famers. Most people don't even know their real first names. Who are they?

Albert Fred Schoendienst, Charles Herbert Ruffing, and Urban Charles Faber.

# # #

Who is the only Hall of Fame pitcher who is under 6' tall?

Whitey Ford, 5'10".

# # #

This Hall of Famer's uniform number matches the number of World Series games he won as a manager. Who is he?

Casey Stengel—37.

# # #

Who is the only Hall of Famer taken by a team in an expansion draft?

>   Hint: Not Richie Ashburn. The Mets purchased him from the Cubs on
>   December 8, 1961.

The correct answer is Hoyt Wilhelm, the Kansas City Royals' 25th draft pick in 1968. Before he could appear in a Royals uniform, he was traded to the Angels for Ed Kirkpatrick and Dennis Poepke.

# # #

TRICK QUESTION DEPT.:

Initially speaking, who is the first Hall of Famer?

Albert Benjamin Chandler—ABC.

# # #

With the possible exception of the Waner brothers, only two Hall of Famers were high school teammates. Who are they?

Harry Heilmann and Joe Cronin, who went to Sacred Heart School in San Francisco.

Loma Linda (California) High School holds the distinction of being the only high school to produce two men who pitched perfect games—Don Larsen and David Wells.

# # #

Who is the only man to pitch to a horse?

> *Hint: He's a Hall of Famer who changed his name—but not because of this stunt.*

Sandy Koufax, born Sanford Braun. (His parents divorced, and his mother married Mr. Koufax.) He pitched to Mr. Ed in the September 29, 1963, episode of the classic TV show, called "Leo Durocher Meets Mr. Ed." Mr. Ed hit an inside-the-park homer, while his friend Wilbur umpired and Durocher came out to argue a call. Also appearing in this episode were Vin Scully and Johnny Roseboro.

# # #

When he is elected to the Hall of Fame, this player will be the first in Cooperstown to play for the same team four different times. Who is he?

Rickey Henderson. In addition to his stints with the Yankees, Blue Jays, Padres, Angels, Mets, and Mariners, he played for the Oakland A's 1979–84, 1989–93, 1994–95, 1998.

# # #

What is the only *football* radio broadcasting team in the *Baseball* Hall of Fame?

Bob Murphy (the Mets' Hall of Fame broadcaster) and Monte Irvin, who teamed to broadcast New York Jets games in 1962.

# # #

"I am a Hall of Famer. During my playing career, I was managed by six other future Hall of Famers. Who am I?"

Al Lopez. His Hall of Fame managers were Wilbert Robinson (Brooklyn Dodgers, 1928, 1930–31), Max Carey (Brooklyn Dodgers, 1932–33), Casey Stengel (Brooklyn Dodgers, 1934–35; Boston Braves, 1938–40), Bill McKechnie (Boston Braves, 1936–37) Frankie Frisch (Pittsburgh Pirates, 1940–46), and Lou Boudreau (Cleveland Indians, 1947).

# # #

Who is the only eligible pitcher to win at least 20 games six times who is not a Hall of Famer?

Wes Ferrell. On his way to 193 career wins and 128 losses, Ferrell won 21 games in 1929, 25 in 1930, 22 in 1931, and 23 games in 1932—all for Cleveland—then won 25 games in 1935 and 20 in 1936 for the Red Sox.

# # #

On April 5, 1974, when this player made his major league debut, he was the youngest player in the majors. The owner who signed him was also the youngest owner.

The two met again on July 25, 1999, in Cooperstown. Who were they?

The player was Robin Yount, who was 19 when he made his debut with the Milwaukee Brewers. The team owner at the time was Allan "Bud" Selig, who was just 39. Selig was the Commissioner of Baseball in 1999, and he officiated at the ceremonies in Cooperstown when Yount was inducted into the Hall of Fame.

# # #

On July 25, 1999, Nolan Ryan, George Brett, and Robin Yount were inducted together into the Hall of Fame. Yount spent his entire career with the Milwaukee Brewers, while Brett's entire career was with the Kansas City Royals. Ryan played for the Mets, Angels, Rangers, and Astros. Ryan, Brett, and Yount were never teammates.

But five other players were teammates of all three. Who are they?

Jim Sundberg, Thad Bosley, Frank DiPino, Ray Sadecki, and Art Kushyer.

	TEAMMATE OF BRETT	RYAN	YOUNT
Sundberg	KC 1985–86	Texas–1989	Milw. 1984
Bosley	KC 1987–88	Angels–1977 Texas–1989–90	Milw. 1981
DiPino	KC 1993	Hous.–1982–86	Milw. 1981
Sadecki	KC 1975–76	Mets–1970–71	Milw. 1976
Kushyer	KC 1978	Angels–1972–73	Milw. 1976

# # #

"I am a baseball Hall of Famer. During World War II in Germany, I received a battlefield commission at the bridge at Remagen, raising me in rank from sergeant to second lieutenant. I was awarded a Silver Star and a Purple Heart. Then I played a German army sergeant on an episode of the television show *Combat.*

Who am I?"

Warren Spahn. The episode was "Glow Against the Sky," filmed in 1963. Spahn's only line in the show was "*Kommen sie!*" He was paid $35 for his work.

# # #

The first black men to play regularly for three major league teams have been enshrined in Cooperstown. Name the men, the teams, and the date of their big league debuts. (OK, just the years.)

Jackie Robinson, Brooklyn Dodgers, April 15, 1947; Larry Doby, Cleveland Indians, July 5, 1947; Ernie Banks, Chicago Cubs, September 17, 1953.

Hank Thompson has the distinction of being the first black man to play for two teams that don't exist any more—the St. Louis Browns (July 17, 1947) and the New York Giants (July 8, 1949).

# # #

Which modern Hall of Famer played for the most major league teams?

Hoyt Wilhelm—nine. New York Giants, Cardinals, Indians, Orioles, White Sox, Angels, Braves, Cubs, and Dodgers.

# # #

How many Hall of Fame pitchers (besides those who worked primarily in the Negro Leagues) lost fewer than 100 big league games?

Just three: Sandy Koufax—87 losses, Addie Joss—97 losses, and Dizzy Dean—83 losses.

# # #

Who is the only Hall of Fame pitcher to hit a home run in the World Series?

Bob Gibson, St. Louis Cardinals, Game 4, 1967.

# # #

Only three Hall of Famers have hit for the cycle in "natural order"—single, double, triple, homer. Who are they?

Tony Lazzeri, Yankees—June 3, 1932; Charlie Gehringer, Tigers—May 27, 1939; Billy Williams, Cubs—July 17, 1966.

# # #

Who is the only man who pitched a perfect game *and* had more than 2,000 hits?

Hint: He's a Hall of Famer.

John Montgomery Ward. His perfect game was on June 17, 1880. He became a position player after hurting his arm and went on to get 2,104 hits.

# # #

Ted Williams is well-known for selecting the wood from which his bats were to be made. But this future Hall of Famer turned his own bat on his own lathe. Who is he?

Elmer Flick.

# # #

Which Columbia College baseball record is still held by Lou Gehrig?

Most strikeouts in a game by a pitcher—17. This record has since been tied.

# # #

When Carlton Fisk was elected to the Hall of Fame in 2000, he had to choose which team's hat would appear on his plaque—the Red Sox (for whom he played for 11 years) or the White Sox (for whom he played another 13). Fisk selected the Red Sox. Which hats did these Hall of Famers select for their plaques: Yogi Berra, Satchel Paige, Eddie Collins, Jimmy Collins, Mordecai Brown, Elmer Flick, Johnny Evers, Frankie Frisch, Charlie Gehringer, Chick Hafey, Harry Heilmann, Harry Hooper, Rogers Hornsby, Catfish Hunter, Joe McGinnity, Joe Medwick, Mel Ott, Ray Schalk, George Sisler, Tris Speaker, Sam Thompson, Joe Tinker, Rube Waddell, Honus Wagner, Ed Walsh.

It's a trick question: The Hall of Famers listed above do not have identifiable team hats on their Hall of Fame plaques. (Some have no hats at all.)

For a list of which Hall of Famer is wearing which cap in his plaque, see http://www.baseballhalloffame.org/hofers_and_honorees/lists/uniform.htm.

# # #

UNENVIABLE RECORDS HELD BY HALL OF FAMERS DEPT.:
BATTING

Most consecutive strikeouts in consecutive plate appearances in a season.

Sandy Koufax—12. At the plate, Koufax went 0 for 1955, striking out in all 12 of his at bats that season.

# # #

Most at bats in a single season without a triple.

Held by future Hall of Famer Cal Ripken, Jr.—646 in 1989.

# # #

Who holds the modern rookie record for being hit by a pitch most often in a single season?

Frank Robinson—20 in 1956.

# # #

Who grounded into the most double plays in a nine-inning game?

Goose Goslin—4, tied with Joe Torre.

# # #

Fewest home runs in a season by the league's home run leader.

Seven, by Sam Crawford of the Detroit Tigers in 1908. Crawford is tied for the American League and major league record.

# # #

Most strikeouts in a career.

The major league and American League marks are held by Reggie Jackson—2,597. Willie Stargell holds the National League record with 1,936.

# # #

Most strikeouts in a nine-inning game.

Five—by Lefty Grove and Larry Doby (tied with many).

PITCHING

Most runs allowed in a career.

The major league record is held by Pud Galvin—3,303. The American League mark of 2,117 was set by Red Ruffing, while the National League mark of 2,037 is held by Burleigh Grimes.

# # #

Most hits allowed in a career.

Cy Young's 7,092. In the American League, the record is 4,920 by Walter Johnson. Pud Galvin holds the National League mark of 5,490.

# # #

Most 1–0 games lost in a career.

Twenty-six—by Walter Johnson.

# # #

Most grand slams given up in a career.

Ten—by Nolan Ryan.

# # #

Most doubles surrendered in one inning.

Six—by Lefty Grove.

# # #

Most home runs allowed in a career.

Robin Roberts's 505. The National League record is also held by a Hall of Famer—Warren Spahn, with 434.

# # #

Most games lost in a career.

Cy Young's 313. You've got to be pretty good to lose 313 games.

# # #

Most consecutive games lost to a single team in a career.

Thirteen. Between April 23, 1966, and July 24, 1969, Don Sutton, then with the Dodgers, just could not beat the Cubs.

# # #

Most walks in a shutout.

Eleven—by Lefty Gomez (tied).

# # #

Most wild pitches in a career.

The major league record is 277, by Nolan Ryan. The National League mark is 200, by Phil Niekro.

# # #

Most wild pitches in an inning.

The modern American League record of 4 was set by Walter Johnson. Phil Niekro holds the modern National League mark, also 4.

# # #

Most hit batsmen in a career.

The American and major league record of 206 was set by Walter Johnson. The modern National League mark of 154 was set by Don Drysdale.

# # #

Most home runs allowed in one inning.

Four—by Catfish Hunter and others.

# # #

Most walks surrendered in a career.

We can say with utter and complete confidence that Nolan Ryan's major league mark of 2,795 walks will, without any doubt or fear of contradiction, last until the end of time. The National League record is 1,717—by Steve Carlton, while the American League mark is 1,775—by Early Wynn. Ryan beats them by over *1,000.*

# # #

Most balks in a career.

Ninety—by Steve Carlton.

FIELDING

Most errors in a nine-inning game.

The American League mark of 5 is held by Nap Lajoie (tied).

# # #

The modern National League record for most errors in a career by a third baseman.

Pie Traynor's 324.

# # #

The modern National League record for most errors in a career by a short-stop.

Honus Wagner—676.

# # #

The American League record for most errors in a career by an outfielder.

Ty Cobb's 271.

# # #

The American League record for most errors in a career by a pitcher.

Ed Walsh—55.

# # #

OUCH!

———————

NOBODY LIKES TO GO ON THE DISABLED LIST. But there is a difference between pulling a muscle or breaking a bone during a game and the injuries the players below suffered off the field.

# # #

Ken Caminiti broke three bones in his back falling out of a hunting blind.

# # #

José Silva, Pirates pitcher, strained a muscle in his neck while reaching for his alarm clock.

# # #

Jeff Nelson broke a toe on a coffee table during the 1998 All-Star break.

# # #

David Segui, Mariners first baseman, injured his knee getting up from a chair in the clubhouse during a rain delay. He believed that the injury was damaged cartilage, although an MRI showed no serious damage.

# # #

Mike DeJean, a pitcher for the 1998 Rockies, punched a locker, broke his hand, and was out for the season.

# # #

Vince Coleman's injury was no laughing matter. He tripped on the tarpaulin at Busch Stadium on October 13, 1985, before Game 4 of the National League Championship Series, and was done for the season. His Cardinals won that series but lost the World Series to the Royals in seven games.

# # #

On June 7, 1983, George Brett broke a toe on his left foot when he accidentally kicked a doorstop in his home while running to watch Bill Buckner, then with the Cubs, bat on television.

# # #

On the second day of the 1970 season, pitcher Cecil Upshaw, dunking an imaginary basketball on a metal awning, caught his right ring finger and severed nerves and arteries.

# # #

Russ Meyer broke a toe kicking a steel locker and injured himself kicking the pitching rubber.

# # #

Shortly after his Cardinals clinched the National League Central title for 2000, catcher Mike Matheny severed two flexor tendons and a nerve on his right index finger on a hunting knife that was given to him as a birthday present. He was out for the remainder of the season, and for post-season play.

# # #

UNBREAKABLE
RECORDS?

00.

Uniform number first worn by Bobo Newsom with the 1943 Washington Nationals. Also worn by Jeff Leonard, José Canseco, and Jack Clark, because he said it looked good on jewelry.

# # #

0.

Number of lefthanded pitchers used by the 1934 Chicago White Sox.

# # #

0.

Number of times the 1932 Yankees were shut out. No other team has gone through an entire season without being shut out.

# # #

0.

Number of players from the host team to appear in an All-Star Game. No Indians played in the 1963 All-Star Game at Municipal Stadium in Cleveland.

# # #

1.

Amount paid, in dollars, as a signing bonus to future Hall of Famer Bob Feller. Of all baseball's records, this one seems sure to stand the test of time.

# # #

1.

Number of games managed for a big league team at the start of a season before throwing in the towel and resigning, by Eddie Sawyer of the 1960 Philadelphia Phillies. "I'm 49 years old and I want to live to be 50," said Sawyer. The team finished 59–95, just 36 games out of first place.

# # #

1.

Number of players who started the Washington Senators' 1946 Opening Day game who had started their 1945 opener.

Who was he?

Catcher Al Evans. With the end of World War II, regulars returned and fill-ins and wartime call-ups were gone.

# # #

1.

Number of starting players in an All-Star Game who are not Hall of Famers.

Of the 18 starters in the 1934 game, only Wally Berger (a career .300 hitter with 242 home runs) is not a Hall of Famer.

# # #

2.

Number of managers arrested during or just after a game. In the aftermath of an August 11, 1999, bench-clearing brawl between the Johnstown (Pennsylvania) Johnnies and the River City (Missouri) Rascals in the Class A Frontier League, the police were summoned. The River City manager, former big leaguer Jack Clark, was arrested and charged with assaulting a police officer, while Malcolm Fichman, the Johnstown manager, was charged with failure to obey a police officer.

# # #

2.

Most grand slams surrendered by one pitcher to one batter in one inning, by Chan Ho Park of the Los Angeles Dodgers to Fernando Tatis of the St. Louis Cardinals on April 23, 1999.

# # #

2.

Number of catchers from the same team to play in one All-Star Game.

Yankee catchers Yogi Berra and Elston Howard both appeared in the first 1961 game—there were two that year—on July 11, 1961, in San Francisco. This had never happened before and has never happened since.

# # #

2.

Number of perfect games managed by one man—Joe Torre of the New York Yankees. The pitchers were David Wells (May 17, 1998) and David Cone (July 18, 1999).

If some future manager is lucky enough to tie this record, Torre could still claim to be the only man to manage perfect games in consecutive years, and in his hometown!

And Torre may always remain the only man to manage a perfect game on his birthday—David Cone's game was on Torre's 59th birthday.

# # #

2.

Number of batters ejected for arguing balls and strikes during one at bat. On August 23, 1952 at the Polo Grounds, Bob Elliott of the Giants was thrown out by home-plate umpire Augie Donatelli for arguing a second-strike call in a game against the Cardinals. Then his replacement, Bobby Hofman, argued the strike-three call and was likewise tossed.

# # #

2.15

Technically, 2 pounds, 15 ounces—probably the lowest birth weight for a major leaguer, Toronto Blue Jays closer Billy Koch, now 6'3" and 200 pounds. He was born December 14, 1974, in Rockville Centre, New York—12 weeks prematurely. On August 3, 1999, he visited the Mercy Medical Center, where he was born (and where he lived for six and a half weeks), and met doctors and nurses who helped him survive. Koch's father, William, is 6'8".

Compare Koch to Lou Gehrig, said to have weighed 14 pounds at birth.

# # #

3.

Number of no-hitters in which one man played on the same date.

Jimmy Austin played in no-hitters on August 30, 1910 (Yankees), on August 30, 1912 (Browns), and on August 30, 1916 (Browns), pitched by Tom Hughes of the New York Highlanders (no hits through nine innings), Earl Hamilton of the Browns, and Dutch Leonard of the Red Sox, respectively.

# # #

3.

Number of Braves teams defeated by one man. Robin Roberts beat the Boston Braves, the Milwaukee Braves, and the Atlanta Braves. Camilo Pascual beat the Athletics in Philadelphia, Kansas City, and Oakland.

# # #

3.

Number of consecutive seasons in which Grover Cleveland Alexander won the Triple Crown of pitching, leading the league in strikeouts, ERA, and wins. He did it in 1915, 1916, and 1917 (plus a fourth Triple Crown in 1920).

# # #

3.

Number of teams owned by one man—Hall of Famer Bill Veeck: the Indians (1946–49), the St. Louis Browns (1951–53), and the Chicago White Sox (1959–61 and 1976–80).

# # #

3.

Number of perfect games broadcast by one man—Vin Scully of the Dodgers. The pitchers were Don Larsen (World Series, Yankees vs. Dodgers, October 8, 1956), Sandy Koufax (Dodgers vs. Cubs, September 9, 1965), and Dennis Martinez (Expos vs. Dodgers, July 28, 1991).

# # #

3.

Number of times one man played on the winning team in perfect games. Paul O'Neill was with the Cincinnati Reds for Tom Browning's perfect game on September 16, 1988, vs. the Dodgers. He was the right fielder with the New York Yankees on May 17, 1998, for David Wells's gem against the Minnesota Twins and for David Cone's perfect game against the Montreal Expos on July 18, 1999.

# # #

3.

Number of times one man played on the *losing* team in perfect games. Alfredo Griffin had an 18-year major league career (24 home runs, .249 batting average) but 100 years from now, this is the "achievement" for which he will be remembered.

Griffin was with Toronto for Indian pitcher Len Barker's gem, May 15, 1981. On September 16, 1988, he was with the Dodgers when Tom Browning was perfect for the Cincinnati Reds. Finally, Griffin was with the Dodgers again for Dennis Martinez's perfect game for the Expos on July 28, 1991.

# # #

3.

Number of perfect games announced by a public-address announcer: by Bob Sheppard of the New York Yankees. Don Larsen's World Series game (October 8, 1956), David Wells's game (May 17, 1998), and David Cone's game (July 18, 1999).

# # #

4.

Number of umpires in one game who could not count to three. On September 9, 1999, during a game between the Expos and the Padres in San Diego, Phil Nevin came up to bat in the top of the seventh inning to face rookie Ted Lilly after Reggie Sanders whiffed *for the third out!* Nobody left the field, and the count went to 2–1 before anybody realized that the inning had actually ended three "pitches" ago. The alert umpires were Jeff Kellogg, Paul Schreiber, Tim Timmons, and 11-year veteran Jerry Layne behind the plate. When Nevin came to the plate, Layne asked him how many outs there were—the scoreboard had been cleared—and Nevin said "Two, right?" Play continued until somebody in the Expos dugout notified the umpiring crew that there were three outs. Said Layne: "In my mind, I thought it was three, but when nobody flinched, I thought 'Not everybody can be wrong.'" The Padres won the game 10–3.

# # #

4.

Number of guys named Kevin involved in one trade: On December 11, 1986, the New York Mets traded Kevin Mitchell, Kevin Brown, and Kevin Armstrong (among others) to the Padres for Kevin McReynolds and others.

# # #

4.

Number of pennants won by a player-manager: Frank Chance of the Chicago Cubs—1906, 1907, 1908, 1910.

# # #

4.

Number of players in one major league game whose fathers were also major leaguers.

On June 18, 1997, in an interleague game, Mariners José Cruz, Jr., and Ken Griffey, Jr., faced Giants Stan Javier (son of Julian) and Barry Bonds (son of Bobby).

# # #

5.

Number of All-Star Games lost by a manager without a single win—by Al Lopez.

The Hall of Famer had the misfortune to manage the losing American League teams in 1955, 1960 (both games), 1964, and 1965.

# # #

5.

Only one pitcher has had at least one World Series win in five consecutive years. Who is he?

Allie Reynolds, New York Yankees, 1949–53.

# # #

6.

Shortest stint, in number of days, serving as captain of the New York Yankees. Babe Ruth was captain from May 20 until May 25, 1922, when he was stripped of that title for going after a heckler in the stands.

# # #

6.

Most RBIs in a game by one player with just one hit, accomplished on June 21, 1972, by Rico Petrocelli of the Red Sox at Fenway Park. He combined two run-scoring sacrifice flies with a grand slam.

# # #

6.14.

Only Dodger radio broadcaster Ross Porter has done the entire play-by-play for a major league game that went for 22 innings, and lasted six hours and 14 minutes. (Dodgers vs. Expos, August 23, 1989.)

# # #

7.

Number of complete consecutive games in which William "Baby Doll" Jacobson played right field for the 1926 Boston Red Sox but did nothing: between June 18 and June 25, he had no putouts and no assists.

# # #

8.

Number of baseballs held in one hand by Bob Link of the 1987 Williamsport Bills.

It is not yet known how many balls can be held in one hand by Antonio Alfonseca, who has six fingers on each hand (and six toes on each foot).

# # #

8.

Number of Mets catchers who threw out baserunners during the 1998 season.

Jorge Fabregas, Todd Hundley, Mike Piazza, Tim Spehr, Todd Pratt, Rick Wilkins, Alberto Castillo, and Jim Tatum.

# # #

11.

Number of times third baseman Al Rosen's nose was broken on the field.

"Hey, Skip, I could've sworn he was going to bunt*!"*

# # #

12.

Number of New York Yankees who played on world championship teams for five years in a row, 1949–53. Hank Bauer, Charlie Silvera, Allie Reynolds, Eddie Lopat, Vic Raschi, Johnny Mize, Gene Woodling, Joe Coleman, Joe Collins, Ralph Houk, Phil Rizzuto, and Yogi Berra.

# # #

12.

Number of different uniform combinations (shirts, pants, and hats) worn by the Arizona Diamondbacks during 1998–their first year.

# # #

13.

Number of consecutive seasons with at least 100 RBIs. Only two men have reached this milestone–Lou Gehrig (1926–38) and Jimmie Foxx (1929–41).

# # #

13.

Most Opening Day starts by brothers without a win. The Niekros, Phil and Joe, started a combined 13 Opening Day games, but wound up with a combined Opening Day record of 0–10.

# # #

13.

Number of batters faced by one pitcher in a complete game–a rain-shortened 4½-inning quickie pitched by Dick Drago of the Kansas City Royals in Baltimore on July 30, 1971. Drago retired 12 batters in four innings, and gave up Frank Robinson's 493rd career home run, as the Royals lost, 1–0, to Jim Palmer and the Orioles. There were just 29 at bats in the entire 48-minute game.

Thanks to David W. Smith of Retrosheet *for this short take.*

# # #

16.

Number of winning All-Star teams played on by Hank Aaron and Willie Mays. They had the advantage of playing in two All-Star Games in 1959, 1960, 1961, and 1962. The second 1961 game, played in Boston on July 31, ended in a 1–1 tie. (This means that they played on 17 nonlosing teams!)

# # #

17.

Number of last-place finishes by a manager–Mr. Connie Mack. It must have been nice to know that no matter where his team finished, even if it finished in last place 17 times, including seven *consecutive* last-place finishes, the owner would not fire him. Mr. Mack *was* the owner.

# # #

20.

Number of different pitchers who won games for the 1999 Philadelphia Phillies.

# # #

20.

Number of pages devoted in a team's media guide to a retired player—by the Texas Rangers for Nolan Ryan in 1999, the year of his induction into the Hall of Fame. The entry has a list of all 1,176 major leaguers he struck out, including Claudell Washington 39 times and 27 Hall of Famers, and notes that he gave up a record 10 grand slams. The 1999 Tampa Bay Devil Rays Media Guide lists every single hit Wade Boggs has had in his career—22 pages worth. Likewise, the 1999 Braves Media Guide devotes 15 pages to Hank Aaron's legendary career, on the 25th anniversary of his breaking Babe Ruth's career home run record. Every one of Aaron's 755 homers is listed.

# # #

27.

In 1946 the Boston Red Sox played 27 doubleheaders without being swept. The Sox swept 14, and split 13.

# # #

34.

Number of death warrants signed by a Hall of Famer—Commissioner Albert B. "Happy" Chandler, when he was governor of Kentucky, 1935–39, 1955–59.

# # #

36.

Number of triples in a single season, by Owen Wilson of the 1912 Pirates. Nobody has come closer than the 26 hit by Wahoo Sam Crawford in 1914.

# # #

44.

Number of World Series games played by one player, all against the same team. Dodger Pee Wee Reese played all his World Series games against the New York Yankees: 1941—5 games, Dodgers lost; 1947—7 games, Dodgers lost; 1949—5 games, Dodgers lost; 1952—7 games, Dodgers lost; 1953—6 games, Dodgers lost; 1955—7 games, Dodgers won; 1956—7 games, Dodgers lost.

# # #

53.

Number of future Hall of Famers who were playing in the big leagues at the same time, 1928–30.

# # #

53.

Number of major league stadiums in which Don Zimmer appeared in uniform as player, coach, and manager.

For the 1998 season, in which he continued to serve as Yankee bench coach, Zimmer selected uniform number 50, in celebration of his 50 years in professional baseball. In 2000, he wore number 52. He played for the Brooklyn and Los Angeles Dodgers, the Mets, Cubs, Reds, and the Washington Senators from 1954 to 1965. From 1972 to 1991, Zimmer managed the Cubs, Red Sox, Rangers, and Padres and also coached for the Expos, Padres, Red Sox, Giants, Rockies, and Yankees.

Stadiums which have been home to more than one big league team, such as Shea Stadium, the Polo Grounds, Dodger Stadium, and Connie Mack Stadium, are listed only once, for their principal team, or the first one during Zimmer's career.

Thanks to Don and Soot Zimmer for helping us with this list.

STADIUM	CITY	TEAM
The Big "A"/Edison Field/ Anaheim Stadium	Anaheim	Angels
Arlington/Turnpike Stadium	Arlington	Rangers
The Astrodome	Houston	Astros
Atlanta/Fulton County Stadium	Atlanta	Braves
The Ballpark in Arlington	Arlington	Rangers
Braves Field	Boston	Braves
Busch Stadium	St. Louis	Cardinals
Candlestick Park/3Com Park	San Francisco	Giants
Cinergy Field/Riverfront Stadium	Cincinnati	Reds
Colt Stadium	Houston	Astros
Comerica Park	Detroit	Tigers
Comiskey Park	Chicago	White Sox
Comiskey Park II	Chicago	White Sox
Connie Mack Stadium/Shibe Park	Philadelphia	Athletics/Phillies
County Stadium	Milwaukee	Braves/Brewers
Coors Field	Denver	Rockies
Crosley Field	Cincinnati	Reds
Dodger Stadium	Los Angeles	Dodgers/Angels
Ebbets Field	Brooklyn	Dodgers
Exhibition Stadium	Toronto	Blue Jays
Fenway Park	Boston	Red Sox
Forbes Field	Pittsburgh	Pirates

Griffith Stadium	Washington, D.C.	Senators
Hubert H. Humphrey Metrodome	Minneapolis	Twins
Jack Murphy Stadium/Qualcomm	San Diego	Padres
Jacobs Field	Cleveland	Indians
Jarry Park	Montreal	Expos
Joe Robbie/Pro Player Stadium	Miami	Marlins
Kingdome	Seattle	Mariners
Los Angeles Coliseum	Los Angeles	Dodgers
Memorial Stadium	Baltimore	Orioles
Metropolitan Stadium	Bloomington	Twins
Mile High Stadium	Denver	Rockies
Municipal Stadium	Cleveland	Indians
Municipal Stadium	Kansas City	Athletics/Royals
Oakland-Alameda County/Network Associates Coliseum	Oakland	Athletics
Olympic Stadium	Montreal	Expos
Oriole Park at Camden Yards	Baltimore	Orioles
Polo Grounds	New York	Giants/Mets
Robert F. Kennedy Stadium	Washington, D.C.	Senators II
Roosevelt Stadium	Jersey City	Dodgers
Royals/Kauffman Stadium	Kansas City	Royals
Safeco Field	Seattle	Mariners
Seals Stadium	San Francisco	Giants
Shea Stadium	New York	Mets/Yankees
Skydome	Toronto	Blue Jays
Sportsman's Park	St. Louis	Cardinals
Tiger Stadium	Detroit	Tigers
Tropicana Field	Tampa Bay	Devil Rays
Turner Field	Atlanta	Braves
Veterans Stadium	Philadelphia	Phillies
Wrigley Field	Chicago	Cubs
Yankee Stadium	New York	Yankees

# # #

58.

Number of years in which Pat Pieper was the public-address announcer at Chicago's Wrigley Field—with only a megaphone, 1916–74.

# # #

64.

Number of games in which Nolan Ryan struck out at least 10 batters.

# # #

100.

Number of years in a contract. When Dave Nilsson of the Milwaukee Brewers bought the entire baseball league in his native Australia for 1,000,000 Australian dollars ($630,000 U.S.) in 1998, he did so with a 100-year contract—and with an option for another 100 years.

# # #

110.

Number of shutouts pitched in a career by Walter Johnson. This record has stood unapproached since Johnson's retirement in 1928.

# # #

114.

Number of bats broken in one season by Pete Incaviglia.

# # #

115.

Number of consecutive games in which Joe Sewell played in 1929 without striking out.

# # #

152.

Most games appeared in by a rookie who never appeared in a big league game after his rookie year, by future Reds and Tigers manager Hall of Famer George "Sparky" Anderson, who played 152 games for the 1959 Phillies—his only major league season. No wonder—he finished the season with a .218 batting average, 34 RBIs, and no home runs.

# # #

177.

Number of runs scored in a single season since 1900, by Babe Ruth in 1921.

# # #

266.

Number of consecutive home runs at the start of a career before hitting a grand slam. This is one of Cal Ripken, Jr.'s most unusual accomplishments, achieved between July 13, 1984, and July 3, 1994. On that date, he hit a grand slam as the Orioles beat the Angels, 10–3, in Baltimore.

# # #

309.

Most triples in a career, by Sam Crawford. This record has stood since 1917, and nobody is even close.

# # #

370.

Number of innings pitched by Walter Johnson for the 1916 Washington Senators without surrendering a home run.

# # #

635.

Number of songs recorded by a baseball team owner—Gene Autry, the Angels' first owner. He recorded the second best selling single of all time, "Rudolph, The Red-Nosed Reindeer" (number 1 is "White Christmas"), and wrote "Here Comes Santa Claus, Right Down Santa Claus Lane." (See http://www.geneautry.com/exl/gene%20autry.htm for a list of Autry's records.)

# # #

749.

Number of complete games in a career, by Cy Young.

# # #

2,597.

Number of strikeouts in a career by a batter—Reggie Jackson. Nobody is within 660 through 1999. And now that Rob Deer has retired . . .

# # #

2,962.

Most games managed in a career without a first-place finish, by Jimmy Dykes. He managed the White Sox, Philadelphia A's, Orioles, Reds, Tigers, and Indians, 1934–46, 1951–54, 1958–61, never finishing higher than third place.

# # #

3,000.

Number of consecutive home games worked for the Baltimore Orioles by Ernie Tyler. He started his career as an usher in 1954, the team's first year in Baltimore after moving from St. Louis. In 1960 he became an umpire attendant, checking uniforms, equipment, and guest tickets. He has not missed a home game since. His sons manage the Orioles clubhouse and the visiting clubhouse. During the game, Ernie has the best seat at Camden Yards—a stool next to the backstop.

# # #

3,664.

Most career plate appearances without being hit by a pitch, by Mark Lemke (Braves, 1988–94).

# # #

3,731.

Most wins in a career by a manager—Mr. Connie Mack.

# # #

6,210.

Smallest crowd ever to see a World Series game. October 14, 1908, at Detroit's Bennett Park.

# # #

39,427.

Number of pairs of eyeglasses given out to fans at Wrigley Field, August 2, 1998. Why, were the sightlines suddenly out of alignment? Was this some sort of jibe at the umpires? No, it was "Harry Caray Day" at Wrigley, and the glasses were replicas of his trademark oversized black-rimmed glasses.

Perhaps, in addition to Caray's favorite "Take Me Out to the Ballgame," the organist played "On a Clear Day, You Can See Forever," "See You Later, Alligator," "You Won't See Me," "C. C. Ryder," "See You in September," or "I Can See Clearly Now."

# # #

47,579.

Number of coupons for free Big Macs awarded in one day.

On May 22, 1999, Mark McGwire became the first player to deposit a home run in "Big Mac Land" at Busch Stadium in St. Louis. His blast entitled all 47,579 ticket holders to free Big Macs at McDonald's.

# # #

92,706.

Largest crowd ever to see a World Series game, October 6, 1959, at the Los Angeles Coliseum.

# # #

EXTRA INNINGS

———

A NUMBER OF PITCHERS have surrendered home runs to the first batter they faced in the big leagues. Likewise, many batters have hit home runs in their first big league at bats. Only one man has done both. Who is he?

Dave Eiland. He broke into the big leagues on August 3, 1988, with the Yankees. The very first batter he faced was Paul Molitor of the Milwaukee Brewers. Molitor homered. Welcome to the big leagues.

By 1992 Eiland—who never batted in the American League—was with the San Diego Padres. In his first major league at bat, on April 10, 1992, Eiland homered off Bobby Ojeda of the Dodgers.

Thanks to David Vincent and Dave Smith for this unique item.

# # #

Only three players have 3,000 hits, 500 stolen bases, and 600 doubles. Who are they?

	HITS	STOLEN BASES	DOUBLES
Paul Molitor	3,319	504	605
Ty Cobb	4,189	892	724
Honus Wagner	3,415	722	640

# # #

"Before I started playing in the big leagues, I worked as an usher at Dodger Stadium. Who am I?"

Rene Gonzales.

# # #

Hall of Fame umpire Tom Connolly ejected this other Hall of Famer on August 30, 1922. Although he umpired for another 10 years, Connolly never ejected anybody else. Who was the last man Connolly ejected?

Babe Ruth. He argued balls and strikes.

# # #

Since 1900 which players with at least 50 stolen bases have had more stolen bases than runs scored in a season?

Lou Brock, Vince Coleman (four times), Ron LeFlore, Miguel Dilone, and Maury Wills. In 1978, when Dilone was with the Oakland A's, he stole 50 bases but scored only 34 runs—a difference of 16, the record.

# # #

Baseball is full of clubs—the 3,000 Hit Club, the 40–40 Club (40 home runs and 40 stolen bases in the same season), the 500 Home Run Club, to name just a few. Put these clubs in order of the number of members in each, as of 1999: 500 home runs, 3,000 hits, 3,000 strikeouts, 300 wins.

3,000 hits—23 members (through 2000)
300 wins—20 members
500 home runs—16 members
3,000 strikeouts—11 members.

# # #

Phil and Joe Niekro's basketball teammate at Bridgeport High School (near their home in Blaine, Ohio) went on to a Hall of Fame career of his own. Who is he?

John Havlicek, enshrined at the Basketball Hall of Fame in Springfield, Massachusetts.

# # #

Why was former Dodger pitcher Balvino Galvez thrown out of the July 31, 1998, game between his Yomiuri Giants and the Hanshin Tigers in Japan's Central League?

Because he threw a ball at an umpire. A Tiger homered after home-plate umpire Atsushi Kittaka called a ball on one of Galvez's pitches. Galvez's outburst came when he was lifted for a reliever after the home run. On his way to the dugout, he fired a pitch at Kittaka.

Galvez was suspended for the remainder of the season, and he returned home to the Dominican Republic.

# # #

This man's minor league career was interrupted by his service in the United States Marine Corps during World War II. Upon his discharge, he went back to the Joplin (Missouri) Miners, in the Class C Western Association, but his route to the majors was blocked by a slightly better player, Mickey Mantle.

So he left baseball in 1950 to pursue a career in law enforcement.

Mantle went on to win the Triple Crown in 1956 and the American League Most Valuable Player award in 1956, 1957, and 1962. In 1974 he was inducted into the Baseball Hall of Fame in Cooperstown.

Mickey Mantle was convincing as himself in the film *Safe at Home*.

This guy? The film about *his* experiences won the Academy Award® for Best Picture of the Year, and the actor playing him won an Oscar® for Best Actor. One of the authors of this book had a cameo role in that movie.

Who is he, what's the name of the movie, and who was the best actor?

The career minor leaguer was Eddie Egan. The movie was *The French Connection*, in which Egan was played by Gene Hackman. Egan had a bit role in the movie, as did Jeffrey Lyons, who played a TV reporter. His one line: "But is the mayor . . . ?" In the sequel, *The French Connection II*, Hackman's character, Popeye Doyle, mutters "Goddamn Mickey Mantle."

# # #

In 1998, Yankees manager Joe Torre and bench coach Don Zimmer combined for 70 years of big league playing, coaching, and managing experience (32 and 38, respectively).

The same year, the manager and bench coach for another team combined for just nine years of major league experience. Which team?

The Anaheim Angels. Manager: Terry Collins (6) and bench coach Joe Madden (3).

# # #

Where did the 1945 St. Louis Cardinals hold spring training?

Thanks to floods and wartime travel restrictions, the Redbirds were forced to hold spring training in St. Louis.

# # #

For 86 years, the 50–50 Club [50 doubles and 50 stolen bases in the same season] had only one member, Tris Speaker. In 1912, with the Boston Red Sox, he hit 53 doubles and stole 52 bases. Who was the second member, thereby making it a real club?

Craig Biggio. He hit 51 doubles and stole 50 bases for the 1998 Houston Astros.

# # #

Bob Montgomery of the Red Sox was the last player permitted to bat in the big leagues without a batting helmet. He wore a protective wafer in his hat. Dodgers third base coach Joey Amalfitano wore one in the coaching box, too.

Some time after batting helmets became mandatory, the rule was revised to require helmets with at least one earflap—to protect the left ear for a righty batter, and the right ear for a lefty. (Batters could, at their option, wear helmets with both earflaps, as switch-hitting Vince Coleman did.) Who was the last player to bat wearing the old-fashioned earflap-less helmet?

Gary Gaetti. (Twins, Angels, Royals, Cardinals, Cubs, Red Sox, 1981–2000.)

# # #

Gus Suhr of the Pirates had a consecutive game playing streak that began on September 11, 1931. It was at 822 games and counting when he missed a game on June 5, 1937. What happened?

He went to his mother's funeral.

# # #

Where did George Lombard (Braves, 1998) sign his first professional contract?

On a ship during his high school senior class cruise to Hawaii. Darrell Porter signed his contract with the Cardinals in December 1980 during his honeymoon cruise to the Caribbean.

# # #

Before the third inning of the Cardinals game against the Dodgers on April 23, 1999, in Los Angeles, how many grand slam homers had Fernando Tatis hit?

Zero.

# # #

How many did he hit during that third inning?

Two—not only tying pitcher Tony Cloninger's record for most grand slams in a *game* by a National Leaguer but *creating* a Major League record: most grand slams by one batter in *one inning*.

# # #

What percentage of Americans are lefthanded?

10 percent.

What percentage of major league batters hit lefthanded?

34 percent, including switch-hitters.

# # #

One year, this team had five regular players hit over .300, including one standout who hit .386 with 40 homers and 170 RBIs; it set a team record for total bases, RBIs, runs, hits, singles, and doubles. Yet the team finished dead last in the league, seven games behind the next highest finisher. Which team achieved this dubious distinction?

The 1930 Philadelphia Phillies. The star was Chuck Klein. The team finished last because its ERA was the worst in the National League—6.71.

# # #

Willie McGee's father, Hurdice, is a deacon of the Pentecostal Church. Each season he anoints his son's hands and feet with sacred oil to prevent injuries. McGee has been on the disabled list 13 times in his career.

# # #

During the 1907 and 1908 seasons, Walter Johnson of the Senators shut out the Highlanders at Hilltop Park in his first four appearances there. Only one other pitcher has ever thrown four consecutive shutouts in his first four starts in a stadium. Who?

Hint: He has the same last name as Walter Johnson.

In his first four starts at home in the Astrodome for the 1998 Houston Astros, Randy Johnson shut out the Phillies, Brewers, Pirates, and Reds consecutively.

# # #

Who was the first man to hit at least 40 homers in consecutive seasons for two different teams?

Andres Galarraga: 1997 Colorado Rockies—41, 1998 Atlanta Braves—44.

# # #

Who played on the most losing World Series teams?

Fred Merkle, Pee Wee Reese, and Terry Pendleton—five each.

# # #

Who went the longest between All-Star Game MVP Awards?

Willie Mays, five years, 1963–68.

# # #

THREE MASCOT STORIES

In 1999 Hamlet the Sea Serpent, mascot of the Lake Elsinore Storm (the Angels affiliate in the Class A Advanced California League)—not to be confused with Hamlet the Pig, who brings new balls to the home-plate umpire for the St. Paul Saints—was ejected from a game and fined $250 for razzing an umpire by putting on a striped shirt and large glasses after a disputed call.

# # #

Who is the only bird to manage a ball game?

Mal Fichman, manager of the Boise Hawks of the Northwest League, was ejected on June 29, 1989, but reappeared on the field in the costume of the team's mascot, Humphrey the Hawk.

# # #

The Rockies list their mascot Dinger in their media guide as though he were a player. After birthdate, height, weight (1.34 "dynotons"), his contract status is listed as "Fourth year of a 74-year contract, signed through 2067."

# # #

WHAT DO I HAVE TO DO TO GET INTO THE HALL OF FAME? DEPT.:

Only six men pitched to Roger Maris and Mark McGwire. Who are they?

Phil Niekro, Joe Niekro, Tommy John, Jim Kaat, Nolan Ryan, and Bert Blyleven.

# # #

These three teammates on the 1969 Yankees were born the very same day. Who are they?

Al Downing, Len Boehmer, and Fred Talbot—all born June 28, 1941.

# # #

On September 18, 1996, Shawn Green of the Toronto Blue Jays stepped up to the plate in a game in Milwaukee. The Brewers catcher was Jesse Levis. The home plate umpire was Al Clark. Even though it was three months to December, they all exchanged New Year's greetings. Why?

Because it was just a few days after Rosh Hashanah, the Jewish New Year, and all three are Jewish—perhaps the only time three Jews stood at a major league home plate at the same time.

# # #

Name the only all-Greek-American battery.

Milt Pappas (born Miltiades Stergios Papastegios) and Gus Triandos, Baltimore Orioles 1957–62.

# # #

Introductions we'd like to have made: Paul Schreiber meet Jim Baumer.

Schreiber was in the majors during the 1920s (Dodgers, 1922–23) and 1940s (Yankees, 1945) but not in the 1930s. Baumer played for the White Sox in 1949 and the Reds in 1961 but not in the 1950s.

# # #

One of the exhibits at the St. Louis Cardinals Hall of Fame in St. Louis is a baseball bat autographed by the crew of a United States Navy coastal mine-hunter. Why?

Because the ship is the USS *Cardinal.* Stan Musial was present at the ship's 1997 launching.

# # #

It's August 27, 1999, and you're the Vero Beach Dodgers, in the Class A Florida State League. You're playing the St. Lucie Mets, but manager Alvaro Espinoza is home with his wife and newborn baby. Whom do you call on to manage?

Hall of Famer Tommy Lasorda, Senior Vice President of the Dodgers, making an evaluation trip. It was Lasorda's first minor league managerial appearance in 27 years, and his first managerial stint at all in 3 years.

# # #

Robin Yount's final game stunk. Explain.

Hall of Famer Robin Yount spent his entire big league career with the Milwaukee Brewers. In his final home game, on September 29, 1993, he came to bat against the Toronto Blue Jays in the bottom of the fifth, with two outs. His at bat was delayed because a skunk ran on the field—a fitting comment for the Brewers' 69–93 record in 1993.

# # #

Which was the first team to have the Rookie of the Year, Cy Young, and Most Valuable Player Awards in the same year?

None—it has not happened yet.

# # #

The Boston Red Sox were so close to winning the World Series of 1986, that in the 10th inning of Game 6, with the Red Sox leading the Mets 3 games to 2, and the score 5–3, the message board at Shea Stadium prematurely (and as it turned out mistakenly) flashed the message: "CONGRATULATIONS BOSTON RED SOX—1986 WORLD CHAMPIONS." Noted baseball writer Marty Appel informs us that it was announced in the Shea press box that Red Sox pitcher Bruce Hurst had been named World Series Most Valuable Player. Then in the 10th inning, Mookie Wilson hit a ball through the legs of Bill Buckner at first base, and the Mets went on to win the game, and two days later the Series. No world championship for the Red Sox, no MVP for Bruce Hurst. And if you scramble the letters in BRUCE HURST, you get B. RUTH CURSE.

# # #

Which single-season offensive record, set by a member of the lowly St. Louis Browns, has stood for 80 years?

Most hits in a season—257, set by George Sisler in 1920.

# # #

Finish this question:

Tony Gwynn got his 2,000th hit August 6, 1993, a single off Bruce Ruffin of the Rockies in the second game of a doubleheader. His mother, Vendella, was especially pleased because it was ____.

her 58th birthday.

YOU MAY ASK, "SO WHAT?" READ ON.

# # #

When did Gwynn get his 3,000th hit?

On August 6, 1999, his mother's 64th birthday. She was part of the group that mobbed Gwynn at Montreal's Olympic Stadium after the hit.

# # #

Joining in the hugs was first-base umpire Kerwin Danley. Why did the usually impassive umpire abandon his professional disinterest and join the hugging?

Because Danley had been a teammate of Gwynn when they played at San Diego State University.

# # #

In 1983 he was the Mets' first-round draft pick and was given a $65,000 signing bonus. He made it to the big leagues in 1986 and went on to a six-year career with the Mets, Padres, Yankees, Orioles, Indians, and Reds. His career ended in 1991 with an injury. But in 1998, he was a New York rookie again. And although he was never an All Star, he became one of New York's finest. Who is he?

Stanley Jefferson. In 1998 the former outfielder was given a new position, as a New York City police officer.

Perhaps he can talk over the old days with Allan Anderson who, as a Minnesota Twin, led the American League with an ERA of 2.45 in 1988. He was with the world champion Twins in 1991 (although he did not play in the Series). He was in the big leagues from 1986 to 1991 with the Twins.

In 1998 Anderson was in training to become a firefighter in Lancaster, Ohio.

# # #

The ball that Mark McGwire hit for home run number 70, on September 27, 1998, was sold at auction for over $3,000,000.

What happened to the ball Babe Ruth hit for his 700th home run in 1934?

Ruth bought it for $20 from Lennie Bielski, the man who had it.

# # #

Who hit the most career home runs as a player-manager?

Joe Cronin—131.

# # #

Every game in the National League was canceled on April 21, 1925. Why?

In honor of Dodgers owner Charlie Ebbets, who was buried that day.

All major league games were also canceled on the day Bud Harrelson was born—June 6, 1944: D-Day.

# # #

Many teams have "official" tie-ins, such as the official hot dog, the official beer, the official soft drink, and so on. The Jimmy Fund is one of the most famous "official" charities affiliated with a major league team. With which team was it first connected?

The Boston Braves. The Fund was founded in 1948. When the Braves moved to Milwaukee in 1953, the Jimmy Fund became the official charity of the Boston Red Sox, raising money for the Dana Farber Cancer Institute in Boston.

# # #

When Greg Vaughn was traded from the San Diego Padres to the Cincinnati Reds after the 1998 season—a season in which he hit 50 home runs and helped the Padres to the World Series—he broke the record for most home runs in a season after which he was traded or sold. Whose record did he break?

Hank Greenberg. In 1946 Greenberg hit 44 homers for the Detroit Tigers. The following January 18, the Tigers sold him to the Pittsburgh Pirates for $75,000, which works out to roughly $1,704.55 per home run.

# # #

Things that have not yet occurred in baseball: a player whose last name starts with the letter X.

# # #

NOW IT CAN BE TOLD DEPT.:

One pressing question left unanswered by *Out of Left Field* was this: First baseman Frank Thomas of the White Sox, 1994 Most Valuable Player in the American League, and first baseman Jeff Bagwell of the Astros, 1994 Most Valuable Player in the National League, were born the very same day—May 27, 1968. Which one is older?

Thanks to Barb Kozuh of Big Hurt Enterprises, Frank Thomas's mother, Charlie Mae, Astros' Super Scout Tom Mooney, and to Jeff Bagwell himself, we now have the answer: Thomas was born at 4:35 A.M., while Bagwell entered the world at 2:03 P.M. Thomas is 9 hours and 28 minutes older.

# # #

DREAM TEAMS

——————

FREDERICK IOTT, BURT HOOTON, Henry Smith, August Fore-man, Joseph Finneran, John Townsend. Commissioner: Albert B. Chandler.

The "I'm just Happy to be here" team. All were known as "Happy." We're sure they'd also like to play with Dave Jolly and John Smiley and be managed by Jolly Cholly Grimm. They can be interviewed by Happy Felton. Do not invite "Sad" Sam Jones to play for this team.

# # #

Earl Wooten, Milciades Noboa, James Walsh, Adalberto Ortiz, George Griffey, Jim Gilliam, Eugene Thompson, Alvin Moore.

All went by the same nickname—"Junior." And don't forget two ballplayers whose first names really were Junior: Kennedy and Felix. The future captain of this team will undoubtedly be Junior Felix's son, Junior Felix, Jr.

# # #

William Woodward, Elwood English, Woodrow Davis, Gregory Williams, Forrest Main, Virgil Abernathy, Thomas Crowson, Elwood Wheaton, Woodrow Rich, Woodrow Williams, Jefferson Upchurch.

The all-"Woody" team. General manager: Branch Rickey. Supersub: Howard Maple. Favorite minor league team: The Oakland Oaks.

# # #

Kenneth Miller, Mizell Platt, Carroll Lockman, William Wietelmann, Harold Ock, Vernon Wilshere, Dorrel Herzog, Ed Ford, Francis Wistert, Lloyd Moore, Edward Ritterson, Theodore Guese, Lawton Witt, Walter Hilcher, Charles Glazner, Richie Ashburn, Charles Alperman, George Kurowski.

The all-"Whitey" team.

# # #

Oscar Knolls, Hubbard Northen, Herbert Andrews, Herbert Perdue, James Hart, Hubert Collins, Henry Pernoll, Harvey Walker, Hubert Pruett.

The all-"Hub" team.

# # #

John Vowinkel, Raymond Jordan, Robert Collins, Richard Conway, Raymond Radcliff, Floyd Wheeler, Alva Williams, Zeriah Hagerman, Virgin Cannell, Glenn Russell, Arthur Reagan, Richard Wade, Walter Coleman, John Egan, Eldon Repulski, Harry Collins, Truett Sewell.

The all-"Rip" team.

# # #

Frederick Clausen, Frederick Fisher, Florian Ackley, Frederick Buelow, Harry Dorish, Frederick Ostermueller, Wilfred Knothe, Frank Henrich, Fred Ingels Peterson, Frederick Scheeren, Frederick Coumbe, Alfred Von Kolnitz, Frederick Mollwitz, Frederick Maiscl.

The all-"Fritz" team.

Plus Fritz (true name "Fritz") Brickell, Fritzie Connally, and Harry, Charlie, and Larry Fritz.

# # #

Alexander Schauer, Ralph Novotney, George Ellis, George Foster, Oscar Peters, Byron Yarrison, Roy Marshall, Floyd Kroh, Albert Walker, Richard Marquard, Frank Dessau, Edward DeGroff, Ernest Vinson, John Ward, Harry Vickers, Walter Lutzke, Oliver Sellers, James Parnham, Charles Kisinger, Walter Manning, Reuben Melton, Reuben Oldring, Jacob Geyer, Reuben Fischer, George Waddell, Welton Ehrhardt, Raymond Bressler, George Walberg, John Clebon Benton.

The all-"Rube" team.

# # #

Frank Willson, George Speer, James McLaughlin, James O'Hara, Norman Elberfeld, Blaine Durbin, Willis Butler, Winfield Camp, Wilfred Carsey, William Summers, Ernest Mohler, Charles Nichols, Clarence Baldwin, William Gleason, Michael Madden.

The all-"Kid" team.

# # #

Babe Ruth, Will Clark, Gene Autry, Stan Musial, Ted Williams, Gary Carter, Ed Charles, George Theodore, Jimmie Foxx, Mark Fidrych, Greg Luzinski, George Scott, Ralph Houk, Harry Walker, Andy Pafko, Tom Hafey, Dave Baldwin, Leo Durocher, Dennis Eckersley, Sal Maglie, Roger Clemens, Branch Rickey, Orlando Hernandez, Orlando Cepeda.

All were known as "The" something. Babe Ruth—"The Bambino," Will "The Thrill" Clark, Gene Autry—"The Cowboy," Stan "The Man" Musial, Ted Williams—"The Kid" (also "The Thumper"), Gary Carter—"The Kid," Ed Charles—"The Glider," George "The Stork" Theodore, Jimmie Foxx—"The Beast," Mark "The Bird" Fidrych, Greg Luzinski—"The Bull," George Scott—"The Boomer," Ralph Houk—"The Major," Harry "The Hat" Walker, Andy Pafko—"The Brow," Tom "The Arm" Hafey, Dave Baldwin—"The Brain," Leo "The Lip" Durocher, Dennis Eckersley—"The Eck," Sal "The Barber" Maglie, Roger Clemens—"The Rocket," Branch Rickey—"The Mahatma," Orlando Hernandez—"El Duque," Orlando Cepeda—"The Baby Bull."

# # #

Duane Sims, Leon Carmel, Duane Maas, Thomas Simpson, Harry Markell, Edwin Snider, Henry Sedgwick, Charles Esper, Charles Farrell, Alexander Reilley, Albert Kelleher, Clair Shirey.

The all-"Duke" team.

# # #

Harold Daugherty, William Land, Roger Cramer, Charles Wood, Horace Ozmer, Elmer Hamann, Roy Miller, William Bass, Albert Waldbauer, Charles Watson, Ralph Carroll, John Lavan, Harry Imlay, Samuel Ralston, William Moskiman, Luther Cook, Dwight Gooden, Yancy Ayers, Harry Shanley, George Medich, James Prothro, George Leitner, James McJames, Frederick Wallace, Leon Martel, Henry McMahon. Harry Tonkin, William Nance, James Casey, Michael Powers, Morris Amole, Frank Reisling, William Marshall, Merle Adkins, Harry Gessler, Guy White, Willard Hazleton, William Scanlan, Eustace Newton, Michael Kennedy, Theodore Sechrist, Edward Farrell, Albert Bushong.

The all-"Doc" team. Honorable mention: Dock [true name] Ellis.

# # #

Robert Fausett, John Martinez, Charles Sweeney, George Weaver, John Gladman, William Ewing, Glenn Varner, Clarence Etchison, John Stanley, Thomas O'Brien, Charles Herzog, Robert Frierson, John Hopkins, Lee Ross, Orlin Rogers, William Washer, John Freeman, William Hooker, Frank Thrasher, Henry Danner, Charles Morrow, George Stanton, Milton West, James Becannon, George Redfern, Baxter Jordan, Clyde Crouse, Alexander Freeman.

The all-"Buck" team.

# # #

Walter Ruether, Frederick Schliebner, Emil Levsen, Harry Schirick, Charles Sterrett, Arthur Meier, Emil Leonard, Bertram Lerchen, William Hinrichs, John Rudolph, Edward Zwilling, Adolf Jordan, Lloyd Dietz, Henry Dotterer, Robert McCall, Frank Henry, Franklin Wetzel, George Distel, Sterling Stryker, Frank Ulrich, William Ussat, Herman Kemner, Charles Schesler, Clarence Hoffman, Robert Holland, Charles Lieber, Allen Romberger, Lambert Meyer, Albert Mele. Broadcaster—Ronald Reagan.

The all-"Dutch" team.

# # #

Connie Mack, Reggie Jackson, Ernie Banks, Bob Uecker, Dave Winfield.

The all "Mister" Team: Mr. Mack, Mr. October, Mr. Cub, Mr. Baseball. Winfield was derogatorily called "Mr. May" by Yankees owner George Steinbrenner when he had a bad World Series in 1981.

# # #

Harry Brecheen, Jim Kaat, Chico Carrasquel, Norman Brashear, Charles Tebeau, Harvey Haddix, John Mize, William Bransfield, Andres Galarraga, Felix Mantilla, Leo Kiely, Felix Millan, Don Hoak.

They all have feline nicknames: The Cat, Kitty, The Caracas Cat, Kitty, Pussy, Kitten, The Big Cat, Kitty, The Big Cat, The Cat, Black Cat, The Cat, Tiger.

Also Jim "Mudcat" Grant, Katsy Keifer, Ray Katt, Guy Bush—"The Mississippi Mudcat," Len "Meow" Gilmore, and Al Kaline—a Tiger for 22 years.

# # #

Charles Adams, Jay Towne, Harold Danzig, William Borton, Ellsworth Dahlgren, Herbert Ellison, Ralph Pinelli, Clarence Twombly, Foster Ganzel, Ernest Phelps, Norman Young, George Ruth, Herbert Barna, Boris Martin, Werner Birrer, Floyd Herman.

The all-"Babe" team.

# # #

Smith, Gene Michael, Charles Hafey, Eddie, Elmer, Cady, George Coffman, John Dempsey, Richard Sisler, Mickey Mantle.

Brick, Stick, Chick, Pick, Flick, Hick, Slick, Rick, Dick, The Mick.

# # #

Wilhelm Remmerswaal, George Mercer, Winford Kellum, Winfield Noyes, Noble Ballou.

The all-"Win" team.

# # #

Wedsel Groom, Morris Hancken, Lewis Gremp, Warren Rosar, John Hassett, John Lewis, Paul Dear, Arthur Crump, John Ryan, Roland Biancalana, Louis Blair, Charles Schultz, Skelton Napier, David Bell, Harold Hunter, Clarence Hicks, Walter Harris, Carl Peterson, Charles Bradford, Everett Lively, Richard Booker, John Kerr, Drew Gilbert, Robert Blattner, Harold Pritchard.

The all-"Buddy" team.

# # #

Albin Carlstrom, Harry Malmberg, Charles Risberg, Erling Larsen, Charlie Silvera, Olaf Henriksen (from Denmark).

The all-"Swede" team.

Surprisingly, neither Eric Erickson, from Göteborg, Sweden, nor Charlie Hallstrom, "The Swedish Wonder," from Jankoping, Sweden, were called "Swede."

# # #

Edward Swander, Arthur Whitney, Clarke Pittinger, Michael Higgins, William Hargrave, Carl Jorgensen, Merrill May, George Woods.

The all-"Pinky" team. (A handful of Pinkys.)

# # #

James Chaplin, 6'1", 195 pounds; Earnest Osborne, 6'4", 215 pounds; Ernest Bonham, 6'2", 215 pounds; and Dawson Graham, 6'2", 185 pounds.

The all-"Tiny" team.

# # #

Robert Detweiler, William Pearce, James Holmes, Joe Medwick, Howard Holmes, Dick Schofield, Sr., William Hemp.

The all-"Ducky" team.

# # #

Gene Vance, Santos Alomar, Alexander Wihtol, Tobias Griffin, Hilario Valdespino, John McDougal, Sandalio Consuegra, Charles Piez, Sanford Koufax, Charles Burk, Vincent Nava, Edmundo Amoros, James Taylor.

The all-"Sandy" team.

# # #

Kip Young, Leon Roberts, Lipman Pike, Leo Durocher, Harry Collins, Ewell Blackwell, Al Rosen, Horace Koehler, Gross, James O'Neill, Philip James, John Collins.

Kip, Bip, Lip, Lip, Rip, Whip, Flip, Pip, Kip, Tip, Skip, Zip. Honorary Manager: Flip Flap Jones.

# # #

Barney Schultz, Tony Curry, Eddie Haas, Kevin McGehee, Ken Griffey, Sr., Storm Davis, Hank Small, Herb Hutson, Doc Medich, Ken Griffey, Jr., Joe Decker, Tom Seaver, Bill Patton, Emerson Dickman, Birdie Tebbetts, Slick Coffman, Dave Koslo, Whitey Kurowski, Sparky Anderson, Bobby Prescott, Red Munger, Pinky Woods, Snuffy Stirnweiss, Paul Pettit.

The all-"George" team.

THIS GAME
MAKES ME HUNGRY

H ERE'S A LIST OF RESTAURANTS owned by or named for major
leaguers.
Former Commissioner and Hall of Famer Albert B. "Happy" Chandler teamed with entertainer Sammy Davis, Jr., to open a chain called Daniel Boone Fried Chicken.

Sammy Sosa's Restaurant (formerly Michael Jordan's) in Chicago.

Sammy Sosa owns a bar, Sammy Hit Club, in his hometown of San Pedro de Macoris, in the Dominican Republic.

Mickey Lolich's donut shop near Detroit.

Jethroe's, in Erie, Pennsylvania, owned by Sam Jethroe.

Art Shamsky's bar in downtown New York.

Tommy Henrich's in Columbus, Ohio, was on East Broad Street.

Stan and Biggies, co-owned by Stan Musial, in St. Louis.

Gorsuch House, on Gorsuch Avenue in Baltimore, owned by Brooks Robinson.

Big Stone Lodge, owned by Randy Jones, in San Diego. He also owned a barbecue restaurant at Qualcomm Stadium.

Dante and Stew's Vino Restorante Italiano, 17th Street, Denver, owned by Dante Bichette.

Mike Schmidt's, at 8th & Market Street in Philadelphia.

Mike Schmidt's Hoagies in Souderton, Pennsylvania.

Mike Shannon's Steak and Seafood, 100 North 7th Street, St. Louis.

Roger Clemens's Fried Chicken in Rhode Island.

Brooks Robinson's Golden Arm in Baltimore.

Rusty Staub's, a ribs restaurant in New York City.

Boog Powell's at Camden Yards.

Frankie Gustine's, one block from Forbes Field in Pittsburgh.

Chuck Tanner's Restaurant, on Route 18, New Castle, Pennsylvania.

There was a Warren Spahn diner on Commonwealth Avenue in Boston, across from Braves Field.

Ozzie Smith's Restaurant & Sports Bar, 645 Westport Plaza, in St. Louis.

Don Mattingly owned Mattingly's 23, a steakhouse in his hometown of Evansville, Indiana. Unfortunately, it lasted only three years.

Babe Ruth's is London's first sports-themed restaurant.

Harry Caray's restaurant, in Chicago, boasts its own Web site, www.harrycarays.com, which displays its gift shop, menu, and history.

Gorman Thomas runs Gorman's Grill at County Stadium in Milwaukee, where he used to play.

Jungle Jim Rivera's Captain's Cabin near Angola, Indiana.

Moose Skowron's Call Me Moose in Cicero, Illinois.

Phil Niekro's in Atlanta.

Bobby Valentine owns Bobby Valentine's Sports Gallery and Cafe in Milford, Norwalk, and Stamford, Connecticut, and Newport, Rhode Island. Arlington, Texas, had one when he managed the Rangers.

Jim Wohlford owned a bakery in his hometown of Atascadero, California, called The Cowboy Cookie & Grub Co.

Wally Burnette, owner of Burnette's grocery and sandwich shop, Blairs, Virginia.

Don Ferrarese, Ferrarese's Family Deli, Victorville, California.

Gene Freese's Third Base cocktail lounge in New Orleans.

Connie Grob: Connie's Home Plate, Middleton, Wisconsin.

Bill's Bar, Yorkville, Ohio, owned by Bill Mazeroski.

# # #

GET A JOB

W HEN THEIR PLAYING CAREERS WERE OVER, and during the off-season, particularly before the free agent era of mega-contracts, many ballplayers had to find real jobs in the real world.

Some ballplayers go into broadcasting, coaching, managing, or front office positions. But others pursue unusual careers. Richie Hebner was so well-known as a grave digger in his father's cemetery business that when he got a hit, the scoreboard at the VET in Philadelphia would show a grave with the exclamation "DIG IT!"

Here's our collection of unusual second occupations of big league ball players, including both Hall of Famers and many who had just a sip of coffee in the majors.

WORKS WELL WITH ANIMALS

Owner of a cattle ranch and deer hunting operation	Norm Charlton, Jerry Grote
Cattle rancher	Dave Philley, Monty Stratton
Elk and mule deer hunting guide	Mike DeJean
Bull farmer	Dave Concepcion
Professional trainer of hunting dogs	Faye Throneberry

Raising horses	Luis Alicea, Joe Adcock, Irv Noren, Gene Woodling (raises Appaloosas), Dave Bristol (cutting horses), Charlie Metro (quarter horse trainer), Ron Allen (trainer), Hank Allen, Ron's brother (trainer of Thoroughbreds, including *Northern Wolf*), Vic Raschi, Dan Plesac (trotters)
Performer in a flea circus	Grover Cleveland Alexander
Taxidermy shop owner	Bill Pecota, Kurt Stillwell
Hog buyer for a meat packer	Jimmy Archer
Mink farmer	Johnny Bucha
Raising roosters for cockfights	Ivan Calderon, Ruben Sierra

# # #

Construction worker	Clay Bellinger (built Giants spring training and minor league park in Scottsdale, Arizona)
Stagehand at the Metropolitan Opera	Rich Aurilia
Nursery worker	Jimmie Foxx
Tugboat worker	Dusty Rhodes
Beer distributor	Roger Maris, Vic Wertz, Buster Adams
Special education teacher	Curtis Pride
Pharmacist	Scott Fredrickson, Sam Crawford
Food vendor at Exhibition Stadium (when he was 15)	Rich Butler
Assistant women's basketball coach at a community college	Randy Myers
Bowling alley operator	Sherm Lollar, Kid Nichols, Ray Schalk, Yogi Berra and Phil Rizzuto, Hugh Duffy, Stan Musial
Assistant biologist for the United States Fish and Wildlife Service	Frank Reberger
Superintendent of Parks, Clark County, Washington	Gerry Staley

City Councilman, Paris, Texas	Dave Philley
Interior decorator	Harry Agganis
Owner, chain of children's stores	Scott Bailes
Assistant Secretary of Commerce and Assistant Secretary of Agriculture	Wilmer "Vinegar Bend" Mizell—also a three-term congressman from North Carolina
Electrician	Phil Plantier
Professional photographer	George Rohe
Diplomat	Thomas Carroll (1955–56, 1959, New York Yankees, Kansas City Athletics). According to the historian of the State Department and Dr. Thomas Mattox, editor of *American Diplomacy*, Carroll is the only former professional baseball player to become a bona fide diplomat. (Sorry, Tommy Lasorda, always referred to as a great "ambassador for the game," does not count.) Carroll served in the U.S. Army before obtaining his bachelor's degree from Notre Dame. He was a political assistant at the United States embassy in Rio de Janeiro, Brazil, in 1963 and a political officer at the embassy in São Paulo in 1965 and in Santiago, Chile, in 1973.
Computer programmer	Art Howe
Snowplow driver, Massachusetts Turnpike	Former Red Sox manager Joe Morgan
Mushroom farmer	Rocky Colavito
Baseball bat manufacturer	George Brett
Manufacturer of lamps made of baseball bats and balls	Al Zarilla
Valet parker	Marty Cordova, Clay Bellinger

Pecan factory quality inspector	Kent Anderson
Pecan farmer	Ken Holloway
Meat inspector	Noodles Hahn
Lumberjack	Rheal Cormier, Rich Rowland
Craps table supervisor	Brynt Alyea
Rice plantation manager	Ted Lyons
Vendor for the Atlanta Hawks	Ed Olwine
Field representative for a congressman	Ed Bailey
Carnival barker	Dean Chance
Bricklayer	Tom Henke
Brickmaker	Whitey Herzog
Real estate agent	Craig Lefferts, Marty Pérez, Joe Gordon, Dave Bergman, umpire Larry McCoy, Moose Skowron, Johnny Allen, Bob Locker
Sofa deliverer	Bryan Harvey
Grain elevator worker	Brooks Kieschnick
Post Office worker	Sal Yvars, Bubba Trammell, Carlos May, Omar "Turk" Lown, Harry Hooper (postmaster)
Baseball card shop worker	Brooks Kieschnick
Christmas tree farmer	Jackie Jensen, Del Ennis, Benny Bengough
Minister	Albie Pearson, Billy Sunday, Al Travers, John Faszholz, Guy Morton, Jr., Bill Greason, Paul Hinrichs, Bobby Richardson, Mike Easler, Louis Bruce
Hairdresser	Bernie Carbo
Talent agent	Art Shamsky
Law enforcement officer/ sheriff	Mickey Owen, Corky Valentine, Jim Romano, John Romonosky, Frank Papish, Curt Raydon, Ray Murray, Frank Fanovich, Dave Melton, Carl Furillo, Jim Greengrass, Dave Skaugstad, Angelo LiPetri, Pete Suder, Bill Harrington, Earl Harrist, Dick Hoover, Don Kaiser, Monte Kennedy, umpire Dale Scott

	(former Sergeant at Arms for the Kentucky State Legislature), Hank Miklos, Virgil Trucks (who wrote citations for the illegal dumping of coal stove ashes into the streets of Birmingham, Alabama, for $25 per week), Claude Passeau, Duff Brumley, Joe Shaute, Grant Bowler, Jack Lynch, Harry Chiti, Mike Budnick
Idaho state legislator	Larry Jackson
Railroad switchman	Virgil Trucks
Car dealer	Chuck Oertel, Lou Stringer, Ted Beard, Gene Bearden, Johnny Callison, Jim Tatum, Artie Wilson, John Romano, Ewell Blackwell, Walt Masterson, Hank Aaron, Smoky Burgess, Swede Risberg, Barney McCoskey, Garland Buckeye
Carpenter/cabinetmaker	Neil Berry, Jim Bloodworth, Johnny Wyrostek, Roger McCardell, Marshall Bridges, Murry Dickson, Elroy Face, Tom Bolton, Happy Felsch, Randy Kutcher, Vern Law
Liquor store owner	Roy Campanella, Vic Raschi, Gus Triandos
Banker	Ellis Burton, Red Wilson, Emil Verban, Casey Stengel, Nolan Ryan, Bob Will, Chet Nichol, Jr., Dick Strahs, Frank Saucier, Hal Newhouser, Cy Williams, Charlie Devens
Professional fly fisherman	Dick Sharon
Golf pro	Vic Lombardi, Bob Greenwood, Ken Harrelson, Frank Sullivan, Sammy White, Jack Sanford, Curt Simmons, Nick Koback, Lou Kretlow, Ralph Terry, Virgil

	Trucks, Jim Umbarger, Bob Repass, Ralph Terry, Ed Levy
Golf course owner/manager	Dick Groat, Bill Mazeroski, Jerry Lynch, Fred Taylor
Fireworks tester	Earl Averill, Sr.
Owner, fireworks factory	Walt Dropo
Dry cleaner	Mike Garcia, Gil McDougald, Walt Masterson, Al Evans
Attorney	Chuck Essegian, George S. Davis, Donn Clendenon, Tony LaRussa, Hughie Jennings, Eddie Grant
Florist	Jay Avrea, Lou Brock, Joe Lefebvre
Upholsterer	Roger Bowman
License plate manufacturing	Denny McLain
Vintner	Dutch Leonard, Tom Seaver, Rusty Staub (whose wine bears the label "Le Grand Orange")
College professor	Tom Upton (math), Dick Smith (physical education)
Math teacher	John Lee Richmond
Substitute teacher	Bryan Little, Mark Brandenburg
Theology teacher	Umpire Al Clark
High school science teacher	Jim Morris (In fact, Morris was teaching high school science just weeks before he made his big league debut with the Tampa Bay Devil Rays.)
Cemetery operator/worker/ mortician	George Susce, Hank "Bow Wow" Arft, Paul Schramka, Frenchy Bordagaray, Charlie Gibson, Eddie Delker
Tennis instructor	Nick Tremark
Alaska Pipeline worker	Johnny Logan
Bookkeeper	Randy Winn, Luis Aparicio
Bouncer	Rick White
Clothing store owner	Leon Wagner—"Buy your rags at Daddy Wags"
Insurance adjuster	Ron Hansen

Stockbroker	Ross Barnes, Huyler Westervelt, Del Ennis, Dave Bergman, Robin Roberts
Clerk for a stockbroker	Yale Murphy
Dodger Stadium usher	René Gonzales
Physical therapist	Tito Landrum
Rehabilitation therapist in a psychiatric hospital	Orlando "El Duque" Hernandez (after he was banned from the Cuban national team as a defection risk)
Deputy court clerk	Jimmie Foxx
Railway car painter	Ernie Burch
Owner, Dinty Moore's corned beef restaurant in Los Angeles	Kitty Brashear
Pullman car conductor	Hick Carpenter
Cigar salesman	John Clarkson
Tour guide at Gettysburg battlefield	Eddie Plank
Coal dealer	Bill Hassamaer
Carriage maker	William Hunter
Composer	Marshall Locke ("Big Rock Candy Mountain")
Diamond broker	Louis Pelouze
Milkman	Candy John Nelson, John Coleman
Professional wrestler	Cal McVey, umpire Ken Kaiser
Basketball referee	umpire Dave Phillips
Pizza deliverer	Todd Pratt
Bridge builder	Nig Cuppy
Superintendent, Missouri State Reformatory	Lyman Drake
Copper miner	Warren Fitzgerald
Plumber	Chick Gandil
Zinc miner	Mickey Mantle
Geologist	Dave Rowe
Racetrack cashier	George Shaffer
Racetrack crier	Jumbo Jim Davis
Parimutuel clerk, taking $50 racetrack bets	Buck Weaver
Trunk maker	Joe Straub

\# \# \#

STUFF NAMED
AFTER BALLPLAYERS
(AND OTHERS)

A NUMBER OF BALLPLAYERS have their own museums:
>   The Bob Feller Museum is near his birthplace in Van Meter, Iowa.
>   The Babe Ruth Birthplace and Museum is in Baltimore.
The Nolan Ryan Museum is in Alvin, Texas.

The Yogi Berra Museum and Learning Center (http://www.yogiberramuseum.com) in Little Falls, New Jersey, is on the campus of Montclair State University and overlooks Yogi Berra Stadium, home of the New Jersey Jackals.

The Ted Williams Museum and Hitters Hall of Fame (twmuseum@hitter.net) is in Hernando, Florida.

The Ty Cobb Museum (http://www.tycobbhealthcare.org) is in Royston, Georgia, near his home.

The 9-foot tall, 915-pound bronze statue of Cal Ripken, Jr., was unveiled on April 2, 1997, at the Ripken Museum (honoring Cal, Sr., Cal, Jr., and Billy) in Cal, Jr.'s hometown of Aberdeen, Maryland, in a wing of City Hall located at 8 Cal Ripken, Jr., Drive.* Plans were announced on January 26, 2000, to build the $25 million, 6,000 seat Cal Ripken Stadium and Youth Baseball Academy in Aberdeen. The stadium will be home to a team in the Atlantic League, and the academy will teach baseball fundamentals. The stadium will be home to the

---

*If you go, make sure to see the ornate grandfather clock, whose plaque announces that it was presented to "Cal Ripkin, Jr." [sic].

World Series of the Babe Ruth League's under-12 division—the Cal Ripken Division. Ripken has pledged $9 million for the project.

# # #

The Roger Maris Museum is between a Spencer Gifts store and a Pet Center in a shopping center in Fargo, North Dakota.

# # #

There used to be a Carl Hubbell Museum in Meeker, Oklahoma.

# # #

There was a Dizzy Dean Hall of Fame in Jackson, Mississippi.

# # #

The Burleigh Grimes Museum was in Wisconsin.

# # #

One of the largest and most unusual baseball monuments in America is in St. Petersburg, Florida, where 85 brass major league–size home plates recount local baseball history, including each major league team to have played a spring training game in St. Petersburg. The plaques line Jim Healey and Jack Lake Baseball Boulevard, named for the local men who inspired it, on First Street South from Al Lang Stadium to Tropicana Field, home of the Devil Rays.

# # #

Which major league stadiums were named after major league players?

Comiskey Park, Bennett Park in Detroit (later the site of Tiger Stadium), named for Charley Bennett, and Connie Mack Stadium.

# # #

Bobby Ojeda helped raise $100,000 from Mets fans to build a group home on a California Indian reservation. In 1999 an adjacent Little League field was named for him.

# # #

May 19, 1998, was proclaimed David Wells Day in New York City, in honor of the Yankee pitcher's historic perfect game the previous day over the Twins.

# # #

Can you name a big leaguer who was named for a big leaguer who was named for a big leaguer?

Mickey Tettleton was named for Mickey Mantle, who was named for Mickey Cochrane.

# # #

The Springfield (Illinois) Capitals of the independent Frontier League play at Robin Roberts Stadium, named for Springfield's great Hall of Fame pitcher.

# # #

National League President Leonard S. Coleman, Jr., was present when a statue of Jackie Robinson was dedicated on February 25, 1998, at the Journal Square train station in Jersey City, New Jersey, where Robinson made his debut in Organized Baseball on April 18, 1946.

On August 27, 1997, at Cairo (Georgia) High School, Governor Zell Miller dedicated a 10-mile stretch of State Highway 93 between Cairo and Beachtom to a Cairo native. It's called the Jackie Robinson Memorial Highway.

On April 21, 1998, the Brooklyn Historical Society erected a marker on the side of a bank building at 215 Montague Street in Brooklyn, site of the Dodgers' business office, commemorating the place where Branch Rickey signed Jackie Robinson to play for the Dodgers.

On October 15, 1999, Stamford, Connecticut, unveiled a 7½-foot tall bronze statue of former Stamford resident Jackie Robinson. It will be installed at Jackie Robinson Park.

# # #

Bridgeport and Hartford, Connecticut, now boast identical monuments to Roberto Clemente. The first was erected in Bridgeport's Seaside Park not long after Clemente's death on New Year's Eve, 1972. A duplicate of the 6-foot granite monument to the first Puerto Rican in the Hall of Fame was of particular interest to the one-third of Hartford's citizens who are Puerto Rican American. But Hartford had no ballpark, and the monument was forgotten, then lost for years. In the fall of 1997, police officers found it in a garbage-strewn lot behind a furniture store in Bridgeport.

The monument was escorted from the lot by the University of Hartford baseball team, who took it to Roberto Clemente Field in Colt Park. There, the monument proclaims: "The test of mankind's progress is not whether we add more to the abundance of those who have much. It is whether we provide enough for those who have too little."

On August 6, 1998, Pittsburgh's 70-year-old Sixth Street Bridge was renamed the Roberto Clemente Bridge. It will provide a direct entrance to PNC Park, the Pirates' new home.

# # #

In 1995 Bogota, New Jersey, named a ballfield after Dodgers broadcaster Vin Scully, who lived there when he broadcast for Brooklyn.

# # #

A 12×15-meter mural depicting Hideo Nomo was created by high school students in Japan's Kouchi Prefecture.

# # #

Tony Gwynn Field is at his alma mater, San Diego State University.

# # #

The official address of PacBell Park, the San Francisco Giants' new stadium, is 24 Willie Mays Plaza. (Mays wore #24.)

# # #

The Tampa Bay Devil Rays erected a plaque honoring Wade Boggs on October 1, 1999, on "Baseball Boulevard" outside Tropicana Field, commemorating his 3,000th hit, which he got for the Devil Rays on August 7, 1999. Born in Omaha, Boggs grew up in Tampa.

The baseball field at Tampa's Plant High School was named for Boggs, one of its alumni.

# # #

The baseball field at Colby College, in Waterville, Maine, is named for "Colby" Jack Coombs.

# # #

On January 30, 1978, the New Athens, Illinois, Central High School dedicated its baseball field in honor of New Athens native Whitey Herzog. A plaque was erected, bearing his image in bronze, and this inscription:

> "Named in honor of Dorrel 'Whitey' Herzog. A 1949 N.A.C.H.S. graduate, Whitey managed the Kansas City Royals to two successive American League Western Division championships. He is recognized for his leadership qualities, for his outstanding ability to identify potential star players, guiding them in their development and motivating them to their best performance as part of a team. 'Whitey''s record is a worthy model for young athletes aspiring to a career in professional sports."

# # #

One of the few baseball monuments to honor a woman is in St. Paul, Minnesota, where a mural of Ila Borders adorns Midway Stadium. Borders was the first woman to play in Organized Ball, when she pitched 14⅓ innings for the Duluth Dukes in the independent Northern League on June 24, 1998.
A biography of Borders can be found at www.dsdukes.com/ila.html. Borders has her own Web site, too: www.ilaborders.com.

# # #

The University of Michigan plays its baseball games at Ray Fisher Stadium, named for the Yankees/Reds pitcher, 1910–20.

# # #

There will be a plaque at Dick Howser Stadium at Florida State University in Tallahassee honoring Fred Hatfield, former big leaguer, and FSU's head baseball coach, 1964–68.

# # #

Art Nehf Field, at the Rose-Hulman Institute of Technology, in Terre Haute, Indiana, was named for the Terre Haute native who pitched for the Boston Braves, New York Giants, and Cincinnati Reds, 1915–29.

# # #

Billy Rogell Drive connects I-94 to Detroit's Metropolitan Wayne County Airport. Rogell was the Tigers shortstop, 1930–39. He served for years as a member of Detroit's City Council. A ceremony at the airport (which Councilman Rogell helped locate in the town of Romulus) displayed Rogell memorabilia.

# # #

Hi Bithorn Stadium in San Juan is named for the Santurce native who was the first Puerto Rican to play in the majors. He pitched for the Cubs and White Sox, 1942–43, 1946–47.

# # #

Harmon Killebrew Drive in Bloomington, Minnesota, is on the former site of Metropolitan Stadium, near the Mall of America.

# # #

A street near the Metrodome in Minneapolis is named Rod Carew Drive.

# # #

The Twins ticket office is at 34 Kirby Puckett Place, part of Chicago Avenue.

# # #

What used to be a lovers' lane in Fargo, North Dakota, has been renamed Roger Maris Drive.

# # #

High school teams in Weiser, Idaho, play at Walter Johnson Field.
    Visiting Coffeyville, Kansas? After you've seen Death Alley, where three members of the Dalton gang died in a shootout on October 5, 1892, see the mural to Walter Johnson. (http://www.coffeyville.com/coffeyville/index.html)

# # #

The baseball team at the University of South Alabama (USA) plays at Eddie Stanky Field. Stanky was the baseball coach at USA.

# # #

Sal Maglie Stadium is in his hometown of Niagara Falls, New York. Maglie (Giants, Indians, Dodgers, Yankees, and Cardinals, 1945, 1950–58), was known for pitching so far inside he "shaved" the batters, hence his nickname "The Barber." Thus the stadium's nickname: "The Barber Shop."

# # #

Perrysburg, Ohio, named its high school baseball field Jim Leyland Field in honor of its alumnus, who has managed the Pirates, the Marlins, and the Rockies.

# # #

On June 19, 1997, the New Jersey legislature honored Larry Doby as a "home-town hero." Doby, born in Camden, South Carolina, grew up in Paterson. It also named part of Route 120, which passes by the Meadowlands Sports Complex, home of the NFL's Giants and Jets, the NBA's Nets, and the NHL's Devils, "Larry Doby Highway."

In 1997 five Larry Doby All-Star Playgrounds were created in Doby's honor in Cleveland, to mark the 50th anniversary of his breaking the American League color line in that city. Camden announced plans for a monument to Doby, and to name a ballfield for him.

# # #

A portrait of Spavinaw, Oklahoma, native Mickey Mantle is permanently displayed at the State Capitol in Oklahoma City. Plans are under way to create a Mickey Mantle museum near Spavinaw.

# # #

In keeping with their tradition of naming streets at their spring training complex in Vero Beach, Florida, after their Hall of Famers, in 1998 the Dodgers dedicated Avenida Jaime Jarrin, in honor of their Spanish-language broadcaster, inducted into the broadcasters' wing at Cooperstown that year.

The game room is the Walt Alston Game Room, not far from the Sandy Koufax Theater and the Roy Campanella Meeting Room.

# # #

Not all baseball monuments, plaques, and statues honor players. A plaque was put up in Brooklyn that said "THIS IS THE FORMER HOME OF EBBETS FIELD: PLEASE NO BALLPLAYING."

# # #

A plaque to Mary Conrad was unveiled at the home-plate entrance to the Ballpark at Arlington on April 13, 1998. Ms. Conrad, who died in 1997, was a lifelong Rangers fan beginning with their first season in 1972.

# # #

In April 1998 the Pennsylvania Historical and Museum Commission announced plans to erect historical markers to Honus Wagner in Allegheny County and to Connie Mack in Philadelphia.

# # #

An 8-foot bronze statue of Kentucky native Harold "Pee Wee" Reese wearing a Brooklyn Dodgers uniform will be erected at Louisville Slugger Field in Louisville, Kentucky, home of the RiverBats, the Milwaukee Brewers' affiliate in the Class AAA International League. After his Hall of Fame playing career, Reese worked for many years as a representative of Hillerich and Bradsby, manufacturers of Louisville Sluggers.

# # #

On April 23, 1998, a plaque was affixed by the private New York City Historical Landmarks Committee to Babe Ruth's home at 345 West 88th Street in Manhattan.

The Alexandria (Louisiana) Aces of the independent Texas-Louisiana League, play their games at Bringhurst Field, located at 1 Babe Ruth Drive.

Babe Ruth and Joe DiMaggio were parishioners at St. Angela Merici Church in the Bronx. Ruth, his wife, and his daughter are among the donors of the church's marble altar, and their names appear on a plaque in the church.

# # #

"I'm a big leaguer. The street on which my parents live was named for my sister. Who are we?"

The street in Martinsburg, West Virginia, on which Scott Bullett's parents live was named Vicky Bullett Street, in honor of the 1988 Olympic gold medal–winning and 1992 bronze medal–winning basketball player. She plays for the Charlotte Sting in the WNBA.

# # #

A citywide drive was conducted in 1965 in Atlantic City, New Jersey, to name a street after Hall of Famer Pop Lloyd, who played there for the Bacharach Giants of the Negro Leagues. Today, Pop Lloyd Boulevard connects Ohio Avenue to Park Place.

# # #

Yuma, Arizona, is the site of the Ray Kroc baseball complex, named for the former owner of the San Diego Padres. It is the training complex for the Yakult Swallows in Japan's Central League.

# # #

On October 29, 1997, a school in Brooklyn was named for Roy Campanella.

# # #

Funds were raised by the George S. Davis Chapter of the Society for American Baseball Research to place a memorial stone at Davis's previously unmarked grave at Philadelphia's Fernwood Cemetery. Davis was elected to the Hall of Fame by the Veterans' Committee in 1998.

# # #

Plans to erect a statue to Hall of Famer Herb Pennock in his native Kennett Square, Pennsylvania, have stirred controversy.

While nobody contests his credentials as a great pitcher (240–161), those opposed to honoring him with a statue point out that as general manager of the 1947 Phillies, he tried to prevent the Dodgers from bringing Jackie Robinson to play in Philadelphia, even threatening to boycott the game if Robinson played. In fact, Robinson did play, and so did the Phillies, but some in and around Kennett Square do not believe that Pennock should be honored. Mayor Charles S. Cramer, Sr., who is black, disagrees and supports the project, noting how much times have changed.

# # #

A bronze statue of Gene Autry, the first owner of the Angels, will be installed at Edison International Field (at 2000 Gene Autry Way) in Anaheim. The statue will be in a courtyard at the stadium, surrounded by replicas of Autry's five stars from the Hollywood Walk of Fame.

Gene Autry Park was dedicated by the Angels in Mesa, Arizona, on March 1, 1985. It was their spring-training home.

Autry also has a town named for him—Gene Autry, Oklahoma.

Autry is the only man to have a number retired in his honor (26), to have a town and a hotel named after him, and to be made an honorary general in the California National Guard.

# # #

A billboard near Tate High School in Gonzalez, Florida, notes that four of its graduates went on to the big leagues: Travis Fryman, Jay Bell, Scotti Madison, and Don Sutton.

# # #

The library at the Steve Garvey Junior High School in Lindsay, California, was named for Tommy Lasorda.

# # #

Norristown, Pennsylvania, has named a small street that leads to a ballfield after Tommy Lasorda, who grew up playing there. So far, nothing has been named for another Norristown native, Lasorda's godson, Mike Piazza.

# # #

The stadium at Cal Poly–San Luis Obispo is named for Ozzie Smith. Smith, who attended the school from 1974 to 1977, donated $1 million to his alma mater.

# # #

Former teammates Bob Feller and Herb Score were present when a Little League field in Chardon, Ohio, was recently named for Mel Harder, Cleveland Indians star from 1928 to 1947.

# # #

Billy Sunday Drive, named for the ballplayer-turned-evangelist, is near his birthplace in Ames, Iowa.

# # #

Temperance, Michigan, has named a ballfield for LeRoy "Tarzan" Parmalee, from nearby Lambertville. He compiled a 59–55 record, 1929–39, pitching for the Giants, Cubs, Cardinals, and Philadelphia A's.

# # #

Keystone Junior College, in La Plume, Pennsylvania, prides itself on being the alma mater of Christy Mathewson. Indeed, in recent years it has held an annual Christy Mathewson Day in honor of the great pitcher near his August 12 birthday. But August 14, 1999, was a memorable day at Keystone for a far different reason. A locked display of Mathewson memorabilia—perhaps one of the finest collections of Mathewson items—was broken into, and priceless items, left to the school by Mathewson's widow, were stolen. Among the missing items were baseball uniforms, his military uniforms, photographs, and books.

The Whittenton Ball Field, now used by the Little League in Taunton, Massachusetts, has a plaque noting that it was the site where Christy Mathewson began his professional career in 1899.

# # #

In May 1973 the Babe Ruth League field in Sylacauga, Alabama, was renamed for Walton "Walt" Cruise, who lived in Sylacauga since he was 6. The 82-year-old Cruise was presented with a commemorative plaque. He played for the Cardinals and Braves, 1914–24. A roommate of Jim Thorpe with the 1919 Braves, Cruise kept the bat he used, going 1 for 9 (a triple) and scoring the only Braves run in the Leon Cadore–Joe Oeschger marathon 26-inning 1–1 tie on May 1, 1920. In September 1967 Cruise donated the glove he used in that game to the Immortal Sports Museum in Pittsburgh.

# # #

Nokomis, Illinois, is the home of a baseball museum honoring three Hall of Famers who were born nearby—Ray Schalk (from Harvel), Red Ruffing (Granville), and Jim Bottomley (Oglesby). Former Cubs pitcher Glen Hobbie was president of the museum.

# # #

Clio, Alabama, renamed the street where he lived as a child "Don Sutton Street" and added "Home of Don Sutton" to the town's water tank.

# # #

Milltown, New Jersey, is planning a plaque at Michelin Field to commemorate Babe Ruth's appearance there in an exhibition game and to commemorate a similar appearance by Casey Stengel.

# # #

Through the efforts of Roseville, Minnesota, historian and author Stew Thornley, commemorative plaques have been erected marking the sites of Nicollet Park, home of the Minneapolis Millers from 1897 to 1955, and Lexington Park, home of the St. Paul Saints from 1897 to 1956.

# # #

There's a George Kell Field in the Hall of Famer's hometown of Swifton, Arkansas. The field is home to the local American Legion team.

# # #

The television exhibition gallery at the Museum of Broadcast Communications, part of the Chicago Cultural Center, was renamed for Jack Brickhouse, long-time broadcaster for the Chicago Cubs, White Sox, Bulls, and Bears.

# # #

A Little League park has been named for Chuck Harmon in his hometown of Washington, Indiana. The town has named a street Harmon Drive in his honor. The city of Golf Manor also named a street for him.

# # #

A youth field in Corkagh Park, Clondalkin, Dublin, Ireland, was dedicated on July 4, 1998, as the "Peter O'Malley Little League Baseball Field," named for the Los Angeles Dodgers Chairman of the Board. O'Malley is also President of the Little League Foundation Board of Trustees. The field is adjacent to the Dodger Baseball Field, for adult games. Both were gifts of the O'Malley family.

# # #

The Aguilas del Zulia in the Venezuelan Baseball League play at Estadio Luis Aparicio El Grande Stadium, while the Caribes play at Estadio Alfonso "Chico" Carrasquel in Puerto La Cruz.

# # #

The city of San Pedro de Macoris announced plans to erect a statue to native son Sammy Sosa in front of its baseball stadium, in recognition of his historic 1998 MVP season with the Cubs, when he hit 66 home runs. A statue of Sosa now stands in the middle of the town square, erected after 1993, Sosa's first 30 home run, 30 stolen base season.

# # #

The University of Oklahoma baseball team plays its games at L. Dale Mitchell Park in Norman.

# # #

Rudy York Road in Cassville, Georgia, is near his birthplace in Rome.

# # #

Germantown, Pennsylvania, is the site of a plaque honoring Connie Mack. It was erected at his home and dedicated in May 1998 by the Philadelphia A's Historical Society.

The Society was also instrumental in funding and dedicating a historical marker at 21st Street and Lehigh, former site of Shibe Park, which was later renamed Connie Mack Stadium.

# # #

The Jimmy Fund, official charity of the Boston Red Sox (375 Longwood Avenue, Boston, MA 02215-5347), sold small statues of Ted Williams. Plans are in the works in Boston for an annual Ted Williams Day in Boston, and to erect a statue of Williams.

# # #

On September 8, 1998, just 16 minutes after Mark McGwire hit his record 62nd home run of the season, Kelly Mueller gave birth to a son at St. Mary's Health Center in Richmond Heights, Missouri. Kelly and her husband, Daniel, of Ballwin, Missouri, named the boy Tyler McGwire Mueller.

A wax statue of Mark McGwire has been added to the Hollywood Wax Museum in Branson, Missouri. The Roger Maris statue was literally melted down for construction of the McGwire statue.

# # #

Signs outside of St. Louis's Busch Stadium renamed "Stadium Plaza" as "McGwire Drive" in September 1998, but the move was only temporary—through the end of the season. Meanwhile, some St. Louis aldermen offered legislation to make the change permanent.

By act of Congress, the part of Interstate 70 that passes through St. Louis, Missouri, has been renamed "Mark McGwire Interstate Route 70."

# # #

The Atlanta Braves have gone out of their way to honor Hank Aaron in and around Turner Field. First, there's the statue. Then there's the ball he hit for his record-breaking 715th career home run, on display in the Ivan Allen, Jr., Braves Museum and Hall of Fame. Hank Aaron Drive runs next to Turner Field. Finally, a plaque in a parking lot adjacent to Turner Field marks the spot where #715 landed in the Braves' former home, Atlanta–Fulton County Stadium.

In 2000 the first 44 people who bought BMWs from the new "Hank Aaron BMW" dealership in Union City, an Atlanta suburb, received Aaron's signature on a plate in the "Signature Series" glove compartment.

# # #

On September 18, 1998, the Pittsburgh Pirates and the Pennsylvania Historical and Museum Commission dedicated a plaque in Three Rivers Stadium parking lot #4 to commemorate the very first World Series, Pittsburgh vs. Boston in 1903.

# # #

The smallest statue we've ever seen is of Roger Clemens—about four inches tall. You can see it in cyberspace at http://www.andyscollectibles.com/inv/clemensstatue.htm.

# # #

In 1998 the national stadium in Managua was named for the first Nicaraguan to play in the American major leagues—Dennis Martinez, who retired just before the 1999 season.

# # #

The Kent State University Golden Flashes play at Gene Michael Stadium.

# # #

The University of Cincinnati Bearcats play at Johnny Bench Field.

# # #

McGraw-Jennings Field at St. Bonaventure College in upstate New York is named after its two most famous alumni: John McGraw and Hughie Jennings. At the field's dedication on June 1, 1927, the Bonnies played against the New York Giants, managed by McGraw. The Giants featured Rogers Hornsby, Mel Ott, and Bill Terry.

# # #

A bronze statue of Enos Slaughter was unveiled outside of Busch Stadium in St. Louis on July 18, 1999. It shows him sliding home with the winning run in the 1946 World Series.

A nearby statue honors George Kissell, who was a minor league instructor for the Cardinals for many years.

The Lou Brock statue was dedicated on August 29, 1999.

Other statues at the stadium honor Cardinal greats Stan Musial, Rogers Hornsby, Dizzy Dean, and Ozzie Smith. Present for the dedication of the Dizzy Dean statue on May 27, 2000, were all four children of his brother Paul "Daffy" Dean and 40 other family members.

On April 18, 1998, the Cardinals unveiled a bronze statue of Bob Gibson at Busch Stadium. Sculptor Harry Weber described capturing Gibson's unique and instantly recognizable angled delivery as quite an engineering feat: "We've got about a ton of bronze hanging out at about a 45 degree angle." The Cardinals are selling 12" replicas of the Gibson statue for $5,000. Profits go to Cardinals Care, the team's charitable organization, which benefits youth groups.

A similar statue of Red Schoendienst was unveiled outside Busch Stadium on April 11, 1999, in recognition of the Hall of Famer's 51 years of service to the Cardinals as player, coach, and manager. On hand for the dedication were Stan Musial, Bob Gibson, Lou Brock, Whitey Herzog, Enos Slaughter, Marty Marion, Bob Forsch, and Danny Cox.

# # #

There's a statue of "Casey at the Bat" outside Tropicana Field in Miami.

# # #

The annual award given to the nation's top college defensive back is named after a mediocre baseball player. Who and why?

Although Jim Thorpe hit only .252 in his six-year big league career with the Giants, Reds, and Braves, his accomplishments on the gridiron were legendary. He helped popularize professional football and was the first commissioner of what became the National Football League. A statue of Thorpe is at the entrance to the pro football Hall of Fame in Canton, Ohio.

A school on the Pine Ridge Indian Reservation in South Dakota is named for Jim Thorpe, of the Sac and Fox tribe.

# # #

One of the largest items named for a ballplayer and perhaps the only non-stationary one was created in January 1999, as Southwest Airlines named one of its Boeing 737-700 planes the *Nolan Ryan Express*. In Dallas and Houston, Ryan signed decals, which featured a baseball with airplane wings, on both sides of the plane's nose. The plane was used to fly Ryan to his 1999 Hall of Fame induction in Cooperstown.

The Alvin (Texas) High School has named its baseball field after native Nolan Ryan.

Alvin Junior College is the site of the Nolan Ryan Center for Continuing Education, funded by the Nolan Ryan Historical Foundation.

Pat Rapp's son Ryan Patrick was named after Nolan Ryan.

There's a statue of Ryan outside the post office in Alvin.

# # #

Oklahoma City's new Bricktown Ballpark on Mickey Mantle Drive, home of the RedHawks, the Rangers' AAA affiliate in the Pacific Coast League, was dedicated on April 17, 1998, with the unveiling of a statue of Mantle. Among Mantle's Yankee teammates present for the dedication were Bobby Murcer, Ryne Duren, Yogi Berra, Ralph Houk, Enos Slaughter, Bobby Richardson, Bobby Brown, Jerry Lumpe, and Whitey Ford. The former players' handprints, preserved in cement, surround the statue.

# # #

Hall of Famer Robin Yount was born at St. Elizabeth Hospital in Danville, Illinois, but his family lived in Covington, Indiana, eight miles away. Neither town has named anything after Yount.

# # #

Who is the only man formally censured by the United States Senate to have a professional baseball stadium named in his honor?

Thomas Dodd. The United States Senator from Connecticut, 1959–71 (and father of Senator Christopher Dodd), was censured by the Senate in a 92–5 vote on June 23, 1967, for diverting $116,000 in campaign contributions. Thomas Dodd Stadium is the home of the Norwich (Connecticut) Navigators, the Yankees affiliate in the AA Eastern League.

# # #

Former infielder and Red Sox manager Joe Morgan and his wife, Dot, told us that there is a Joe Morgan baseball field in his native Walpole, Massachusetts.

# # #

The Pacific Coast League Historical Society has placed a plaque in the shape of home plate on the site of Gilmore Field, home of the old Hollywood Stars. The site is now the home of *Vibe*, at Studio 46, part of CBS Television City.

# # #

There's a Jim "Junior" Gilliam Park in Los Angeles, near LaBrea Avenue, south of Rodeo.

# # #

The Little Padres Park at the Jackie Robinson Family YMCA in San Diego was dedicated on Robinson's birthday, January 31, 1997. It is the home of a new Little League.

# # #

At spring training in 1998, the Red Sox named the entrance to their minor league facility in Fort Myers, Florida, after Charlie Wagner, who has been with the team as player, coach, and scout since 1938.

# # #

The University of South Carolina at Aiken refurbished its ballpark and named it after an alumnus, Roberto Hernandez.

# # #

The largest athletic complex in the city of Central Falls, Rhode Island, was named after Arizona Diamondbacks Executive Vice President Roland A. Hemond, who was born there. In an interview on June 25, 1999, during Cardinal José Jimenez's no-hitter against the Diamondbacks at the BOB, Hemond told us that the Curtis Bay, Maryland, Coast Guard station has named a softball field for Hemond, a Coast Guard veteran.

# # #

Arizona's Scottsdale Stadium (spring training home of the Giants) salutes Billy Martin with a plaque. Also honored is Jim Palmer, who played high school ball in Scottsdale.

# # #

The Marine Parkway Memorial Bridge, which connects Brooklyn, New York, to the Rockaways, is named for Gil Hodges. A sign and a bust of Hodges are at the Brooklyn entrance to the bridge. A school and a park are also named for the late Brooklyn Dodgers star and Mets manager, who lived in Brooklyn. A playground, at Fourth Avenue and Enton Place in Brooklyn—site of the old Washington Park ballfield—is named for Hodges.

A bronze bust of Hodges was erected in 1997 in the rotunda of the Pike County Courthouse in Petersburg, Indiana. A native of Princeton, Indiana (which has named a ballfield after him), Hodges grew up and went to school in Petersburg.

# # #

Perryton, Texas, named its high school field Mike Hargrove Field after its alumnus. Surprisingly, Hargrove did not play baseball in high school.

# # #

Perhaps this chapter should be retitled STUFF AND PEOPLE NAMED AFTER BALLPLAYERS: Rafael Palmeiro named his first child Patrick Ryne, after former Cubs teammate Ryne Sandberg.

Tim Raines's son André is named after André Dawson, Raines's Expos teammate 1979–86. Dawson is young André's godfather.

Curt Schilling, who devotes time and money to fight Lou Gehrig's Disease, named his son Gehrig.

Luis Aparicio named a son after his White Sox teammate and fellow Hall of Famer Nellie Fox.

George Brett named his son Robin after Robin Yount. The two were great friends, but they were never teammates. Yount spent his entire career with the Milwaukee Brewers, and Brett's entire playing career was with the Kansas City Royals. Robin Brett was there when his father and Yount were both inducted into the Hall of Fame in Cooperstown, New York, on July 25, 1999.

# # #

Signs north and south of Glen Dale, West Virginia, proclaim it BIRTHPLACE OF GEORGE BRETT—BASEBALL HALL OF FAME.

# # #

Raul Mondesi—who has two sons named Raul—provides funds and equipment for the 500 children in the Raul Mondesi League in his native Dominican Republic.

# # #

Eric Young had a ballpark built and named for him while he was with the Rockies. Other Rockies who have contributed funds to restore youth fields named for them include Ellis Burks, in Colorado Springs, Pedro Astacio in his native Dominican Republic, Jerry Dipoto, in Littleton, and Larry Walker, in Denver and Ft. Collins.

# # #

The Texas Rangers have instituted a program, similar to the Rockies', of building youth ballparks and naming them after Rangers. The Johnny Oates Texas Rangers Youth Ballpark is in West Dallas. The Ivan Rodriguez Youth Ballpark in North Fort Worth was completed in 1998. There's a Juan Gonzalez/Texas Ranger Youth Ballpark in southeast Dallas and a Will Clark youth ballpark in Fort Worth.

# # #

In 1999 the Red Sox named a youth baseball field at Ramsey Park in Roxbury, Massachusetts, about a mile from Fenway Park, after their great slugger and former batting coach Jim Rice. Funds for the design and construction of the park came from the Sox' share of proceeds from the All-Star Workout Day and home run contest. The field includes a miniature version of Fenway Park's "Green Monster," dugouts, a backstop, bullpens, foul poles, lights, scoreboard, fencing, bleachers, an irrigation and drainage system, public-address system, restrooms, and a concession stand.

# # #

In 1997 the Red Sox named the main field at their minor league spring training complex in Fort Myers, Florida, after their long-time coach Eddie Popowski.

# # #

The entire Hermanos Unidos de Queens Little League was renamed the Tony Fernandez Little League.

# # #

Bristol, Connecticut, is the home of the A. Bartlett Giamatti Little League complex, named for the former Commissioner of Baseball.

# # #

The Siegfried Line, the Mason-Dixon Line, the Maginot Line, and now, the Mendoza Line. Mario Mendoza holds the ignominious honor of having an entire line named after him—the Mendoza Line. During his great playing career, George Brett was quoted as saying that the first thing he did when reading the sports pages of his newspaper every day was check to see who was below the Mendoza Line—i.e., batting below .200.

From 1974 to 1982, Mendoza played for the Mariners, Pirates, and Rangers. His career average of .215 does not adequately reflect his five seasons below his own line.

# # #

The San Diego Padres have named an annual award for Clyde McCullough, who spent nearly 50 years in baseball. Originally given to their best rookie, since 1990 the Clyde McCullough Award has been given to the Padres' best pitcher. Winners include John Kruk, Benito Santiago, Roberto Alomar, Andy Benes twice and Trevor Hoffman—a three-time winner.

# # #

The Mets have named two areas at Shea Stadium after their first manager. The parking area adjacent to the stadium is Casey Stengel Plaza, and a restaurant in the stadium is Casey's Club.

# # #

The statue of Walter Johnson at Griffith Stadium in Washington, D.C., which President Harry S. Truman dedicated in 1947, was moved to Walter Johnson High School in Bethesda, Maryland.

# # #

This chapter notes the statues, plaques, monuments, schools, stadiums, fields, museums, halls of fame, streets, etc. named after baseball players. But two players have had the extremely unusual distinction of having medical procedures named for them. (Medical procedures are frequently named for the doctors who perfected them, e.g., the Heimlich Maneuver.) Who are these players and what are the procedures?

The first is "Tommy John" surgery. Technically, this is a "reconstruction of the ulnar collateral ligament of the elbow."

One of the first people, and probably the first ballplayer, to undergo a precursor of Tommy John surgery was Harry Hulihan. Vermont baseball historian John Bennett informed us that Hulihan, a native of Rutland, Vermont, pitched seven games for the 1922 Boston Braves before an arm injury ended his career. Before he quit after the season, Hulihan underwent tendon graft surgery, a radical procedure for the 1920s. A tendon was taken from his hip and placed in his left arm. He never pitched again in the majors.

Dr. Frank W. Jobe, who performed the surgery on John and perfected the operation, estimated for us that between 1,000 and 2,000 such operations have been performed. Among the players who have had this career-saving surgery are Doug Linton, David Wells, Tom Candiotti, Jason Isringhausen, Darren Dreifort, Pedro Borbon, Jeff Wallace, Tim Worrell, Bill Pulsipher, Norm Charlton, Ken Ryan, Jeff Wallace, Eric Gagne, Steve Karsay, Cal Eldred, Butch Henry, Steve Sparks, Billy Brewer, Jose Mesa, Tom Gordon, David Palmer, Mike Holtz, Scott Schoeneweis, Al Reyes, Jay Buhner, Bobby Muñoz, Kerry Wood, Paul Wilson, Mark Wohlers, Billy Koch, John Smoltz, Scott Erickson, Rudy Seanez, Sean Spencer Yankee prospect Sam Marsonek, and Jay Payton—twice!

The second medical procedure named for a pitcher who went on to an extremely successful career after the procedure is the "Orel Hershiser Procedure"—technically the "anterior capsulolabral reconstruction of the shoulder joint."

The procedures are detailed in "Ligamentous and Posterior Compartment Injuries" in the October 1995 issue of *Operative Techniques in Upper Extremity Sports Injuries.*

Thanks to Dr. Jobe, who developed these surgical techniques, for providing us with this information.

# # #

Three big leaguers were honored in 1999 with their own brand of cereal: Proceeds from Roberto Clemente's Commemorative Slugger Cereal will benefit the Roberto Clemente Foundation. There are Sammy Sosa and Derek Jeter cereals, too.

Note: Monster Crunch Cereal is also available—it's named after the Red Sox mascot Wally the Green Monster.

# # #

There's a Casey Stengel ballpark in Glendale, California, where he lived.

# # #

The road into Forrest City, Arkansas, proclaims it to be the HOMETOWN OF DON KESSINGER.

# # #

Miami has named a street for Havana native and current Miami resident José Canseco.

# # #

There's a Mo Vaughn Youth Center in Dorchester, Massachusetts.

# # #

In 1985 the Casey Stengel baseball league in which Frank White played was renamed the Frank White League.

# # #

On June 25, 1999, the Kansas City Royals unveiled statues of their late owners, Ewing and Muriel Kauffman, outside Gate "A" at Kauffman Stadium.

# # #

Dartmouth College plays its home games at Red Rolfe Field, so named in 1971. Rolfe was a 1931 graduate of Dartmouth, and after his career as a player for the Yankees and manager of the Tigers he became Dartmouth's Director of Athletics in Hanover, New Hampshire, 1954–67.

The Ivy League is divided into two divisions—the Red Rolfe Division (Harvard, Yale, Dartmouth, Brown), and the Lou Gehrig Division (Columbia, Princeton, Cornell, Pennsylvania).

# # #

The right field foul pole at Fenway Park is known as the "Pesky Pole" because of the propensity of Johnny Pesky, Red Sox shortstop (1942, 1946–52) and later both coach (1975–84) and manager (1963–64, 1980), to hook home runs around it. Bob Feller told us that the name was given by Indians pitcher Mel Harder.

# # #

Duffy's Cliff was a mound that extended from the left field flagpole to center field at Fenway Park, 1912–33. Duffy Lewis was expert at playing balls hit there.

# # #

Comerica Park, new home of the Detroit Tigers, is the site of the Tigers' Walk of Fame, featuring larger-than-life action statues of the five great Tiger Hall of Famers—Ty Cobb, Charlie Gehringer, Al Kaline, Hank Greenberg swinging, and Hal Newhouser.

Apparently reacting to some criticism that the statues honored only white men, the Tigers belatedly decided to retire #23 for Willie Horton and to add his statue to those of Cobb, Gehringer, Greenberg, Newhouser, and Kaline—each of whom had already been inducted into the National Baseball Hall of Fame in Cooperstown, and had his number retired by the Tigers.

# # #

On May 13, 1952, pitcher Ron Necciai of the Bristol (Connecticut) Twins in the Class D Appalachian League faced the Welch Miners. He struck out 27—the only professional ballplayer ever to accomplish this extraordinary feat. In the process, he gave catcher Harry Dunlap his own record—26 putouts. (Necciai fielded a ground ball and struck out four in one inning.) Necciai's major league career (12 games, 1–6, 1 hit, 1 RBI) with the 1952 Pittsburgh Pirates was cut short by ulcers and a torn rotator cuff.

Forty years later, after Necciai threw out the first pitch for the Bristol Sox before a game against the Kingsport Mets, the Sox unveiled a bronze plaque commemorating Necciai's unique and unforgettable achievement.

# # #

The Creten, Minnesota, high school honored one of its great alumni by putting Paul Molitor's name on its backstop.

# # #

The Bethesda, Maryland, Community Baseball Club created Shirley Povich Field, named for the *Washington Post's* great sportswriter. The 750-seat field, with a concrete grandstand, will be home to the Bethesda Big Train (named for Walter Johnson) of the Clark C. Griffith Collegiate Baseball League.

# # #

There's a Joe DiMaggio Children's Hospital, part of Memorial Healthcare System, in Hollywood, Florida.

Joe DiMaggio Park in Chicago, Illinois, was dedicated in 1998.

The Yankees will place a bronze bust of Joe DiMaggio outside Yankee Stadium.

Hollywood, Florida, will dedicate a 24-acre park in honor of Joe DiMaggio, who lived there in his later years.

Manhattan's West Side Highway was renamed the "Joe DiMaggio Highway" on April 23, 1999, the day a monument to the Yankee Clipper was dedicated at Yankee Stadium's "Monument Park." The monument now stands beside those to Babe Ruth, Lou Gehrig, Miller Huggins, and Mickey Mantle.

Joe DiMaggio was present when a 12-foot, 16,000-pound statue of him was unveiled on May 18, 1991, outside the National Italian American Sports Hall of Fame in Arlington Heights, Illinois.

# # #

Seats at the end of each row at Seattle's new Safeco Field bear a cast-iron image of Seattle native Fred Hutchinson. Hutchinson pitched for the Tigers and managed the Tigers, Cardinals, and Reds, whom he led to a world championship in 1961. He died of cancer in 1965. Seattle is the home of the Fred Hutchinson Cancer Research Center, the only National Cancer Institute–designated cancer center in the Pacific Northwest.

# # #

Al Kaline hit the box seat railing in foul territory at Tiger Stadium so often that a row of seats was removed. It was known as "Kaline's Corner."

# # #

By tradition, the Hughie Jennings Memorial Lecture at the University of Maryland School of Law in Baltimore is given on Opening Day and is devoted to the confluence of law and baseball. Hall of Famer Jennings was also a lawyer.

# # #

Amherst, New Hampshire, has not yet named anything for its native Hall of Famer Frank Selee.

# # #

A marker on the site of Tiger Stadium, at the corner of Michigan and Trumball, names it as a registered Michigan Historic Site:

"TIGER STADIUM"

Baseball has been played on this site since before 1900, and it has been the home of the Detroit Tigers from their start as a charter member of the American League in 1901. Standing on the location of an early haymarket, the stadium has been enlarged and renamed several times. Once called Bennett Park with wooden stands for 10,000, it became Navin Field in 1912 when seating was increased to 23,000 and home plate was moved from what is now right field to its present location. Major alterations later expanded its capacity to more than 54,000, and in 1938 the structure became Briggs Stadium. Lights were installed in 1948 and in 1961 the name was changed to Tiger Stadium. The site of many championship sporting events, the evolution of this stadium is a tribute to Detroit's support of professional athletics.

The Tigers moved into new Comerica Park for the 2000 season.

# # #

Lou Costello Park is at the corner of Ellison Street and Tony Lalaman Boulevard in his native Paterson, New Jersey. It features a statue of Costello, whose "Who's on First?" comedy routine with his partner, Bud Abbott, is an immortal piece of baseball lore. The slightly larger than life statue shows Costello with a baseball bat on his shoulder.

# # #

In 1973 an elementary school in Chicago was named for Wendell Smith, Hall of Fame sportswriter who roomed with Jackie Robinson during his first tumultuous year in the majors.

University of Notre Dame gives an annual award named for Smith.

# # #

In recognition of his contributions to the rehabilitation of the baseball field used by Phoenix House—a drug rehabilitation center in California's Orange County—the field was named for Gary DiSarcina.

# # #

The Little League field in East Whittier, California, was named for Darin Erstad, who helped provide funds to refurbish it.

# # #

Houston's Independent School District named a baseball field in honor of Ray Knoblauch, father of Chuck, in recognition of his contributions to amateur baseball in Houston.

# # #

The first new statue to be installed at PNC park, the new home of the Pittsburgh Pirates, will be a 12′ tall bronze likeness of Willie Stargell. It will join statues of Pirates greats Honus Wagner and Roberto Clemente. The Stargell statue—at the left field entrance to PNC on Federal Street—will be created by Susan Wagner, who sculpted the statue of Clemente.

# # #

ON THE COVER

━━━━━━━

THAT'S JULIO CRUZ ON THE COVER. A native of Brooklyn, Cruz broke into the majors with Seattle on July 4, 1977. The slick-fielding second baseman and Gold Glover spent eight years with the Mariners, then three with the White Sox.

The photo was taken during batting practice before a White Sox–Royals game on August 22, 1983, in Kansas City.

Cruz told us that the "reason it was easy to balance the baseball at the end of my bat was because the bat was cupped out at the end of the barrel. The reason for a cupped bat is so that the weight can be distributed evenly in the bat . . . The reason I could balance a bat on my nose is that my nose is flat due to too many bad hops caught with my nose and not my glove."

Julio's brothers Hector and Tommy also played in the major leagues.

In addition to his charity work, Julio is now the head baseball coach at Eastside Catholic High School—the Crusaders—in Bellevue, Washington.

ABOUT THE AUTHORS

Jeffrey Lyons is the entertainment critic for WNBC-TV in New York City and host of the nationally syndicated radio feature *The Lyons Den*. He has been a guest broadcaster for the Boston Red Sox and is a columnist for the Red Sox fan magazine *Diehard*.

Douglas B. Lyons, Jeffrey's younger brother, is a criminal lawyer in New York City. Jeffrey's first words to Douglas, when Jeffrey was three and Douglas was four days old, were "Are you a Dodger fan?"